BIOLOGICAL AND NEUROPSYCHOLOGICAL MECHANISMS

Life-Span Developmental Psychology

The West Virginia University Conferences on Life-Span Developmental Psychology

Datan/Greene/Reese: Life-Span Developmental Psychology: Intergenerational Relations

Cummings/Greene/Karraker: Life-Span Developmental Psychology: Perspectives on Stress and Coping

Puckett/Reese: Mechanisms of Everyday Cognition

Cohen/Reese: Life-Span Developmental Psychology: Methodological Contributions

Reese/Franzen: Biological and Neuropsychological Mechanisms: Life-Span Developmental Psychology

BIOLOGICAL AND NEUROPSYCHOLOGICAL MECHANISMS

Life-Span Developmental Psychology

Edited by

Hayne W. Reese
West Virginia University

Michael D. Franzen
Department of Psychiatry
and Allegheny Neuropsychiatric Institute
Allegheny General Hospital, Pittsburgh

LEA LAWRENCE ERLBAUM ASSOCIATES, PUBLISHERS
1997 Mahwah, New Jersey

Lawrence Erlbaum Associates, Inc., Publishers
10 Industrial Avenue
Mahwah, New Jersey 07430

Cover design by Cris Horvath

Library of Congress Cataloging-in-Publication Data

Biological and neuropsychological mechanisms : life-span developmental
    psychology / edited by Hayne W. Reese, Michael D. Franzen.
        p.   cm.
    "The chapters in this volume evolved from oral presentations given
at the Thirteenth West Virginia University Conference on Life-Span
Developmental Psychology, held in Morgantown, West Virginia" — Pref.
    Includes bibliographical references and index.
    ISBN 0-8058-1152-4 (alk. paper)
    1. Developmental psychology — Congresses.   2. Developmental
psychobiology — Congresses.   3. Neuropsychology — Congresses.
I. Reese, Hayne Waring.   II. Franzen, Michael D.
III. West Virginia University Conference on Life-Span
Developmental Psychology (13th : 1992 : Morgantown, W. Va.)
    [DNLM: 1. Neuropsychology — congresses.   2. Human Development —
congresses.   3. Cognition — physiology — congresses.   4. Personality
Development — congresses.   WL 103.5 B615 1996]
BF712.5.B56 1996
155 — dc20
DNLM/DLC   96-17641
for Library of Congress   CIP

Books published by Lawrence Erlbaum Associates are printed on acid-free paper, and their bindings are chosen for strength and durability.

Printed in the United States of America
10 9 8 7 6 5 4 3 2 1

Contents

Preface

The chapters in this volume evolved from oral presentations given at the Thirteenth West Virginia University Conference on Life-Span Developmental Psychology, held in Morgantown, West Virginia. Consistent with preceding volumes in this series, the contributors represent a variety of disciplines related to the theme of the conference and the ensuing volume: In the present instance, the theme is biological and neuropsychological mechanisms in life-span psychological development, and the disciplines represented are behavioral medicine, neurology, neuropsychology, psychophysiology, and psychology. The theme is expressed in theories and findings about genetic and environmental mechanisms (Sandra Scarr), brain mechanisms (Marcel Kinsbourne; Dennis Molfese, Victoria Molfese, Leslie Gill, & Sharon Benshoff; Charles Nelson), relations of physiological functioning in infancy to later development (Stephen Porges & Jane Doussard-Roosevelt), physiological risk factors in infancy (David Tupper), adolescence (Robert McCaffrey & Catherine Forneris), old age (Robert Keefover & Eric Rankin), methodological and data analytic problems (John Nesselroade & Jack McArdle), and issues about the validity of neuropsychological assessment (Michael Franzen & Peter Arnett).

This volume starts with overviews of theoretical and methodological issues (Scarr; Nesselroade & McArdle; Franzen & Arnett) and continues with chapters dealing with selected portions of the life span — four chapters on mechanisms in infancy (Molfese et al.; Nelson; Tupper; Porges & Doussard-Roosevelt), two chapters on mechanisms in childhood and adolescence (Kinsbourne; McCaffrey & Forneris), and one chapter on mechanisms in adulthood and old age (Keefover & Rankin). The disproportionate emphasis on infancy reflects our belief that biological and neuropsychological mechanisms operating in that age period have especially important implications for the rest of the life span. However, the underemphasis in this volume on adulthood and old age does not indicate any doubts on our part as to the significance of biological and neuropsychological mechanisms in that age. Three papers given at the conference dealt with adulthood and old age; however, the author of one paper had agreed to contribute to the conference but not to the published proceedings, and the author of another was unable to prepare a chapter for publication because of ill health.

The success of the Thirteenth West Virginia University Life-Span Developmental Conference must be shared among and attributed to many persons. The idea for the conference originated with Hayne W. Reese, Centennial Professor and Director of the Developmental Training Program in the Department of Psychology. Financial support was provided through the generosity of Barry A. Edelstein from the chair's office in the Department of Psychology, James M. Stevenson from the chair's office in the Department of Behavioral Medicine and Psychiatry, the Office of the Associate Provost for Research and Graduate Studies administered by William E. Vehse, and the National Institute of Mental Health (Grant T32 MH18374).

The daily activities of the conference would not have been possible without the assistance of our student aides. Our most special thanks go to these graduate students, who served as guides, transporters, and assistants for speakers and attendees: Patrick T. Davies, Keith T. Jones, Frank H. Jurden, Liang-Jei Lee, Elizabeth R. Levelle, Lillian M. Michalko, Eileen J. Reamy, Kelly S. Simpson, M. Joy Stewart, Ruth H. Tunick, and especially, Edie Jo Hall and Constance E. Toffle, who served as aides-in-chief. We also acknowledge with deep gratitude the secretarial aid of Ann Davis and Sandy Townsend and the management of records and funds by Janet Stalewski.

—Hayne W. Reese
—Michael D. Franzen

List of Contributors

Peter Arnett, Department of Psychology, Washington State University

Sharon Benshoff, Department of Psychology, Southern Illinois University at Carbondale

Jane A. Doussard-Roosevelt, Institute for Child Study, University of Maryland

Catherine A. Forneris, Department of Psychology, University at Albany, State University of New York

Michael D. Franzen, Department of Psychiatry and Allegheny Neuropsychiatric Institute, Allegheny General Hospital, Pittsburgh

Leslie A. Gill, Department of Psychology, Southern Illinois University at Carbondale

Robert W. Keefover, Department of Neurology, School of Medicine, West Virginia University

Marcel Kinsbourne, New School for Social Research, New York

John J. McArdle, Department of Psychology, University of Virginia

Robert J. McCaffrey, Department of Psychology, University at Albany, State University of New York

Dennis L. Molfese, Behavioral and Social Sciences, School of Medicine, Southern Illinois University at Carbondale

Victoria J. Molfese, Department of Psychology, Southern Illinois University at Carbondale

Charles A. Nelson, Institute of Child Development, University of Minnesota

John R. Nesselroade, Department of Psychology, University of Virginia

Stephen W. Porges, Institute for Child Study, University of Maryland

Eric D. Rankin, Department of Behavioral Medicine and Psychiatry, School of Medicine, West Virginia University

Hayne W. Reese, Department of Psychology, West Virginia University

Sandra Scarr, Professor Emerita, University of Virginia; Chairman and CEO, KinderCare Learning Centers, Inc., Montgomery, AL

David E. Tupper, Department of Neurology, Hennepin County Medical Center, Minneapolis

1 The Development of Individual Differences in Intelligence and Personality

Sandra Scarr
University of Virginia
KinderCare Learning Centers, Inc., Montgomery, AL

A theory that explains becoming human, becoming a member of a culture and society, and becoming a unique human being must call on diverse theoretical resources in the biological and social sciences. To integrate such diverse concepts requires the umbrella of evolutionary theory, which alone can encompass so many levels of analysis (Scarr, 1993). In this chapter, I present an elaboration of the theory of genotype → environment effects (Scarr & McCartney, 1983) that was developed in my presidential address to the Society for Research in Child Development (Scarr, 1992) and, further, in replies to critics of that article (Scarr, 1993).

The major theses of the theory are: (a) an evolutionary perspective can unite the study of both species-typical development and individual variation; (b) environments within the normal species range are, of course, required for species-normal development, but research in modern societies suggests that individual variation among children reared in those environments arise primarily from genetic variation and from individually experienced environments, not from objectively measured environments; (c) environments should be seen as opportunities for experiences that are constructed by persons in developmentally changing and individually different ways; and (d) within dominant cultures in modern Western and Asian societies most differences in development are not due to differences in environmental opportunities.

Evolution and Psychology

Darwinian evolutionary theory has two simple principles: genetic variation and natural selection. Evolutionary theory's central principle is that gene frequencies in breeding populations change from generation to generation because environments affect differentially individuals' reproductive success. The next generation more closely resembles the successful breeders and nurturers of the preceding generation, because their genes are more frequent in the offspring generation. Generational changes in gene distributions lead to changes in behavioral phenotype distributions across species' histories, because different phenotypes arise from different genotypes. Selection acts at the level of individual phenotypes, which more and less contribute to the next generation, and thereby indirectly affects gene distributions. If there were no genetic variation, there could be no evolution.

The role of evolution in the study of human development seems confusing to many psychologists. Today's psychology is struggling to escape its impoverished past — 50 years of naive behaviorism, built on a theory of deprivation effects, spelled out in unlikely scenarios. If an experimental manipulation, usually a deprivation of normal, species-typical experience (e.g., patterned visual experience or maternal rearing) could be shown to prevent normal development (e.g., vision or social behavior), then the environmental control of such developmental patterns was inferred. The fact that normal members of the species (e.g., cats or rhesus macaques) would have universal access to those experiences (e.g., patterned visual stimuli or maternal contact) did not deter psychologists from explaining normal human variation in terms of the effects of their deprivation experiments on other species. This grand non sequitur dominated psychology during the 20th century. Exclusive attention to proximal mechanisms of development, based on manipulation of deprivations of normal experience, has blinded developmental theory to understanding the history and nature of development, human and otherwise.

Evolutionary psychology makes different assumptions and therefore asks different questions. It assumes a human species history that shaped human learning patterns and emotional expressions. It assumes the presence of genetic variability in the most basic human traits, or else evolution could not have occurred and individuals would not differ. It assumes that those experiences that are required for species-normal development are widely available to biologically normal members of the species. If failure to encounter experiences that are essential for normal sensory, cognitive, emotional, and social development results in the failure to develop into normal species members, then those experiences must have been readily available in human history, or another evolutionary mechanism would have developed (e.g., internally guided development or elimination of that aspect of development through selection). If essential experiences are denied, whether through biological defects or through social environmental maladaptation (e.g., wars, famines, severe neglect, and abuse), then individual development will be negatively affected. Individual differences can, and do, arise from such deprivations in a minority of cases, both historically and internationally at the present time. Just as severe cases of visual impairment and brain damage cannot explain normal variation in visual acuity or intelligence, so severe deprivations of experience cannot explain normal individual differences in most populations. In the big picture of human development, such social and biological misfortunes do not provide the underlying principles of normal human variation. Rather, genetic and environmental variations in a normal species range are the theoretical principles that explain why differences in intelligence and personality arise. The implications of evolution for theories of development are profound and are the subject of this chapter.

A CONTEMPORARY SYNTHESIS

In 1941 (Dobzhansky, 1941), the New Synthesis of modern genetics and evolutionary theory was hammered out to the great benefit of biology. Theory and mechanism were joined (Mayr, 1970). More than 50 years later, we need a synthesis of theory in the biological and social sciences that evaluates the roles of culture, society (including socialization), and biology as coacting determinants in shaping human development. We need to work out theory and mechanism of development. For too long psychologists have argued nature versus nurture, biology versus culture, as though one cause excluded others. The major parameters of a synthetic theory are expressed here in 20 propositions that subsume the major observations about human development (Scarr, 1993):

On Development

1. Development in all species is a probablistic course of genetically programmed change across the life span whose expression is affected by environments from the cellular to the global level. Environments that do not provide opportunities for species-normal development (see #16 later) inhibit genetic expression; environments that do not provide culturally normal opportunities for development (see #17 later) may shift development to culturally abnormal paths.

2. The course of human development itself evolved across species history. All periods of the life span have been subject to selection and are genetically variable to some extent (e.g., timing of birth, speech, menarche, menopause). Intellectual and personality development are general behavioral tendencies that have evolved and shape what is learned. Develop-

mental patterns are as species typical as any other aspect of morphology and behavior.

3. Evolution, through coadapted gene complexes, shaped general patterns of human behavior and development (e.g., general intelligence, emotionality), as well as specific behaviors (e.g., eye blinks, smiles). Behavioral phenotypes can be defined at different levels of generality, but there are positive correlations among specific behaviors that yield more general patterns that are characterized by genetic individual variability.

On Behavioral Evolution

4. All animal (human and other) behavior is the product of evolution. Evolution is an historical process of selective and random forces acting on genetic variation within each species from one generation to the next.

5. All animals (including humans) show versatility and adaptability in behavior. Honey bees learn to anticipate experimental moves of their honey sources (Degler, 1991). Learning is a common feature of all species – not learning to solve human problems but solving problems of their own, related to survival and fitness. Biology defines what can be learned, when it can be learned, how likely behaviors are to occur, and what is reinforcing.

6. Inclusive fitness explains much about social behavior, altruism toward kin, and self-sacrifice in favor of close relatives (Haldane remarked, sardonically, that he would sacrifice himself for three brothers and nine cousins; Mayr, 1970). Reciprocity among nonkin can be seen as tit for tat: Minnesota farmers send hay to drought-stricken Georgia; Georgia farmers reciprocate when Minnesota needs hay. Alliances of nonkin (friends) are found among other species (e.g., chimpanzees; Goodall, as cited in Degler, 1991).

7. Genetic commonalities determine similarities among species members in morphology and behavior around the world.

8. Genetic variability determines some to much of what is observed in all species as normal morphological and behavioral variation as well as abnormal characteristics.

On Culture

9. Culture defines the content of what is to be valued and acquired; biology provides the motivation and intelligence for learning it. Cultures define what is desirable to be learned, what is to be believed, and how to behave. Cultural diversity and genetic diversity coexist in the human species.

10. Cultures set a range of opportunities for development; they define the limits of what is desirable, "normal" individual variation, and what is

"abnormal" in that culture (although there is some cultural consensus that some forms of deviance and psychopathology are abnormal).

On Society

11. Human societies evolved with social behaviors, kinship recognition, prolonged infancy, and so forth. Human society is a product of human evolution, just as packs of wolves, hives of bees, and prides of lions evolved with their behaviors.

12. Societies stratify opportunities for development; they determine access to cultural knowledge and developmental supports, or lack of same. Industrial and postindustrial societies stratify opportunities less by tradition and more by achievement than preindustrial societies.

13. Social groups from the family to the body politic socialize the young to live by cultural values. Cultural knowledge is transmitted by adults and peers across an individual's life span. Children are usually the focus of societies' efforts to socialize culturally approved ways of being, believing, and behaving. In societies not in turmoil, the family, however culturally defined, is usually the major agent of socialization efforts.

14. Access to dominant cultural knowledge and supports is often less available for racial and ethnic minorities with distinctive cultures of their own.

On Environments

15. Environments provide a range of opportunities for development; the same environments do not have the same effects on all individuals, because individuals construct different experiences from the same environmental opportunities, based on their prior experiences and on their genotypes.

16. Environments must provide opportunities that are necessary for normal species-typical development, or else individuals will not become normal members of the human species. Most species-typical developments are maturationally driven changes that find opportunities in every culture for their full development (e.g., language, locomotor skills, sensorimotor and concrete-operational intelligence). Cultural practices that appear dissimilar provide functionally equivalent opportunities for species-normal development.

17. Environments must also include opportunities to acquire developmentally appropriate cultural knowledge, or else individuals will not be considered culturally normal. Cultural values about desirable human traits and socialization practices are ends and means, respectively; they vary among cultures within the species-normal range. Cultural beliefs about behavior and socialization practices that deviate substantially from what is

culturally normal will lead to individual development that is not culturally acceptable, even if it is species normal (and culturally normal in another context).

18. Given equal access to cultural knowledge and to other environmental opportunities for experience, genetic individual variation determines the many aspects of individual differences that are manifested in what is learned when, and by whom.

19. Given limited access to cultural knowledge and to essential opportunities for experience, individual differences may reflect those differences in opportunities to learn.

20. Individuals' unique experiences are, most often, positively correlated with their own characteristics (e.g., good readers read more; attractive children receive more positive attention), but there can be instances of negative correlations (poor readers are given intensive reading interventions; peer-rejected children are taught social skills) and genotype-environment interactions (only good readers profit from advanced instruction; only fine athletes respond to opportunities to try out for the varsity team).

Human development is naturally a product of biology, culture, and society, acting in concert. By species-normal criteria, individual patterns of development are more likely to be influenced by genetic differences than by differences in opportunities that cultural and social environments afford. All societies not in turmoil afford children opportunities to become normal members of the species. By culture-normal criteria, the location of the individual in the social structure may have important effects on access to opportunities that lead to culturally defined normal development.

NONLINEAR EFFECTS ON DEVELOPMENT

Role of Environments

Environments provide opportunities for development to occur. The range and variety of opportunities provided are important, because below some threshold there are insufficient opportunities for adequate, species-normal development to occur. Gottlieb (1976) provided useful distinctions about the possible roles of genes and environments in development. The functions are to induce, maintain, and elaborate developmental change. There is a great deal of evidence that the induction of developmental change (also called experience expectant development; Wachs, 1992) is a maturational process by which the organism becomes receptive to environmental inputs that were previously present but had no effect or a different effect on development. The example of the effect of human speech on infant speech development comes readily to mind. In the first months, infants are sensitive to phonological elements of adult speech but not to syntactic or semantic aspects of speech; in the second year, however, meaningful utterances come to be understood and produced in communicative interchanges with adults. Normal species environments are required to maintain and elaborate maturationally initiated changes; profoundly deaf infants cease babbling around the end of the first year, presumably for lack of environmental input that comes to hearing infants from others' and their own sounds. Further, deaf infants' speech is not elaborated for the same reasons. Speech is an example of experience dependent developments (Wachs, 1992).

Gottlieb (1991) argued that canalization (restriction of possible developmental outcomes) is due not only to genes but also to experiential components at all levels of developmental system. This is theoretically true and empirically true under extreme, species abnormal conditions (and, I would add, when the organism is species-abnormal; e.g., deafened chicks or profoundly deaf children do not recognize species-typical calls or maintain vocalizations, respectively). Gottlieb did not distinguish what actually happens in the real world from what can be produced experimentally. By studying artificially handicapped, abnormal organisms reared under extreme experimental conditions, Gottlieb illustrated one mechanism by which species-typical behaviors may be produced, but he did not illuminate how normal variation in species behaviors actually occurs. By implying that experimentally produced results generalize to real-world variation, Gottlieb repeated the errors of a proximal, nonevolutionary psychology that was typical earlier in the 20th century. His animal models may apply to children with profound sensory deficits and those severely deprived of species-normal experience to explain normal individual variation. Extreme experimental manipulations can illuminate mechanisms by which defective development can occur, even though it seldom does. Who would deny that such organismic and environmental events can produce abnormal development? In their reply to Gottlieb, Turkheimer and Gottesman (1991) commented:

> Consider the reaction norm for duckling sensitivity to maternal chicken calls. Across a broad range of genotypes and naturally occurring environments, it is relatively flat, as it must be to ensure survival of the ducklings. . . . Now consider psychometric intelligence in humans. . . . Along the environmental axis, the reaction norm for intelligence is flat across a wide range of normal family environments but drops off drastically at the very low end of the environmental continuum, as illustrated in [Fig. 1.1].

> . . . the description of the reaction norm for intelligence is almost identical to the description of the reaction norm for duckling sensitivity to chicken calls, and one might conclude that "normal family environment" plays a crucial

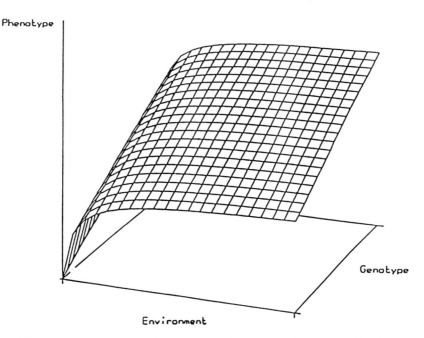

FIG. 1.1.   Hypothetical reaction surface for intelligence, showing a positive linear slope along the genetic axis and sharp decline in the range of very poor environments (Turkheimer & Gottesman, 1991).

role: Without it, intelligence cannot develop at all, regardless of genotypic potential. (pp. 18–19)

With normal family environments, be they duckling or human, youngsters are unlikely to differ much because of variations in those environments. Only extremely poor environments (or impaired organisms) prevent normal species-typical development by depriving the young of opportunities that environment must afford if development is to occur. These are the very features that cultures everywhere provide in a form that meets the needs of experience-expectant and experience-dependent developments. From an evolutionary perspective, the culturally universal availability of developmentally appropriate environments is a tautology; how could it be otherwise, if that culture is to survive?

Specific Parental Practices

Socialization researchers claim that the details of childrearing are crucial for normal human development. Mothers (or other caregivers) must provide specific kinds of interactions to promote specific features of normal language and cognitive development (Wachs, 1992). From an evolutionary perspective, this is highly unlikely. Are there societies with biologically intact children who cannot solve infant intelligence problems or do not engage in symbolic play, regardless of their culture of rearing?

Evolution cannot require exquisitely specific environments for species-normal development unless they are universally available, or there would not be many normal members of the species. If specific environmental events are necessary for normal development (to induce, maintain, or enhance developmental changes; Gottlieb, 1976), they must be widely available to species members in all cultures, or else those developments must be unimportant to survival, because they would have been selected against. All species must be either (a) prepared to develop the characteristic from endogenous sources or (b) prepared to respond to widely available environmental opportunities — to know it and respond to it when it is encountered. Most early developments are species-typical, universal responses of human infants and young children to widely varying, but functionally equivalent, culturally sanctioned, environmental opportunities to acquire species-normal behaviors. There are many different routes through early childhood.

Surely, some individual ducks and some human parents do fail to provide developmentally appropriate environments, and their offspring do not become species normal. Selection acts against such individuals. If children did not have parents or other caregivers, they would not survive. But how much do differences among parents affect differences among their children — genetically and environmentally? This is the empirical question addressed by behavior genetic studies, an important question that is not addressed by extreme manipulations of the rearing environment or the integrity of the organism, as Gottlieb did, or by socialization studies that include only biological families.

Correlations of Genes and Environments in Families

Socialization studies, many of which are described by Baumrind (1993) and Hoffman (1991), hopelessly confound genetic transmission of parental to child characteristics with socialization practices, because they are all studies of biological families. With these data, there are no ways to test competing theories about sources of individual differences — environmental, genetic, or both (Scarr, in press).

In fact, there is considerable evidence that popular measures of family "environments," such as the HOME Scale and the Family Environment Scales (FES), are confounded by genetic differences among parents

(Bouchard & McGue, 1990; Jang, 1993; Plomin, 1994; Plomin & Berge-man, 1991; Plomin, Loehlin, & DeFries, 1985; Plomin, McClearn, Peder-sen, Nesselroade, & Bergeman, 1989a, 1989b; Plomin & Neiderhiser, 1992; Reiss et al., 1994; Rowe, 1981, 1983). By comparing the similarities in perceptions of the family environment among families with genetically identical twins, first-degree relatives, and adopted relatives, behavior genetic analyses show that genetic similarities affect the similarity of perceptions of relationships in the family on major dimensions of parenting (warmth and control) and on intellectual stimulation in the home.

Most striking is the finding that, as adults, identical twins reared apart (MZAs) perceived their rearing families to have been as similar as those of fraternal twins reared together, even though the MZAs were reporting on different families! The MZAs were not as similar as the MZs reared together but considerably more similar than DZs reared apart. Thus, the heritability estimates for various FES scales for the adult twins rearing environments ranged from .15 to .35 (Plomin et al., 1989b). When reporting on rearing practices with their own children, the adult MZAs were as similar as adult MZTs (those pairs reared together), and both MZ groups reported more similar childrearing practices than DZ twins (Plomin et al., 1989a). Heritabilities of the FES scales for adult twins rating their offspring families ranged from .12 to .40 (median = .26). Both parents' and offspring's perceptions, measured when the offspring were adolescents to older adults, show that 25%–50% of the variability in measures of perceived family environments are due to genetic variability.

Perhaps, one could dismiss these results as perceptions of the family environment, showing merely that genetic differences affect people's per-ceptions of relationships and emotional climates in their homes (actually getting socialization researchers to admit that much would be a triumph for empirical theory testing). Fortunately, there are four observational studies of parent–child interactions that provide similar evidence of genetic effects on family environment. In the largest study ever done of genetic contribu-tions to family environments, Reiss, Hetherington, and Plomin (reported in Plomin, 1994) sampled intact families with identical and fraternal twins and biological siblings, and stepfamilies with genetically unrelated siblings, half siblings, and full siblings. They found large effects for genetic differences (52%–64% of the variance) in adolescents' positivity and negativity in interactions with family members, scored from videotaped observations. That is, similarity in family interactions was primarily related to the genetic similarity of the participants. Strangely enough, the shared environment (all of the sibling and twin pairs in this study were reared in the same homes) accounted for only 0%–23% of the variance in adolescents' interactions. Nonshared environments, those that are unique to individuals and not due to either genetic or environmental relatedness, and measurement error accounted for 25%–37% of the variation in observed interactions. Parental

TABLE 1.1

NEAD Model-Fitting Components of Variance of Composites of Videotaped Observations Derived From a Measurement Model

Respondent	Target	Measure	e^2n	e^2s	h^2
Child	Mother	Positivity	.35*	.06	.59*
		Negativity	.37*	.15	.48*
Child	Father	Positivity	.36*	.00	.64*
		Negativity	.25*	.23*	.52*
Mother	Child	Positivity	.19*	.63*	.18*
		Negativity	.29*	.34*	.38*
		Control	.58*	.42*	.00
Father	Child	Positivity	.19*	.63*	.18*
		Negativity	.34*	.42*	.24*
		Control	.25*	.51*	.24*

Note: Model-fitting estimates of nonshared environment/error (e^2n), shared environment (e^2s), and heritability (h^2).

*$p < .05$.

positivity and negativity in interactions with their adolescent children showed more shared environmental effect (34%–63%) and lesser effects of genetic differences among the children (0%–38%) and nonshared environments (19%–34%). These results are shown in Table 1.1.

Additional data about genetic effects on other aspects of children's rearing environments are also revealing. Peer relationships and the choice of peers have been shown to be genetically variable (Plomin, 1994; Rowe, 1981, 1983). Perhaps this result is not surprising, because children do choose their peers, whereas they cannot choose their family members. Whereas genotype-environment correlations in biologically related families may be of the passive type, peer relations may show the active and reactive types (Plomin, 1994). Adolescents' ratings of positive peer and teacher relationships were moderately heritable (.31 and .38), but parents' ratings of their adolescents' popularity with peers and the delinquent, drug abusing, or college-bound orientation of peers showed more heritability than parent ratings of the family environment. For separate mother and father ratings, the heritabilities of peer popularity were .62 and .73; for peer college orientation, .73 and .85; for peer delinquency, .70 and .49, and for peer substance abuse, .72 and .74 (Plomin, 1994, Table 3.5, p. 86). Effects of shared environments on adolescents' peer relationships, based on the correlations of genetically unrelated siblings in the same family, were small to moderate (.00 to .42, median = .13).

Plomin (1994) summarized the research on genetic and environmental effects on self-report and observations measures of the family environment.

Genetic effects are not just limited to children's perceptions of their family environment. Parents' perceptions of their parenting implicate genetic contributions even in child-based genetic designs (i.e., twins are the children in the family). In child-based genetic designs, genetic effects can be detected only to the extent that parents' perceptions of their parenting reflect genetically influenced characteristics of their children.

Finally, evidence of genetic effects emerges from four observational studies of parenting and sibling behavior using child-based genetic designs. The results from these observational studies suggest that the genetic contribution to measures of the family environment is not limited to subjective processes involved in questionnaires. Genetic effects appear to be not just in the eye of the beholder but also in the behavior of the individual. (pp. 79–80)

The implication of this rather recent research for studies of family environmental effects on children's personality and intellectual development is profound. In socialization studies, ubiquitous correlations between parent characteristics and features of the parent-provided home with child development have been erroneously explained as a causal effect of home environments on children. In fact, observations from behavior genetic studies, which vary genetic and environmental relatedness of participants, have shown that the correlation between parental and home characteristics and children's development is explained primarily not by the home environment but by genetic resemblance among family members. When only biologically related families have been studied, this genetic effect of parents on children (and siblings on each other) has been misinterpreted, with important misinferences for developmental theory and for intervention efforts to change some parents' childrearing practices.

Similarity in intelligence and personality among biological family members does not arise from growing up or living in the same household (Plomin & Daniels, 1987; Scarr & Grajek, 1982; Scarr & Ricciuti, 1991). Even socialization researchers now say that they do not expect that living in the same family makes siblings or parents and children similar to each other (Baumrind, 1993; Bronfenbrenner, Lenzenweger, & Ceci, 1993; Hoffman, 1991), because each person perceives and reacts to the family environment in different ways (for the theory, see Scarr & McCartney, 1983). The observed family correlations are not in dispute, but the causal mechanisms by which family members do and do not resemble each other are very hotly contested.

Correlations of Relatives: Personality and IQ

Loehlin and Rowe (1992) recently summarized the effects of genetic and environmental differences on individual variation on the "Big Five" personality dimensions, the factors that emerge repeatedly from self-reports and ratings of personality in five languages, around the world. The Big Five are extroversion–introversion, agreeableness (altruism, nurturance), conscientiousness, neuroticism–anxiety, and intellectual openness.

The results, shown in Table 1.2, are very consistent across personality measures: Unshared environments within families and measurement error account for about one half of the variation; 43% of the variance is due to genetic variation and 6% to shared family environments. Dozens of twin, family, and adoption studies of sources of individual variation in personality measures support these results. Results of studies of self-reported personality leads behavior genetic researchers to conclude that about one half of the reliable variation is due to genetic variability and about half to environmental differences unique to individuals and not shared with other family members. Yet, psychology has thousands of studies focused on the alleged effects of shared environments on personality — all based on biological relatives. It is extremely difficult to bring the behavior genetic results on personality to the attention of socialization researchers, whose theory cannot accommodate these findings.

Let us look at the data on intelligence. Theories, whether socialization or behavior genetic, must fit the observations. Bouchard and colleagues (Bouchard, Lykken, Tellegen, & McGue, in press) provided a stunning summary of the pattern of family correlations for adults in their samples of five critical kinships, under two rearing conditions — same and different families (see Fig. 1.2).

These observations yield broad heritabilities (including nonadditive genetic effects) of .70 to .94 for IQ differences in White North American and European populations from which the samples were drawn. Estimates of IQ heritability in these populations can be as low as .50 (Plomin, in press), if one includes data on large numbers of young adopted siblings, whose IQ correlation averages .24, versus five studies of late adolescent and young adult siblings (adopted in infancy), whose IQ correlation is 0. If one includes only data from older adolescents and adults for all family relationships, the heritability of IQ in North American and Western

TABLE 1.2
Parameter Estimates for "Big Five" Personality Dimensions

Dimension	Unshared Environment	Broad Sense h^2	Narrow Sense h^2	Siblings' Shared Environment
I. Extraversion	.49	.49	.32	.02
II. Agreeableness	.52	.39	.29	.09
III. Conscientiousness	.55	.40	.22	.05
IV. Emotional Stability	.52	.41	.27	.07
V. Intellectual Openness	.49	.45	.43	.06
MEAN	.51	.43	.31	.06

Note: Loehlin & Rowe, 1992.

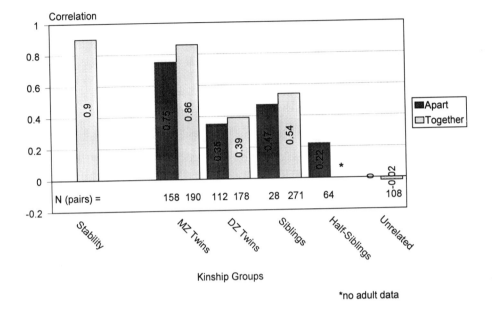

FIG. 1.2. IQ correlations and sample sizes for adult data from five kinship groups reared apart and together (Bouchard, Lykken, Tellegen, & McGue, in press).

European populations is 70%–90% (Bouchard & McGue, 1990; Scarr, in press). As McCartney (McCartney, Harris, & Bernieri, 1990) showed, heritabilities for IQ increase from childhood to adulthood, in keeping with our theory that older adolescents and adults increasingly express their genetic variability as they choose environments and create their own experiences (Scarr, 1992; Scarr & McCartney, 1983).

Differences in socialization history had negligible effects on the IQ results (Bouchard et al., in press). The implication of these results is that any redistribution of existing environments considered favorable to those in environments considered unfavorable can have limited effects on culturally approved intellectual development, because environments experienced by these samples are largely functionally equivalent. Although estimates of environmental variance (e^2) range from .06–.30, unique individual experiences, which cannot be programmed, comprise most of e^2.

Continued Resistance

Socialization researchers invent ad hoc reasons to exclude behavior genetic results from theoretical consideration (Baumrind, 1993; Hoffman, 1991; Jackson, 1993; Wachs, 1992, 1993), because they say samples of families of twins, adoptive families, half siblings, and so forth are too odd to support generalizations of the results to "normal" families. Family processes are too subtle to be measured, too variable from one family to another to be truly studied. Ad hoc fairy tales about birth order (see Ernst & Angst, 1985), gender differences, and family dynamics—mostly untested or untestable hypotheses—are generated as needed to explain away any genetic results (Rowe, 1994).

Limitations in the generalization of behavior genetic studies to the populations studied is understood but mooted by the replications of results across many modern Western and Asian societies. The assertion that behavior genetic studies are based on "extraordinary populations" (Baumrind, 1993, p. 7) of "atypical individuals" (Jackson, 1993, p. 25) is simply not the case. Samples of families in behavior genetic studies include ordinary biological ones, stepparent families (who are hardly rare today), families of adult twins, families with twin offspring (who are not abnormal), and adoptive families, whose parents are on average quite normal but infertile, whose adopted children were born prior to the wide availability of abortion (in the United States, 1973), and who were an intellectual cross section of the U. S. population (Scarr & Weinberg, 1978).

A commonly voiced objection to behavior genetic designs is that parents, twins, and adoptees all know their respective statuses and may have expectations about how similar they "should" be, or that the sibling pairs, with genetic correlations from 1 to 0, may be treated more and less alike, according to expectations about their similarity. Behavior genetic studies have addressed these concerns with bias in studies of family resemblances. First, in twin studies, co-twins who are treated more alike (dressed the same, same room, same classroom, etc.) are not behaviorally more alike than other twins who are treated more differently (Loehlin & Nichols, 1976). Thus, although MZ twins are treated, on average, more similarly than DZ twins, that does not constitute a bias in the twin method, when more similar treatment among MZs and DZs does not affect behavioral similarity. Second, not all parents are correctly informed about the zygocity of their twins; several studies have shown that twins' behavioral resemblance is in accord with their actual, not their mistaken, zygocity (Goodman & Stevenson, 1991; Scarr, 1968; Scarr & Carter-Saltzman, 1979). Third, in adoption studies, perceived family resemblances were found to be greater in biologically related than in adoptive families, but parents' and adolescents' perceived similarities were not related to measured resemblances on personality and IQ measures, although perceptions were related to similarities in social attitudes (Scarr, Scarf, & Weinberg, 1980). Thus, neither differential treatment nor perceived similarities seem to bias family resemblances in intelligence or personality.

It is hard to imagine a research design that could meet all of the actual and potential objections of socialization researchers. At least, adequate designs must include siblings with different degrees of genetic and environmental relatedness, if their hypotheses are to be tested at all. The outcome of rejecting informative results is that socialization theories are not, and cannot be, tested. Thus, socialization processes, as currently proposed, are not even scientific theories (Scarr, in press).

GENETICS AND INTERVENTIONS

Biology was thrown out of the social sciences in the 1920s for political reasons, because cultural and social explanation seemed to free humans from their animal natures and challenge the social and economic status quo. There is still considerable backlash against what some believe to be undesirable political implications of evolutionary and biological ideas (Degler, 1991). "The nature–nurture issue is inherently political with implications both for research funding priorities and public policy programs which may lean towards or away from analysis of the role of environmental factors in developmental outcomes and the search for interventions that promote optimal development" (Baumrind, personal communication, October 4, 1992).

The rejection of evolutionary and other biological thought in the social sciences has resulted in a seeming conflict between biological determinism and social improvement. Child developmentalists were and are concerned about the applications of knowledge to the betterment of humankind, especially the young. Biological, especially genetic, explanation appeared fatalistic: Biology was a dead-end destiny for the poor, for social outcasts, and for their generations to come. Social environmental explanations seemed to offer the hope of improvement within a single generation for the poor and outcast and bright futures for generations to come. Reform-minded social scientists embraced a kind of cultural explanation that excluded biology (Degler, 1991).

For political reasons, cultural and social environmental explanations replaced, rather than augmented, biological explanations of human behavior and development in the middle of the 20th century (Degler, 1991). Behaviorism, with its exclusive focus on proximal causes of learning, seemed to promise endless optimism about behavioral change. Given a properly executed reinforcement schedule, or proper habit training, any desirable developmental outcome was within reach for any child. Some psychologists, such as Frank Logan (1971), never abandoned evolutionary explanations of animal behavior; others, such as the Brelands (Breland & Breland, 1961), found that trained animals reverted to species-typical behaviors despite the best laid reinforcement schedules.

Behavior geneticists became an active minority in the social sciences in the 1960s, with the publication of the first textbook (Fuller & Thompson, 1960), and have continued to work on questions of individual variability in behavior and development on a path blazed by differential psychologists (Cronbach, 1957). It was not until 1975, with the publication of E. O. Wilson's monumental *Sociobiology*, that evolutionary biology directly challenged the hegemony of cultural/social environmentalism in the social sciences. But the social sciences have not yet accepted new knowledge from the biological sciences. Social reformers still oppose genetic and biological hypotheses because they believe they cause pessimism for social change.

> For psychologists, as for medical researchers, the purpose of identifying undesirable predispositions of individuals *should be* [italics added] to devise more effective health-promoting interventions, not to discourage such attempts on the supposition that these predispositions are *genetically based and therefore intractable* [italics added]. . . .Given limited resources, many socialization researchers choose to focus on those factors that are most susceptible to change — on how parents and educators can provide optimum environments for optimum development or optimum human behaviors. (Baumrind, 1993, p. 1313)

One can disagree both with the value assumptions of this statement and with its factual base. First, one might want to know the scientific truth about behavior and development per se, because deceit does not enhance the scientific enterprise. Second, if some predisposition were found to be "genetically based" (presumably, genetically variable), denying that result would not enhance intervention efforts. Third, genetic does not mean intractable! Baumrind herself offered several examples of treatments for genetic disorders, and the list of identified genetic disorders for which treatments are available, or nearly available, is growing enormously.

Like many socialization researchers. Baumrind seemed to fear the misuse of genetic information to discourage intervention efforts. Few would disagree that there is much to be done for children in this world, and perhaps doing anything is better than doing nothing. More optimistically, one would hope that more knowledge of genetic as well as nonshared environmental factors in development would help us to design and implement more effective intervention strategies — ones that could actually have some beneficial effects for the participants. To be effective, interventions must fit the needs of the participants. For children whose environments are very deprived or disrupted, we do not need further research to tell us that providing environmental opportunities in the normal, stable range will be beneficial.

For children whose environments are in the species- and culturally normal range (see Scarr, 1993), variation among children in intelligence and personality may or may not be affected by interventions that are planned without regard to genetic individuality (Buss, 1992). In some cases, through instruction, specific skill levels can be increased for a group, usually without affecting the distribution of individual differences. In other cases, resistance to intervention, with negligible to small but statistically significant effects, is more typical of the results from our best-laid intervention plans (Ramey & Ramey, 1990). One is hard pressed to think of a single social science intervention for people in ordinary environments that has had more than trivial effects.

The best evidence from behavior genetics (Plomin, 1990, 1994; Plomin & McClearn, 1993; Reiss et al., 1994; Scarr, 1993, in press; Wachs & Plomin, 1991) is that the human world is made up of genetic differences, nonshared experiences, and genotype-environment correlations, whereby people are born to, evoke, select, and create environments that are correlated with their own personalities and intelligence. Only in randomized experiments can these ubiquitous person–environment correlations be reduced or eliminated. Life is not a randomized trial.

What we observe to be correlations among family members results primarily from their genetic resemblance, not from any shared environments. To a great extent, each individual perceives, interprets, and gives private meaning to his or her own unique version of experience, regardless of how much the environment may be overtly shared with others. Although socialization researchers seem to favor gene–environment interactions (e.g., Baumrind, 1993), a closer look at what seem to be genotype or person × environment interactions often reveals correlations of environments with characteristics we have just discovered (Rowe & Waldman, 1993; Rutter & Pickles, 1991).

If we conceive of the environment as a broad set of opportunities that should be available to every developing person, then we will let each person select from that array of opportunities those experiences that are most compatible (interesting, satisfying, challenging) to his or her own personality and intelligence. Interventions, therefore, become assurances of opportunities and encouragement to make choices that are compatible with one's own characteristics. Ironically, the more socially and economically just a society is, the higher the heritabilities are for measured traits. Higher heritabilities of academic achievement were found with more equal educational opportunities in Norway (Sundet, Tambs, Magnus, & Berg, 1988), Denmark (Teasdale & Owen, 1985), Sweden (Fischbein, 1980; Pedersen, Plomin, Nesselroade, & McClearn, 1992; Thompson, Detterman, & Plomin, 1993), and the United States (Scarr, 1971, 1981). The heritability of educational achievements rose with more equal opportunities, whether the opportunities differences had been experienced by social class, gender, or ethnicity. More equal opportunities reduce arbitrary environmental differences, thereby highlighting genetic variability.

If we want a developmental theory that accounts for observations about family effects on children, it behooves us to include genetic variation, nonshared environments, and genotype-environment correlations. Evidence shows that family resemblances are due largely to genetic similarity among people born into the same families. Small common environmental effects — those due to being reared in the same family — have been found, and they would doubtlessly be larger if very deprived families were included. For most families in North American and European populations, however, environmental differences among them have very small effects on their children's development. If socialization researchers wish to dispute these conclusions, they must test their ideas with informative research designs. Advocacy for social reform cannot be substituted for scientific theory and research. Respect for individual diversity would be a desirable outcome of this debate.

REFERENCES

Baumrind, D. (1993). The average expectable environment is not good enough: A response to Scarr. *Child Development, 64*, 1299–1317.

Bouchard, T. J., Jr., Lykken, D. T., Tellegen, A., & McGue, M. (in press). Genes, drives, environment and experience: EPD theory — revised. In C. Benbow & D. Lubinski (Eds.), *From psychometrics to giftedness: Essays in honor of Julian Stanley.* Baltimore: Johns Hopkins University Press.

Bouchard, T. J., Jr., & McGue, M. (1990). Genetic and rearing environmental influences on adult personality: An analysis of adopted twins reared apart. *Journal of Personality, 58,* 263–292.

Breland, K., & Breland, M. (1961). The misbehavior of organisms. *American Psychologist, 16,* 681–684.

Bronfenbrenner, U., Lenzenweger, M. F., & Ceci, S. J. (1993). *Heredity, environment and the question "how?": A new theoretical perspective for the 1990s.* Unpublished manuscript.

Buss, D. M. (1992). *Strategic individual differences: The evolutionary psychology of selection, evocation, and manipulation.* Manuscript prepared for the Dahlem Workshop: What are the Mechanisms Mediating the Genetic and Environmental Determinants of Behavior?, Dahlem, Germany.

Cronbach, L. J. (1957). Two disciplines of scientific psychology. *American Psychologist, 12,* 671–684.

Degler, C. N. (1991). *In search of human nature: The decline and revival of Darwinism in American social thought.* New York: Oxford University Press.

Dobzhansky, T. (1941). *Genetics and the origin of species.* New York: Columbia University Press.

Ernst, S., & Angst, J. (1985). *Birth order.* Frankfurt: Springer-Verlag.

Fischbein, S. (1980). IQ and social class. *Intelligence, 4,* 51–63.

Fuller, J. , & Thompson, R. (1960). *Foundations of behavior genetics.* St Louis, MO: Mosby.

Goodman, R., & Stevenson, J. (1991). Parental criticism and warmth toward unrecognized monozygotic twins. *Behavior and Brain Sciences, 14*, 394–395.

Gottlieb, G. (1976). Conceptions of prenatal behavior: Behavioral embryology. *Psychological Review, 83*, 215–234.

Gottlieb, G. (1991). Experiential canalization of behavioral development: Theory. *Developmental Psychology, 27*(1), 4–13.

Hoffman, L. W. (1991). The influence of family environments on personality: Accounting for sibling differences. *Psychological Bulletin, 110*, 187–203.

Jackson, J. K. (1993). Human behavioral genetics, Scarr's theory, and her views on interventions: A critical review and commentary on their implications for African American children. *Child Development, 64*, 1318–1332.

Jang, K. L. (1993). *A behavioral genetic analysis of personality, personality disorder, the environment, and the search for sources of nonshared environmental influences.* Unpublished doctoral dissertation, The University of Western Ontario, London, Ontario.

Loehlin, J. C., & Nichols, R. C. (1976). *Heredity, environment, and personality.* Austin: University of Texas Press.

Loehlin, J. C., & Rowe, D. R. (1992). Genes and environment and personality development. In G. L. Capara & G. L. Van Heck (Eds.), *Modern personality psychology: Critical reviews and new directions* (pp. 353–370). New York: Harvester/Wheatsheaf.

Logan, F. (1971). The snark is a boojum. *American Psychologist, 26*, 143–150.

Mayr, E. (1970). *Populations, species, and evolution.* Cambridge, MA: Harvard University Press.

McCartney, K., Harris, M. J., & Bernieri, F. (1990). Growing up and growing apart: A developmental meta-analysis of twin studies. *Psychological Bulletin, 107*, 226–237.

Pedersen, N. L., Plomin, R., Nesselroade, J. R., & McClearn, G. E. (1992). A quantitative genetic analysis of cognitive abilities during the second half of the lifespan. *Psychological Science, 3*, 346–353.

Plomin, R. (1990). The role of inheritance in behavior. *Science, 248*, 183–188.

Plomin, R. (1994). *Genetics and experience: The interplay between nature and nurture.* Thousand Oaks, CA: Sage.

Plomin, R. (in press). Nature, nurture, and development. In R. J. Sternberg (Ed.), *Encyclopaedia of human intelligence.* New York: Macmillan.

Plomin, R., & Bergeman, C. (1991). The nature of nurture: Genetic influences on "environmental" measures. *Behavior and Brain Sciences, 14*, 414–424.

Plomin, R., & Daniels, D. (1987). Why are children in the same family so different from one another? *Behavioral and Brain Sciences, 10*, 1–60.

Plomin, R., Loehlin, J. C., & DeFries, J. C. (1985). Genetic and environmental components of "environmental" influences. *Developmental Psychology, 21*, 391–402.

Plomin, R., & McClearn, G. E. (Eds.). (1993). *Nature, nurture, and psychology.* Washington, DC: American Psychological Association.

Plomin, R., McClearn, G. E., Pedersen, N. L., Nesselroade, J. R., & Bergeman, C. S. (1989a). Genetic influences on adults' ratings of their current environment. *Journal of Marriage and the Family, 51*, 791–803.

Plomin, R., McClearn, G. E., Pedersen, N. L., Nesselroade, J. R., & Bergeman, C. S. (1989b). Genetic influence on childhood family environment perceived retrospectively from the last half of the lifespan. *Developmental Psychology, 24*, 738–745.

Plomin, R., & Neiderhiser, J. M. (1992). Genetics and experience. *Current Directions in Psychological Science, 1*, 160–164.

Ramey, C. T., & Ramey, S. L. (1990). Intensive educational intervention for children of poverty. *Intelligence, 14*(1), 1–9.

Reiss, D., Plomin, R., Hetherington, E. M., Howe, G., Rovine, M., Tryon, A., & Stanley, M. (1994). The separate world of teenage siblings: An introduction to the study of the nonshared environment and adolescent development. In E. M. Hetherington, D. Reiss, &

R. Plomin (Eds.), *Separate social worlds of siblings: Impact of nonshared environment on development*. Hillsdale, NJ: Lawrence Erlbaum Associates.

Rowe, D. C. (1981). Environmental and genetic influences on dimensions of perceived parenting: A twin study. *Developmental Psychology, 17*, 203–208.

Rowe, D. C. (1983). A biometrical analysis of perceptions of family environment: A study of twin and singleton sibling kinships. *Child Development, 54*, 416–423.

Rowe, D. (1994). *The myth of family influences*. New York: Guilford.

Rowe, D., & Waldman, I. D. (1993). The question "how" reconsidered. In R. Plomin & G. E. McClearn (Eds.), *Nature, nurture, and psychology*. Washington, DC: American Psychological Association.

Rutter, M., & Pickles, A. (1991). Person–environment interactions: Concepts, mechanisms, and implications for data analysis. In T. D. Wachs & R. Plomin (Eds.), *Conceptualization and measurement of organism–environment interaction*. Washington, DC: American Psychological Association.

Scarr, S. (1968). Environmental bias in twin studies. *Eugenics Quarterly, 15*, 34–40.

Scarr, S. (1971). Race, social class, and IQ. *Science, 174*, 1285–1295.

Scarr, S. (1981). *Race, social class and individual differences in IQ*. Hillsdale, NJ: Lawrence Erlbaum Associates.

Scarr, S. (1992). Developmental theories for the 1990s: Development and individual differences. *Child Development, 63*, 1–19.

Scarr, S. (1993). Biological and cultural diversity: The legacy of Darwin for development. *Child Development, 64*, 1333–1353.

Scarr, S. (in press). Socialization and behavior genetic theories of intelligence: Truce and reconciliation. In R. J. Sternberg & E. Grigorenko (Eds.), *Intelligence: Heredity and environments*. New York: Cambridge University Press.

Scarr, S., & Carter-Saltzman, S. L. (1979). Twin method: Defense of a critical assumption. *Behavior Genetics, 9*, 527–542.

Scarr, S., & Grajek, S. (1982). Similarities and differences among siblings. In M. E. Lamb & B. Sutton-Smith (Eds.), *Sibling relationships* (pp. 357–381). Hillsdale, NJ: Lawrence Erlbaum Associates.

Scarr, S., & McCartney, K. (1983). How people make their own environments: A theory of genotype→environment effects. *Child Development, 54*, 424–435.

Scarr, S., & Ricciuti, A. (1991). What effects do parents have on their children? In L. Okagaki & R. J. Sternberg (Eds.), *Determiners of development* (pp. 3–23). Hillsdale, NJ: Lawrence Erlbaum Associates.

Scarr, S., Scarf, E., Weinberg, R. A. (1980). Perceived and actual similarities in biological and adoptive families: Does perceived similarity bias genetic influence? *Behavior Genetics, 10*, 445–458.

Scarr, S., & Weinberg, R. A. (1978). The influence of "family background" on intellectual attainment. *American Sociological Review, 43*, 674–692.

Sundet, J. M., Tambs, K., Magnus, P., & Berg, K. (1988). On the question of secular trends in the heritability of intelligence: A study of Norwegian twins. *Intelligence, 12*, 47–59.

Teasdale, T. W., & Owen, D. R. (1985). Heredity and familial environment in intelligence and educational level—a sibling study. *Nature, 309*, 620–622.

Thompson, L. A., Detterman, D. K., & Plomin, R. (1993). Cognitive abilities and scholastic achievement: Genetic overlap but environmental differences. *Psychological Science, 3*, 158–165.

Turkheimer, E., & Gottesman, I. I. (1991). Individual differences and the canalization of human behavior. *Developmental Psychology, 27*, 18–22.

Wachs, T. D. (1992). *The nature of nurture: Vol. 3. Individual Differences and Development Series*. Newbury Park, CA: Sage.

Wachs, T. D. (1993). The nature–nurture gap: What we have here is a failure to collaborate.

In R. Plomin & G. McClearn (Eds.), *Nature, nurture, and psychology*. Washington, DC: American Psychological Association.

Wachs, T. D., & Plomin, R. (Eds.). (1991). *Conceptualization and measurement of organism-environment interaction*. Washington, DC: American Psychological Association.

Wilson, E. O. (1975). *Sociobiology*. Cambridge, MA: Harvard University Press.

2

On the Mismatching of Levels of Abstraction in Mathematical–Statistical Model Fitting

John R. Nesselroade
John J. McArdle
University of Virginia

In "Are Theories of Learning Necessary?", Skinner (1950) used the term *theory* to refer to "any explanation of an observed fact which appeals to events taking place somewhere else, at some other level of observation, described in different terms, and measured, if at all, in different dimensions" (p. 193). Skinner thus identified several levels of abstraction between observable events and the explanations for those events, and he questioned the value of such multilevel explanatory systems. Hebb (1949), Reese and Overton (1970), and others elucidated the formal representations and empirical requirements for a "model." Cattell (1966b, 1966c) discussed the form of a model, especially one based on formal mathematical and statistical features (see also Leamer, 1978; Salmon, 1971). Following these latter notions we presume that there is merit in fitting abstract models to empirical data, but we take a critical look at some issues that arise because of the involvement of model fitting with different levels of abstraction of concepts and relationships.

The Growth of Model Fitting

Mathematical–statistical model fitting of data was given considerable attention in the 1940s and 1950s. Although modeling seemed to be a major "growth industry" in physics, chemistry, economics, and biology it did not become so in psychology and sociology until the later 1960s. The delay is somewhat surprising because the need was certainly there — the problems facing psychology and sociology were no simpler than those in the other disciplines. Doubtless, there were many reasons for this longer lag time, one of which was the lack of sufficiently powerful computational machinery available to the interested psychologist and sociologist. Another was the deeply entrenched research and graduate training focus on using data to reject or accept null hypotheses rather than to assess the plausibility and goodness of fit of explanatory models (Cohen, 1994; Morrison & Henkel, 1970; Mosteller & Tukey, 1977). Since the 1960s, we have witnessed a surge of interest in mathematical–statistical modeling of behavioral and social science phenomena. Increased interest in mathematical–statistical modeling is as evident in the study of development and change as it is in any area of psychology. Indeed, students of development are participating actively in a stunning increase in both the amount of mathematical–statistical modeling and in the level of comprehensiveness and sophistication of its use (see, e.g., Bollen & Long, 1993; Collins & Horn, 1991; Connell & Tanaka, 1987; Hertzog & Schaie, 1988; Horn & McArdle, 1980).

Instead of going to the "calculator room" as was common in the 1940s and 1950s or the "comp center" as was the case in the 1960s and 1970s, we now sit in our own offices before our private video display terminal and "estimate models." Attracted as if by electronic pheromones, modelers fly with abandon to their consoles and attach themselves, separating when they are convinced that another important line of work has been perpetrated. Perhaps this development is not too surprising. After all, the personal computer that now appears on any secretary's desk is more than 100 times more powerful than those of the largest computer centers of the late 1960s, and the software is far more "user friendly." Perhaps even more important, granting agencies are not reluctant to fund such activities.

The quite noticeable changes in our observable mathematical–statistical modeling behavior have included important alterations in the way data analyses are conceptualized and discussed. From some quarters, there has been a strong push away from loosely defined analytical models in favor of those that are more explicitly and precisely specified. For example, models that in the past were called analyses of variance and exploratory factor analyses, even at times with some reverence, are now often denigrated by reviewers. Some of the the more respectful critics point out that these models are instances of saturated linear comparisons and unrestricted factor analyses (McArdle & Nesselroade, 1994). Rotationally indeterminant factor models now often are supplanted by highly constrained comparisons and what are loosely labeled "confirmatory factor analysis " models. Instead of testing hypothesized "no differences," more and more investigators are now testing the goodness of fit between a precisely specified model and empirical data, examining how satisfactorily that model accounts for variation in variables of theoretical interest and providing confidence boundaries around these statements.

Although the newer modeling and estimation procedures continue to be confined largely to relatively simple linear, additive models, their capabilities for representing more complex relationships (e.g., incorporating nonlinear constraints in the specification of the models being fitted) are growing. Indeed, the current formulations and accompanying computational machinery are quite impressive, even by 1990 standards. Despite the elegance of the methods and techniques available for representing reality in mathematical and statistical models, however, it is important to remember that mathematical and statistical modeling procedures are the tools and not the craftsmen; they are the instruments and not the musicians. As with quality tools and fine musical instruments, full realization of the promise of these analytic devices requires a high level of familiarity and knowledge on the part of users. The more skillfully these implements are used, the more impressive and valuable are the outcomes that they help to produce, and the greater will be the gains from applying them to substantive problems and issues. Thus, the old adage, "technology does not produce science," continues to accrue validity.

Focus of the Chapter

A benefit of the currently available modeling innovations has been that users are forced to provide an explicit rendering of hypothesized interrelationships among implicated concepts and variables in order to invoke the computational machinery that yields estimates of the model's parameters. A drawback, however, is that even "half-baked" notions can be lent an air of considerable respectability when put in the guise of an explicit model, just as a mediocre composition can be made to sound acceptable (or at least better) when performed on fine musical instruments by a competent, formally attired orchestra.

The primary objective of this chapter is to identify and discuss selected matters that we believe are germane to the productive application of mathematical–statistical model fitting procedures. The ideas that we emphasize have substantial histories in the psychological literature (e.g., attitude–behavior and treatment–outcome relationships) from which important lessons can be learned, but in the contemporary modeling context, these discussions have not yet received the attention that we believe they merit.

Our principal contention is that one of the activities necessary to realize the best that current mathematical–statistical modeling procedures have to offer is to attend explicitly to the matter of tailoring concepts to relational statements in regard to their levels of abstraction. The tailoring must take into account one's theory-driven objectives. In current parlance, the tailoring is an aspect of model specification. It is on this matter that we try to center the present discussion most directly. Admittedly, there is likely to be an iterative, successive approximation character to any fruitful application of modeling procedures in a given substantive domain as theory and data are used to exploit each other (Cattell, 1966c; Leamer, 1978). But persistence in the efforts to forge stronger and stronger links both between observable and latent variables and among latent variables is a key element of scientific research and a constant reminder that validation of models is a never-ending process.

Consider some common examples of what we mean by levels of abstraction of concepts and relationships and the matter of mismatch between them. One does not attempt to explain the workings of a radio or television set to a 4-year-old child using concepts such as differences in potential, micromhos of conductance, or phase shifts. Such concepts are not a good match to relationship statements of the form "the signal goes in there and the sound comes out here." As central as the abstract concepts are to the design of electronic circuitry, their level of abstraction is not suited to the conceptual machinery of the 4-year-old. Similarly, one does not recite principles of lift and drag to a 6-year-old child who is experiencing difficulty keeping a kite aloft. Depending on the child's age, this kind of explanation may come later when the kite is lost and the child is trying hard to hold back the flow of tears. In some sense, the child's behavior determines the appropriate level of explanation, but how do we know just what is appropriate in a given circumstance?

To take yet another example, when one is trying to construct an explanatory account of dividend size for stockholders, it seems far more appropriate to focus on the relationship between magnitude of a company's annual stock dividend and its amount of annual sales than between magnitude of the annual stock dividend and annual level of "extraversion" of members of the sales force. Even if extraversion is a valuable component of successful selling, the relational coefficient between it and annual sales is certainly not the most appropriate parameter estimate to report to disappointed stockholders (unless they all happen to be differential psychologists). Here, we usually count on the stockholders to tell us if we are at an appropriate level of explanation.

The value of a mathematical–statistical model rests to a considerable extent on the match between the structural model (e.g., a structural–causal set of relationships) and the latent variables to which it is being applied. Are the substantive concepts at the optimal level of abstraction for the nature of the relationships embodied in the structural model? Such a question underscores the important role that latent variables play in using abstract relationships to account for observable manifestations. But such relationships are what theory is about. How do we know when we have achieved a "good" match? Usually we only have the consensus of a local group of scholars. However, we do have at least one superordinate concept—

factorial invariance (McArdle & Cattell, 1994; Meredith, 1964, 1993; Thurstone, 1957)—that can be used both as a hammer (to impose conditions that data may or may not meet) and as a chisel (to separate quantitative and qualitative differences and changes) in shaping models of reality from the standpoint of matching of levels of abstraction. Other promising tools and concepts are mentioned later in the chapter.

In model building and theory testing there should be deliberate, explicit concern for possible discrepancies among levels of abstraction and for the implications of those discrepancies. Admittedly, what are discrepancies for one purpose might not be for another. We offer some examples that illustrate the importance of the match in levels of abstraction and examine the concepts in relation to three areas that are germane to the interests of developmentalists where mathematical–statistical modeling is prevalent — factor analysis, personality measurement, and behavior genetics.

On purely technical grounds, we acknowledge that the match of levels of abstraction of concepts and relationships might not be critical per se to the estimation process. As long as the model is identified, generally its parameters can be estimated, regardless of how ill-specified the model might be (e.g., McArdle & Prescott, 1992). Interpreting the level of model–data congruence in relation to the further elaboration of explanatory frameworks is another story. The match between levels of abstraction is critical to the interpretation and evaluation of the outcome of the model fitting exercise, the further evolution and elaboration of an explanatory scheme, and the advancement of an area. In common parlance, "Sure, it can be estimated, but can sense be made out of it?" What we aim to do is to point the way to more deliberate exploration of the matter of match between levels of abstraction in concepts and relationships to help further the use of model fitting in applications of particular interest to developmentalists.

COMPLETENESS OF DATA USED IN MODELING SCHEMES

Before proceeding to a more systematic examination of examples pertinent to the notion of match between the levels of abstraction of concepts and relationships found in the psychological literature, we briefly consider some more general aspects of the empirical substrate of model fitting. These concerns are addressed for the purpose of laying useful groundwork for subsequent consideration of the levels of abstraction issues that follow.

The data used in modeling schemes arise in the context of a research design, however well or poorly conceived it may be. Elsewhere, the concepts of selection and selection effects (Aitken, 1934; Lawley, 1943–1944; Meredith, 1964, 1993; Pearson, 1903) have been used to emphasize the fact that empirical research always involves limited (selected) data and that the resulting selection effects impinge on the inferences one draws from those data (Horn & McArdle, 1992; McArdle, 1994, 1995; McArdle & Cattell, 1994; McArdle & Nesselroade, 1994; Nesselroade, 1983, 1991a; Nesselroade & Jones, 1991). Here we briefly review the key arguments in relation to the concerns of the present chapter.

The principal idea is that research design is a multimodal selection operation, the modalities of which are persons, variables, and occasions of measurement and other bounding dimensions of the data manifold described by Cattell (1952b, 1966a). The specific array of data obtained in a given empirical study is the product of a set of selection operations defined on one or more of these modalities. The general idea is portrayed in Fig. 2.1. When empirical data are collected, they are invariably selected from a vast universe of potential observations. As a consequence of the selection operations that define a specific collection of data, the obtained data

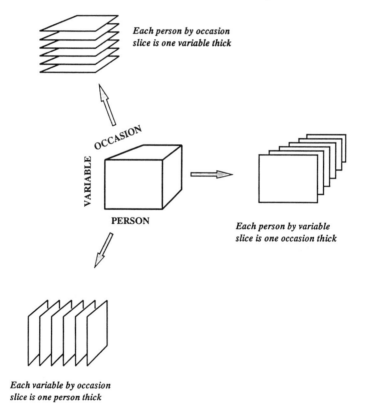

FIG. 2.1.   Research design and data collection: "Slicing" the data box.

inevitably harbor selection effects with respect to those dimensions along which selection occurred. On the one hand, these selection effects jeopardize the external validity of the conclusions one reaches about relationships from an examination of those data. On the other hand, a better understanding of their nature may enable investigators to design research with deliberately placed "holes" for more economical but still valid data collection (for a review, see McArdle, 1994).

Suppose one's data are derived from a design that involves a large, exquisitely representative sample of persons. Such representative sampling with respect to persons is very expensive, so typically one must compromise with regard to other data modalities, for example, by using a minimum set of variables to identify key concepts or measuring the persons only one time. A large scale survey, for instance, might involve measuring broad-gauge concepts such as anxiety or extraversion with two or three self-report items. The resulting data are very narrowly selected with respect to the variables dimension of the data box, and this variable selection jeopardizes estimates of relationships of anxiety or extraversion thus measured to other concepts and variables. Hence, the matter of levels of abstraction of concepts is inextricably tied to the concerns of selection of data with respect to choice of variables. Just as obviously, data reflecting only one time of measurement (cross-sectional data) are very narrowly selected with respect to the occasions dimension of the data box, and the selection effects that inhere in the data because of the severe selection with respect to time virtually eliminate meaningful discussion of stability and change and curtail the discovery of time-based relationships among the variables.

We elaborate a little more concerning each of the three selection modalities: persons, variables, and occasions of measurement. It is selection with respect to the variables dimension of the data box that leads most directly into the issues of concern for this chapter, although from the perspective of a developmentalist, it is difficult to exaggerate the threat of selection effects due to selection with respect to the occasions dimension.

Person Selection

Whether one uses convenience samples or broadly constituted ones, unless some representative sampling scheme is employed, the data that are used in model fitting will reflect the effects of selection with respect to persons. These effects, in turn, can affect the model-fitting process in a variety of ways. We need not say much more about selection with respect to the persons dimension of the data box here. It is with respect to this modality of selection that researchers seem to be the most sensitive and for which the most notable progress has been made in specifying how adjustments can be made in current modeling practice (e.g., Berk, 1983; Heckman, 1979; Heckman & Robb, 1986; Muthèn, 1984; Rubin, 1987).

Variable Selection

It is with respect to the variables dimension of the data box that selection effects may well take their greatest toll with respect to model-fitting exercises, in part because the tools for assessing and correcting for such selection effects are not nearly as well articulated and rigorous as they are for the effects due to selection with respect to the persons dimension of the data box. In the case of latent variable modeling, the appropriateness of the choices of observed variables or indicators to mark the latent variables has long been understood to dictate the limits of usefulness and generality of the model-fitting outcomes (e.g., Cattell, 1952a). Moreover, the omission of key variables from model specification and observation is known to bias the remaining parameter estimates in deleterious ways (e.g., Goldberger, 1972). The mathematical and statistical tools for minimizing the effects of these problems may still be somewhat deficient, but the general issue of how to build strong, convincing links between observed and unobserved variables — and thereby among unobserved variables — has been a concern for many decades (e.g., Cattell, 1952b; Humphreys, 1962; Thurstone, 1938).

Occasion Selection

Many important concepts and relationships are defined in relation to time, a fact that pertains to their levels of abstraction. Elsewhere (Nesselroade, 1983; Nesselroade & Jones, 1991), it has been argued that, for developmentalists, selection with respect to occasions of measurement is one of the most influential aspects of research design. A single occasion of measurement, for example, as in cross-sectional research designs, represents an extreme case of selection with respect to the occasions modality of the data box. Indeed, from this perspective, one of the primary differences between cross-sectional and longitudinal research designs is the degree of severity of selection with respect to occasions. Regarding selection with respect to occasions, cross-sectional and longitudinal designs can be argued to be quantitatively, but not qualitatively, different.

A simple longitudinal design of two occasions of measurement (e.g., pre–post designs) represents a slightly more generous selection of data with respect to the occasions modality — but how much more generous is it? According to Rogosa (1988), it may not be much more generous in the framework of conventional panel designs. But if the two times of measurement are selected with differing time lags, the limitations can be diminished (see McArdle & Woodcock, 1996). The nature of selection with respect to the occasions dimension of the data box and the accompanying selection effects has not yet been formulated with the level of mathematical and statistical rigor as is the case for selection with respect to the persons modality, but the general selection formulations implicate it as a serious design concern.

MATCHES AND MISMATCHES IN LEVELS OF ABSTRACTION

Factor Analytic Models

A distinction found in the modeling literature that bears directly on the matter of levels of abstraction has been referred to as the measurement versus the structural model (e.g., Jöreskog & Sörbom, 1979) and as the outer model versus the inner model (e.g., Lohmöller, 1989; Wold, 1975). The measurement or outer model, which links manifest and latent variables, by definition involves concepts at different levels of abstraction. The structural or inner model consists of the latent variables and the relational statements among them. The distinction between measurement and structural or inner and outer models is not required for purely mathematical or statistical reasons per se (for proof, see McArdle & McDonald, 1984), but there is no doubt that the distinction is a fundamental aspect of contemporary modeling philosophy. Without this particular difference in level of abstraction, modeling by means of latent variables would have no future because there would be no way to devise empirical tests of deductions stemming from the model.

Examples to be presented later involve both measurement and structural aspects of modeling. In the measurement model case, the presence of different levels of abstraction of concepts and variables is understood; indeed, it is a deliberate feature of the modeling. Nevertheless, the possible range of matches between levels of abstraction of concepts, variables, and the relational statements connecting them is wide and deserves explicit discussion. The structural or inner model is very much at the center of the issues on which we are focusing.

The relationships between latent and manifest variables are reflected in regession-like weights (e.g., factor loadings) in some cases and in correlation coefficients (e.g., factor structure values) in others (see, e.g., McArdle, 1994). The factor analytic literature since the 1940s contains some of the most enlightening discussions of the measurement model. The discussions are found in that literature because one of the primary uses of factor analysis is to examine relationships between observed and latent variables (e.g., the information contained in the factor pattern and factor structure matrices). This venerable goal remains salient today despite great advances in the methods and techniques of factor analysis (McArdle & Cattell, 1994).

To get a fix on the key issues, it is useful to remind ourselves of what was being attempted by factor analysts in the middle decades of the 20th century. In brief, many of them were trying to specify certain content areas and to delineate a basic set of dimensions—a reference frame—that spanned those content domains, for example, as general traits of interindividual differences in human abilities. Some content areas (e.g., human abilities) were broad in conception; others were relatively narrow (e.g., honesty). In personality research, for example, investigators such as Cattell (1950), Eysenck (1952), and Guilford (1959) sought to identify major personality dimensions that "spanned the space" of personality. Indeed, this general line of inquiry continues even today as witnessed by contemporary efforts to clarify further the nature and generality of the "Big Five" personality traits (e.g., Goldberg, 1993; McCrae, 1989; cf. Block, 1995; Mershon & Gorsuch, 1988).

Illustrative is the work of Raymond B. Cattell (1950, 1957), who over 6 decades has been intent on unearthing a set of basic dimensions or factors from a domain of observable variables to represent human personality (see, e.g., Angleitner, 1991). Cattell had to address two major problems before factor analysis could be used to approach this task efficiently. The first was the circumscription of the domain of content, and the second was the inclusion of that content in a representative manner in empirical research. Cattell argued that "everyday" language was the place to start in defining the domain of personality because it would mirror all the important aspects of behavior (e.g., all those aspects noticeable enough to have earned a verbal label). This argument is now referred to as *the lexical hypothesis* (Goldberg, 1990). Cattell took the extant list of more than 4,000 trait adjectives that had been compiled by Allport and Odbert (1936) as the first approximation to the domain—the *personality sphere.* These adjectives were the basis for developing the personality dimensions found, for example, in self-report measures such as the 16 Personality Factor (16PF) test (Cattell, Eber, & Tatsuoka, 1970) and were also used as the basis for a series of studies based on behavior ratings. Block (1995) summarized and critiqued Cattell's and others' efforts to determine personality structure by this approach.

Other researchers also have argued for the validity of content domain specification and representation in the establishment of psychological concepts (e.g., Cronbach & Meehl, 1955; Humphreys, 1962; Nunnally, 1967). Humphreys (1962), for example, argued that domain identification and representative sampling schemes such as Cattell developed were steps in the right direction but did not satisfactorily resolve the density and sampling of variables questions. He further elaborated the organization of domains and how the construction of measures should be based on principles that matched the level of abstraction of the variables to one's purposes. Humphreys illustrated the basic ideas using tools (saws, hammers, wrenches, etc.) as a domain and developed his arguments around familiar aspects of these items. His proposals gave further substance to the importance of distinguishing among levels of abstraction of concepts and their roles in relational statements. For instance, hand tools is a more inclusive class than either saws or wrenches. The manifest variable *number of teeth* is more sensibly related to the concept *saws* directly and to the concept *hand tools* indirectly by means of the saws concept, rather than directly related to hand tools. Although one could describe other handtools (e.g., wrenches) as having zero saw teeth, zero saw teeth in a wrench does not mean the same thing as zero saw teeth in a saw.

As we noted in the introductory section, the validity of a mathematical-statistical model rests somewhat on the match among the levels of abstraction of the structural model and the variables. We now turn to some other examples that further illustrate the importance of this match in levels of abstraction. To conclude, we examine these ideas specifically in relation to behavior genetics modeling.

There are many examples of matching (and mismatching) of levels of abstraction of concepts and relationships in the behavioral and social sciences. Because of its explicit mathematical–statistical properties, the factor analysis model was used previously to illustrate some key concepts pertinent to the theme of this chapter. We again draw from that literature to render more concrete the notion of disparity among levels of abstraction of concepts and relationships in the realm of mathematical–statistical modeling.

Personality Measurement

Through the application of the factor model, a number of important structural discoveries have been made, especially in the domains of temperament and human abilities. In the course of this work, a number of issues arose concerning the level of abstraction of concepts and relationships as they pertain to the modeling of observed variables. The theory of fluid and crystallized intelligence (Horn & Cattell, 1966), for example, resulted from dissatisfaction with the level of abstraction represented by Spearman's concept of general intelligence vis-à-vis that of actual test performance.

Different Levels of Abstraction. In the personality domain, Cattell (1957) distinguished among life-record (L) data, questionnaire (Q) data, and objective performance test (T) data as the products of three distinct and important media of observation employed by students of behavior. He argued that part of the proof of the fundamental nature of putative basic personality factors was that they would be detectable across the different observational media. Thus, he argued that one should be able empirically to align or "match" factors as the same whether they were obtained from L, Q, or T data. Cattell's initial attempts to provide this evidence of generality were challenged and the success of attempts to match personality factors across observational media was enthusiastically debated in the early 1960s (e.g., Becker, 1960; Cattell, 1961; Peterson, 1965).

In the aftermath of the discussions, there emerged a conception that illustrates the levels of abstraction notion very directly and that has helped considerably in the evaluation of subsequent personality and ability trait research. Cattell (1965) articulated a distinction between *order* and *stratum* in describing the nature of factors. Order had to do with the mechanics of factor analyzing data. The initial factors were first-order factors. If the intercorrelations of those first-order factors were themselves factored, the factors obtained were second-order factors, and so on. Stratum characterized the level of the factors in the theoretical scheme in which they were embedded. First-stratum factors, for instance, occupied the first level of abstraction in a theoretical scheme that linked multiple levels of factors to observable measures. Thus, depending on the level of abstraction represented in the variables being factor analyzed (e.g., single items vs. scale scores), one could obtain second-stratum factors in a first-order analysis or in a second-order analysis.

More concretely, what in Cattell's scheme were the second-stratum concepts of extraversion and anxiety could be obtained as first-order factors if one factored the scales (sums of item subsets) of the 16PF or as second-order factors if one factored the items of the 16PF. For example, the counterparts of the broad second-stratum factors of extraversion and anxiety that were found at the first order when T data were factored appeared at the second order when questionnaire items were factored. Thus, Cattell argued that until the proper level of abstraction of concepts (factor strata) was resolved, the theoretically specified relationships (factor isomorphism across media of observation) could not be evaluated against empirical data.

Consistency and Generality of Personality Traits.   Another example of the salience of matching levels of abstraction of concepts and relationships comes from the literature on trait consistency and generality. Characterizing the personality, attitudinal, and evaluation literature since the 1960s have been the debates about the small to middling correlations usually found between measures of personality traits and measures of behaviors purported to be influenced by those traits (e.g., Epstein, 1983; Epstein & O'Brien, 1985; Mischel, 1968; Mischel & Peake, 1982; Steyer, 1987; Steyer

& Schmitt, 1990), between expressed attitudes and behaviors (Fishbein & Ajzen, 1974), and between treatments and outcomes in evaluation research (Wittmann, 1988a, 1988b, 1991). Ranging through these discussions is a series of proposals and counter proposals concerning the role of data aggregation in empirical tests of the hypothesized linkages between broad dispositions and more specific behaviors in personality and attitudinal research and between generalized treatments and relatively specific outcomes in evaluation studies. Researchers have investigated the pros and cons of a variety of ways to aggregate information to explore the limits of these relationships. The issues have centered around aggregation of information in relation to different concepts of reliability and validity, and the exchanges among protagonists have helped to clarify a number of issues in important ways.

Various investigators have tried to formalize the nature of relationships across domains under appropriate aggregation of variables in ways that might lead to the expected relationships among different classes of variables. Wittmann's (1988a, 1988b, 1991) synthesis, which involves multiple data box representations and a multivariate generalization of the concept of reliability, emphasized the levels of abstraction issues under discussion. He used Brunswik's "lens model" to illustrate how *symmetry* and *asymmetry* apply to the matching of concepts in levels of abstraction when the objective is to optimize predictability.

Wittmann's argument is represented in Fig. 2.2. Empirical work supports Wittmann's (1988a, 1988b) contention that more symmetric choices of variables in regard to generality or level of abstraction on the antecedent and outcome sides of equations will lead to considerably stronger relationships. For example, from the domain of evaluation research, Wittmann illustrated how outcome criteria can be tailored to input variables to match them in level of abstraction and, thereby, yield correlations in the .70–.80 range instead of the usually found .20–.30 range. Wittmann's examples of mismatches include linking broad social programs on the treatment side with specific indicators on the outcome side or, equally unpromising, (mis)matching highly specific treatments with global measures of outcome.

More concretely, in relation to Fig. 2.2, health interventions might range from very national ones such as healthy behavior suggestions delivered via the mass media (e.g., as Level 3 predictors) through state-wide, school-based physical exercise programs (as Level 2 predictors) to local applications of fluoride in community water supplies (as Level 1 predictors). Examined outcomes might range from very general assessments of overall health via epidemiological statistics (e.g., as Level 3 criteria) to performance on physical fitness tests for teenagers (as Level 2 criteria) to incidence of tooth decay in children (as Level 1 criteria). Although the Level 3 teatment (mass media health suggestions) might exert some positive influence on the

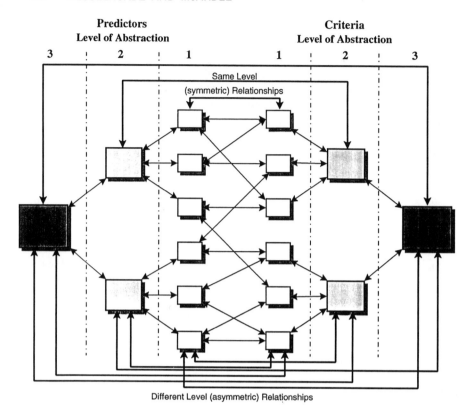

FIG. 2.2.   Symmetric and asymmetric relationships among levels of abstraction (after Wittmann, 1991).

Level 1 outcome (incidence of tooth decay in children), the relationship is bound to be less dramatic than that commonly reported between the introduction of fluoride and the incidence of tooth decay in children. By the same token, the local introduction of fluoride in water supplies cannot be expected to exert a major effect on general assessments of overall health.

More recently, Brody (1994) made arguments similar to Wittmann's regarding achieving increased estimates of heritability coefficients by means of more aggregation of measures. However, aggregation purely for the sake of increasing the magnitude of stability and other kinds of validity coefficients without concern for relationships that the very act of aggregation may be obscuring is naive. The literature on the trait-state distinction in personality research, for example, contains many examples of how extreme enthusiasm for high stability coefficients, sometimes obtainable by gross aggregation of scores over time, has tended to detract from the systematic examination of personality functioning (Nesselroade, 1988; Nesselroade & Boker, 1994).

Behavior Genetics Modeling

In the remainder of this chapter, we examine some issues of match and mismatch in a salient arena of application of mathematical-statistical modeling—behavior genetics. We draw attention explicitly to the levels of abstraction issue and examine the role it plays in estimating the parameters of pertinent models.

Since the 1970s, mathematical-statistical modeling has been increasingly used in behavior genetics research (e.g., Boomsma & Molenaar, 1986; Dolan, 1990; Martin & Eaves, 1977; McArdle & Goldsmith, 1990; Neale & Cardon, 1992). Some part of this increase is due to the ease with which both simple and complex biometric genetic models can be fitted to data using, for example, LISREL and other computer programs. Also, some part of the growth is due to a more general awareness of the potential value of genetic information as illustrated, for example, by the level of federal support received by the Human Genome Project.

Models of the impingement of genetic and environmental influences on phenotypic variables, some simple, some complicated and elaborate, have been fitted to both cross-sectional and longitudinal data. Not surprisingly, there have been disagreements concerning the use of behavior-genetic models for understanding behavioral and psychological phenomena, both statistically and substantively and in both stability and change contexts. It is our contention that the bases for some of the disagreements can be attributed to the levels of abstraction issues identified previously. What one researcher regards as an optimal combination of levels of abstraction is regarded by another to mix them up, thereby yielding peculiar information. We explore this notion, in part to see if some light can be shed on the future conduct of behavior genetics analysis of psychological/behavioral variables. A couple of examples clarify the importance of the matching of levels of abstraction ideas in the context of behavior genetics models.

Attitudes and Heritability.   Tesser (1993) analyzed responses to a series of attitude items in terms of relationships between the heritabilities of the responses to the items and other item characteristics including response latencies and resistance to change. He concluded that the data were consistent with an interpretation that attitudes manifesting higher heritabilities were "stronger" than attitudes of lower heritability. "Stronger" meant that pertinent items were responded to more quickly, were more difficult to change, and were more consequential in attraction among individuals.

Tesser (1993) asked rhetorically whether these data suggested that there is a gene for specific attitudes analogous to a gene for eye color. His answer was: "I doubt it. However, one can imagine a number of mechanisms by which more directly heritable physical differences might play themselves out in specific attitudes in a particular cultural milieu" (p. 139). Tesser identified sensory structures, body chemistry, intelligence, temperament and activity level, and conditionability as examples of more directly heritable differences. Thus, in relation to Fig. 2.2, Tesser identified several different levels of abstraction of concepts on the outcome side—for example, eye color versus conditionability versus attitudes—and identified those at one level (eye color) as more directly related to genetic influences than those found at other levels.

Televison Viewing and Heritability. Plomin, Corley, Defries, and Fulker (1990, 1992) and Prescott, Johnson, and McArdle (1991) had an exchange concerning the former's conclusions regarding behavior genetics modeling of the influences on television viewing in early childhood. Several aspects were highlighted, but the question of Prescott et al. (1991), "Does viewing time reflect passivity, need for stimulation, or some other characteristic of adaptive significance?" (p. 431), illustrates once more the issue of level of abstraction of concepts and the matter of matching them to the set of relationships being modeled. The response of Plomin et al. (1992), "Behavioral genetic research is a reasonable first step in answering questions about the origins of individual differences, and such research is heuristic, raising other interesting questions of the sort listed" (p. 76), reinforces the previous emphasis on the successive approximation and gradual model refinement that appear necessary to scientific advance.

The examples involving attitudes and heritability and television viewing and heritability highlight the following fact. The phenotypic variance of any variable that one chooses to study can be decomposed biometrically into different sources of variance and the results summarized with statements such as "x is largely genetic" or "y is largely environmental." Such decomposition of phenotypic variance into different sources is always possible regardless of the level of abstraction of the particular variable relative to the levels of abstraction of biological and other behavioral/psychological variables that might be implicated. As was mentioned earlier, parameters of identified models can be estimated, but interpretation of the estimates can require additional information. When levels of abstraction are mixed, it is possible that some relevant information will be confounded in misleading ways with the levels of measurement.

Just what outcomes, such as those described previously, mean in terms of mechanisms, levels of abstraction, and complexity of relationships is the kind of information that needs ultimately to be sought if behavior genetics analysis is to contribute in a major way to our understanding of ontogeny across the life span. Developing valid models of the interrelationships among biological and behavioral phenomena rests heavily on explicit regard for the matching of levels of abstraction of the relationships and their referent concepts on both the biological and behavioral sides.

Matching Levels of Abstraction.   What are the essential dimensions of concepts in relation to the questions being examined here? We have mentioned some existing taxonomies of abstractions that bear on the problem. These include the hierarchical and the reticular frameworks found in the factor analytic literature (Cattell, 1965) and the notions of symmetry and asymmetry discussed by Wittmann (1988a, 1988b, 1991). The general issue concerns how the matching of levels of abstraction of concepts bears on the fitting of behavior genetics models to data. Stated another way, what is the nature of the relationship between levels of abstraction of concepts and relationships and the interpretation of outcomes when behavior genetics models are fitted to behavioral and psychological variables? For example, given the current state of behavior genetics models with regard to levels of abstractions of the concepts on the antecedent side — genetic and environmental information — are there more or less appropriate levels of abstraction for variables on the outcomes (phenotypic) side? Which criteria can be developed for ascertaining the answer in a given circumstance?

These issues can be illustrated at several levels using the basic concepts of structural factor analysis illustrated in Fig. 2.3 and 2.4. At a first level, consider the standard univariate biometric model. As Fig. 2.3 illustrates, this model assumes that a measured variable (Y) is a function of three or more uncorrelated latent components: (a) additive genetic influences (A), (b) unspecified influences common (C) to all members of the same family, and (c) largely unspecified nongenetic or environmental influences including errors of measurement (E). Information from members of different family configurations (MZ and DZ twins, parents and children, adopted and biological family members, etc.) is used to estimate the parameters of

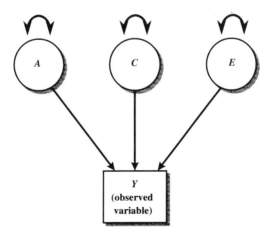

FIG. 2.3.   Univariate biometric model (A = additive genetic influences, C = unspecified influences common to members of the same family, E = largely unspecified nongenetic or environmental influences including errors of measurement).

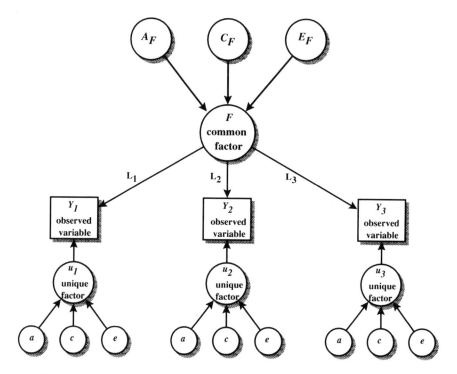

FIG. 2.4.   Multivariate psychometric common factor model (A_F = additive genetic influences on the common factor, C_F = unspecified influences that are common to members of the same family acting on the common factor, E_F = largely unspecified nongenetic or environmental influences including error of measurement acting on the common factor).

the model. The resulting parameters of the model are often reported directly or as a complex, explained variance ratio $\sigma^2_A/(\sigma^2_A + \sigma^2_C + \sigma^2_E)$, termed the *heritability coefficient*. The denominator of the heritability coefficient is directly assessable only in toto, as variance in the phenotype, with the component variances being estimable only indirectly.

As with the use of most complex mathematical–statistical models, the validity of statements about behavior genetic influences based on heritability estimates is subject to several concerns. The usual sampling limitations of any explained variance ratio apply to heritability, and confidence boundaries for the estimates are critical to their interpretation. Also, heritability estimates are obtained under multiple latent variable assumptions about orthogonality, linearity, homoscedasticity, covariances, and interactions. These assumptions are often untested and, in some cases, untestable, a limitation that is often ignored in subsequent discussions. Yet, it is on the basis of the heritability estimate that claims such as "x is largely genetic" or "y is largely environmental" that were mentioned previously are rested.

Most important, however, from the perspective of this chapter, is the fact that heritability estimates may be biased by the levels of abstraction involved in the modeling. To illustrate, consider the model that is presented in Fig. 2.4. This model renders explicit an additional level of abstraction by including the latent variable F (a common factor) between the two levels of abstraction that are represented in Fig. 2.3. For example, measures of primary mental abilities are commonly a focus of behavior genetics investigations. Considerable evidence exists (Horn & Cattell, 1966) that there is at least one additional level of abstraction — for example, fluid and crystallized intelligence factors — intervening between the ability test scores and the A, C, and E of Fig. 2.3 and 2.4. F in Fig. 2.4 is a function of the orthogonal A, C, and E, and the observed variables, Y_k, are functions of the common factor F with factor loadings, L_k, and their respective unique factors, u_k. If this model represents the "true" relationship among different levels of abstraction, then the parameter estimates of the model in Fig. 2.3 are statistically biased, and the heritability estimate would be biased as well.[1] The heritability of the common factor, which now contains no random measurement error (see McArdle & Goldsmith, 1990), depends on three influences A_f, C_f, and E_f. However, if this model is correctly specified, then the variance of any observed variable, Y_k, is also a function of the biometric components of the unique factor (which does contain random measurement error). For any Y_k, the degree to which the modeling approach represented in Fig. 2.3 approximates the values of those variances of interest shown in Fig. 2.4, namely A_f, C_f, and E_f, is a direct function of the size of the loading L_k. The common factor model represented in Fig. 2.4 can be falsified by a multivariate data set, but the univariate representation of Fig. 2.3 does not afford that scientifically desirable possibility. In general, only minor aspects of the univariate biometric model can be rejected at this level of measurement.

The factor-based model of Fig. 2.4 reflects one of the most fundamental concepts in behavioral analysis — all measured scores are composed, in part, of one or more common factors, and the common factors are involved in the chain of structural influences and effects. In this model, the common factors reflect the geneotypic and environmental influences, and these influences are measured in the observed variables in a way consistent with the strength of the relationship between the variables and the factors (for more details, see McArdle & Goldsmith, 1990). In the history of behavior genetic analyses, however, a variety of alternative multivariate models have been postulated. One classical alternative model (first presented by Loehlin

---

[1]The MATHEMATICA computer program for the symbolic evaluation of the bias in these models can be obtained as an ASCII file under the subdirectory \PUBLIC_ ACCESS\JRN\LEVELS1994 from the Anonymous FTP server at the University of Virginia (VIRGINIA.EDU).

& Vandenberg, 1968; Martin & Eaves, 1977) suggests that all variables are influenced by the same additive genetic factor (A) and some other (orthogonal) nongenetic factor (E). This biometric-factor concept might be an appropriate interpretation of the genotypic action at some level of abstraction. One interesting feature of these two models is that the psychometric genetic model (Fig. 2.4) requires parameters that are a subset of the biometric factors concept. Thus, these competing alternatives may be adequately tested at any well-defined level of measurement (for details, see McArdle & Goldsmith, 1990), and the test provides an important clue to the appropriate level of abstraction.

At any level of abstraction, however, the potential relationship between these kinds of latent variables and genetic information needs to be considered carefully (McArdle, 1994). Many examples of striking genotypic behavioral influences are reported in the literature (see any issue of the journal *Behavior Genetics*). Another often overlooked point is that the genetic information in a standard biometric model is obtained only as a latent "genotype" that is estimated under restrictive assumptions (orthogonality, linearity, homoscedasticity, no interactions, etc.). This level of evidence is not the same as, nor does it give the necessary empirical basis for, the existence of a "gene" in the sense defined and used in molecular biology. Behavioral geneticists have recognized this level of abstraction problem and made a first move toward a more fundamental level of analysis (e.g., DNA analysis using quantitative trait loci; Plomin et al., 1994) However, direct relationships between genetic information at low levels of abstraction (e.g., chromosomal information) and important behavioral tendencies, especially within the normal response range, at a higher level of abstraction remain to be demonstrated. This last statement is issued more as a challenge to, than an indictment of, those attempting to explore the biological/behavioral interface.

CONCLUSION

In concluding this chapter, there are several points that we wish to emphasize. Our emphases are intended to further the use of mathematical--statistical modeling in the social and behavioral sciences. Seen from the somewhat historical perspective we have tried to develop, there are reasons to be concerned with the matter of level of abstraction of concepts in relation to mathematical–statistical models and the implications that derive from them. These modeling procedures have moved us away from a focus on the null hypothesis to looking more at the production and evaluation of viable alternative hypotheses. This shift in emphasis has had several positive effects, including attracting more thought to the way even simple statistical analyses are conducted. For example, with proper design considerations, error variance can now be isolated so that estimates of interrelationships among variables are "automatically" corrected for attenuation due to measurement errors.

The examples we have mentioned from the personality domain illustrate several key points bearing on the present discussion. First, the history of psychology reflects concern with the question of matching level of abstraction between concepts and relationships in the development of formal mathematical–statistical models. Second, different configurations of abstraction levels in concepts and relational statements are possible and the choice can be guided by notions such as symmetry elaborated by Wittmann (1988a, 1988b, 1991) and others. Third, there is evidence to suggest that when, in light of one's purposes, an optimal match between levels of abstraction of concepts and relationships in modeling is sought, there can be striking increases in the strength of empirically estimated relationship. Unfortunately, no approach to determining an optimal match of levels of abstraction of concepts and relationships is generally accepted, although Wittmann's use of the concept of symmetry is promising in this regard. Moreover, some of the analytical tools discussed by Wittmann (1988b), such as set correlations, appear suited to evaluating the appropriateness of putative matches in levels of abstraction between predictors and criteria. These particular waters are being further "muddied" by indications that behavioral consistency may be found at the level of interindividual differences in patterns of intraindividual variability (Nesselroade, 1991b; Shoda, Mischel, & Wright, 1994)

We reiterate that aggregating information merely to maximize predictive validity is not the solution to every problem regarding aggregation. Deliberately specified differences in level of abstraction can be a key feature of modeling, as is the case, for example, of measurement models as referenced previously and in multitrait–multimethod analyses (e.g., Widaman, 1985).

From our perspective, one of the most valuable contributions that the structural modeling advances since the 1970s have given is the clarification of measurement issues and procedures by means of the measurement model and its distinction from the structural model in the framework of structural modeling programs. This has helped to clarify important issues of two of the pillars of modern psychological measurement — reliability and validity in their several guises (Cronbach & Meehl, 1955; McArdle & Prescott, 1992). Further, the formalization of the measurement model has made it possible to distinguish rigorously and explicitly among levels of abstraction in the concepts presumed to lie behind the observable measures.

There is no doubt that ascertainment of optimal levels of abstraction of concepts and relationships as discussed here is a part of the evolutionary stance we have to take with theory development in science. One has to find a "toe hold" and work from there. What we have tried to do is sensitize investigators to the idea that level of abstraction should be part of their conscious concerns when they are engaged in testing and improving their models. Having a testable hypothesis is an important concern whether the researcher is engaged in confirmatory or exploratory analysis. We believe, moreover, that testing hypotheses about the level of factorial invariance (abstraction) is among the most important experiments of all. Failing to be aware of this matter can seriously impede the development of better fitting models.

The evolutionary-developmental process of model elaboration has to include increased attention to the various modes of data selection discussed earlier. A given set of observable variables will mark some levels of abstraction much more validly than others. For example, medical doctors listen to self-reports of patients but tend not to act precipitously on those reports until they have supplemented them with other kinds of diagnostic information. Similarly, short shrift can no longer be given to the occasions dimension of the data box. Extending definitions and models over the repeated measurements dimension constitutes an important step toward the implementation of dynamic representations of interesting phenomena.

What do the next couple of decades hold for psychology with regard to mathematical–statistical modeling? Whether or not one accepts the progression of scientific maturation presented by West (1985), it is difficult for developmentalists to deny the appeal of being able to represent their substantive phenomena in rigorous dynamic formulations. And in fact, there are indications in the literature that mathematical dynamic representations of social and behavioral phenomena are just around the corner (e.g., Arminger, 1986; Baltes, 1987). Building and testing dynamic formulations of any meaning and significance involve, of necessity, mathematical-statistical modeling. Just as surely, these activities will force us to confront explicitly the matter of levels of abstraction in teaming concepts with relational statements.

ACKNOWLEDGMENTS

The generous support of the Max Planck Institute for Human Development and Education and the MacArthur Foundation Research Network on Successful Aging in the preparation of this manuscript is gratefully acknowledged by the first author. Research by the second author was supported by a grant from the National Institute on Aging (AG- 07137). We also thank Werner W. Wittmann for his valuable comments on an earlier version of the chapter.

REFERENCES

Aitken, A. C. (1934). Note on selection from a multivariate normal population. *Proceedings of the Edinburgh Mathematical Society, 4*, 106–110.

Allport, G. W., & Odbert, H. S. (1936). Trait names: A psycho-lexical study. *Psychological Monographs, 47,* (211), 1–171.

Angleitner, A. (1991). Personality psychology: Trends and developments. *European Journal of Personality, 5*, 185–197.

Arminger, G. (1986). Linear stochastic differential equation models for panel data with unobserved variables. In N. B. Tuma (Ed.), *Sociological methodology* (Vol. 16, pp. 187–213). Washington, DC: American Sociological Association.

Baltes, P. B. (1987). Theoretical propositions of life-span developmental psychology: On the dynamics between growth and decline. *Developmental Psychology, 23*(5), 611–626.

Becker, W. C. (1960). The matching of behavior rating and questionnaire personality factors. *Psychological Bulletin, 57*, 201–212.

Berk, R. A. (1983). An introduction to sample selection bias in sociological data. *American Sociological Review, 48*, 386–398.

Block, J. (1995). A contrarian view of the five-factor approach to personality description. *American Psychologist, 117*, 187–215.

Bollen, K. A., & Long, J. S. (1993). *Testing structural equation models*. Newbury Park, CA: Sage.

Boomsma, D. I., & Molenaar, P. C. M. (1986). Using LISREL to analyze genetic and environmental covariance structure. *Behavior Genetics, 16*, 237–250.

Brody, N. (1994). Heritability of traits. *Psychological Inquiry, 5*, 117–119.

Cattell, R. B. (1950). *Personality*. New York: McGraw-Hill.

Cattell, R. B. (1952a). *Factor analysis: An introduction and manual for the psychologist and social scientist*. New York: Harper.

Cattell, R. B. (1952b). The three basic factor analytic research designs — their interrelations and derivatives. *Psychological Bulletin, 49*, 499–520.

Cattell, R. B. (1957). *Personality and motivation structure and measurement*. Yonkers, NY: World Book.

Cattell, R. B. (1961). Theory of situational, instrument, second order, and refraction factors in personality structure research. *Psychological Bulletin, 58*, 160–174.

Cattell, R. B. (1965). Higher order factor structures and reticular-vs.-hierarchical formulae for their interpretation. In C. Banks & C. L. Broadhurst (Eds.), *Studies in psychology in honor of Sir Cyril Burt* (pp. 223–266). London: University of London Press.

Cattell, R. B. (1966a). The data box: Its ordering of total resources in terms of possible relational systems. In R. B. Cattell (Ed.), *Handbook of multivariate experimental psychology* (pp. 67–128). Chicago: Rand McNally.

Cattell, R. B. (1966b). The meaning and strategic use of factor analysis. In R. B. Cattell (Ed.), *Handbook of multivariate experimental psychology* (pp. 174–243). Chicago: Rand McNally.

Cattell, R. B. (1966c). Psychological theory and scientific method. In R. B. Cattell (Ed.), *Handbook of multivariate experimental psychology* (pp. 1–18). Chicago: Rand McNally.

Cattell, R. B., Eber, H. W., & Tatsuoka, M. M. (1970). *The 16 personality factor test handbook*. Champaign, IL: Institute for Ability and Personality Testing.

Cohen, J. (1994). The earth is round (*p* < .05). *American Psychologist, 49*, 997–1003.

Connell, J. P., & Tanaka, J. S. (Eds.). (1987). Special section on structural equation modeling. *Child Development 58*(1), 1–75.

Cronbach, L. J., & Meehl, P. (1955). Construct validity in psychological tests. *Psychological Bulletin, 52*, 281–302.

Dolan, C. V. (1990). *Biometric decomposition of phenotypic means in human samples.* Unpublished doctoral dissertation, University of Amsterdam, The Netherlands.

Epstein, S. (1983). Aggregation and beyond: Some basic issues on the prediction of behavior. *Journal of Personality, 51,* 360–392.

Epstein, S., & O'Brien, E. J. (1985). The person–situation debate in historical and current perspective. *Psychological Bulletin, 98,* 513–537.

Eysenck, H. J. (1952). *The scientific study of personality.* London: Routledge & Kegan Paul.

Fishbein, M. L., & Ajzen, I. (1974). Attitudes towards objects as predictors of single and multiple behavioral criteria. *Psychological Review, 81,* 59–74.

Goldberg, L. R. (1990). An alternative description of personality: The big-five factor structure. *Journal of Personality and Social Psychology, 59,* 1216–1229.

Goldberg, L. R. (1993). The structure of phenotypic personality traits. *American Psychologist, 48,* 26–34.

Goldberger, A. S. (1972). Structural equation models: An overview. In A. S. Goldberger & O. D. Duncan (Eds.), *Structural equation models in the social sciences* (pp. 1–18). New York: Academic Press.

Guilford, J. P. (1959). *Personality.* New York: McGraw-Hill.

Hebb, D. O. (1949). *The organization of behavior.* New York: Wiley.

Heckman, J. J. (1979). Sample selection bias as a specification error. *Econometrika, 45,* 153–161.

Heckman, J., & Robb, R. (1986). Alternative methods for solving the problem of selection bias in evaluating the impact of treatments on outcomes. In H. Wainer (Ed.), *Drawing inferences from self-selected samples* (pp. 63–107). New York: Springer.

Hertzog, C., & Schaie, K. W. (1988). Stability and change in adult intelligence: 2. Simultaneous analysis of longitudinal means and covariance structures. *Psychology and Aging, 3,* 122–130.

Horn, J. L., & Cattell, R. B. (1966). Refinement and test of the theory of fluid and crystallized intelligence. *Journal of Educational Psychology, 57,* 253–270.

Horn, J. L., & McArdle, J. J. (1980). Perspectives on mathematical/statistical model building (MASMOB) in research on aging. In L. W. Poon (Ed.), *Aging in the 1980s: Psychological issues* (pp. 503–541). Washington, DC: American Psychological Association.

Horn, J. L., & McArdle, J. J. (1992). A practical guide to measurement invariance in research on aging. *Experimental Aging Research, 18*(3), 117–144.

Humphreys, L. G. (1962). The organization of human abilities. *American Psychologist, 17,* 475–483.

Jöreskog, K. G,. & Sörbom, D. (1979). *Advances in factor analysis and structural equation models.* Cambridge, MA: Abt.

Lawley, D. N. (1943–1944). A note on Karl Pearson's selection formulae. *Proceedings of the Royal Society of Edinburgh* (Section A), *62,* 28–30.

Leamer, E. E. (1978). *Specification searches: Ad hoc inference with nonexperimental data.* New York: Wiley.

Loehlin, J. C., & Vandenberg, S. G. (1968). Genetic and environmental components in the covariation of cognitive abilities: An additive model. In S. G. Vandenberg (Ed.), *Progess in human behavior genetics* (pp. 261–285). Baltimore: Johns Hopkins University Press.

Lohmöller, J.-B. (1989). *Latent variable path modeling with partial least squares.* Heidelberg, Germany: Physica-Verlag.

Martin, N. G., & Eaves, L. J. (1977). The genetical analysis of covariance structures. *Heredity, 38,* 79–95.

McArdle, J. J. (1994). Factor analysis. In R. J. Sternberg (Ed.), *The encyclopedia of intelligence* (pp. 422–430). New York: Macmillan.

McArdle, J. J. (1995). Structural factor analysis experiments with incomplete data. *Multivariate Behavioral Research, 29*(4), 409–454.

McArdle, J. J., & Cattell, R. B. (1994). Structural equation models of factorial invariance in parallel proportional profiles and oblique confactor problems. *Multivariate Behavioral Research, 29*(1), 63–113.

McArdle, J. J., & Goldsmith, H. H. (1990). Alternative common factor models for multivariate biometric analyses. *Behavior Genetics, 20,* 569–608.

McArdle, J. J., & McDonald, R. P. (1984). Some algebraic properties of the Reticular Action Model for moment structures. *The British Journal of Mathematical and Statistical Psychology, 37,* 234–251.

McArdle, J. J., & Nesselroade, J. R. (1994). Structuring data to study development and change. In S. H. Cohen & H. W. Reese (Eds.), *Life-span developmental psychology: Methodological contributions* (pp. 223–267). Hillsdale, NJ: Lawrence Erlbaum Associates.

McArdle, J. J., & Prescott, C. A. (1992). Age-based construct validation using structural equation models. *Experimental Aging Research, 18*(3), 87–115.

McArdle, J. J., & Woodcock, R. W. (1996). *Extending test-retest data to examine developmental time-lag components.* Unpublished manuscript, Department of Psychology, University of Virginia.

McCrae, R. R. (1989). Why I advocate the five-factor model: Joint factor analyses of the NEO-PI with other instruments. In D. M. Buss & N. Cantor (Eds.), *Personality psychology: Recent trends and emerging directions* (pp. 237–245). New York: Springer.

Meredith, W. (1964). Notes on factorial invariance. *Psychometrika, 29,* 177–185.

Meredith, W. (1993). Measurement invariance, factor analysis and factorial invariance. *Psychometrika, 58,* 525–543.

Mershon, B., & Gorsuch, R. L. (1988). Number of factors in the personality sphere: Does increase in factors increase predictability in real-life criteria? *Journal of Personality and Social Psychology, 55*(4), 675–680.

Mischel, W. (1968). *Personality and assessment.* New York: Wiley.

Mischel, W., & Peake, P. K. (1982). Beyond déjà vu in the search for cross-situational consistency. *Psychological Review, 89,* 730–755.

Morrison, D. F., & Henkel, R. E. (Eds.). (1970). *The significance test controversy – A reader.* Chicago: Aldine.

Mosteller, F., & Tukey, J. W. (1977). *Data analysis and regression: A second course in statistics.* Reading, MA: Addison-Wesley.

Muthèn, B. (1984). A general structural equation model with dichotomous, ordered categorical and continuous latent variable indicators. *Psychometrika, 49,* 115–132.

Neale, M. C., & Cardon, L. R. (1992). *Methodology for genetic studies of twins and families.* Boston: Kluwer Academic.

Nesselroade, J. R. (1983). Temporal selection and factorial invariance in the study of development and change. In P. B. Baltes & O. G. Brim, Jr. (Eds.), *Life-span development and behavior* (Vol. 5, pp. 60–87). New York: Academic Press.

Nesselroade, J. R. (1988). Some implications of the trait-state distinction for the study of development over the life-span: The case of personality. In P. B. Baltes, D. L. Featherman, & R. M. Lerner (Eds.), *Life-span development and behavior* (Vol. 8, pp. 163–189). Hillsdale, NJ: Lawrence Erlbaum Associates.

Nesselroade, J. R. (1991a). Interindividual differences in intraindividual change. In L. M. Collins & J. L. Horn (Eds.), *Best methods for the analysis of change: Recent advances, unanswered questions, future directions* (pp. 92–105). Washington, DC: American Psychological Association.

Nesselroade, J. R. (1991b). The warp and the woof of the developmental fabric. In R. Downs, L. Liben, & D. S. Palermo (Eds.), *Visions of aesthetics, the environment, & development: The legacy of Joachim F. Wohlwill* (pp. 213–240). Hillsdale, NJ: Lawrence Erlbaum Associates.

Nesselroade, J. R., & Boker, S. M. (1994). Assessing constancy and change. In T. F.

Heatherton & J. L. Weinberger (Eds.), *Can personality change?* (pp. 121–147). Washington, DC: American Psychological Association.

Nesselroade, J. R., & Jones, C. J. (1991). Multi-modal selection effects in the study of adult development: A perspective on multivariate, replicated, single-subject, repeated measures. *Experimental Aging Research, 11*, 21–27.

Nunnally, J. C. (1967). *Psychometric theory*. New York: McGraw-Hill.

Pearson, K. (1903). On the influence of natural selection on the variability and correlation of organs. *Philosophical Transactions of the Royal Society of London* (Section A), *200*, 1–66.

Peterson, D. R. (1965). The scope and generality of verbally defined personality factors. *Psychological Review, 72*, 48–59.

Plomin, R., Corley, R., DeFries, J. C., & Fulker, D. W. (1990). Individual differences in television viewing in early childhood: Nature as well as nurture. *Psychological Science, 1*, 371–377.

Plomin, R., Corley, R., DeFries, J. C., & Fulker, D. W. (1992). Children's television viewing: Response to Prescott et al. *Psychological Science, 3*, 75–76.

Plomin, R., McClearn, G. E., Smith, D. L., Vignitti, S., Chorney, M. J., Chorney, K., Vendetti, C. P., Karsada, S., Thompson, L. A., Detterman, D. K., Daniles, J., Owen, M., & McGuffin, P. (1994). DNA markers associated with high versus low IQ: The IQ quantitative trait loci (QTL) project. *Behavior Genetics, 24*(2), 107–118.

Prescott, C. C., Johnson, R. C., & McArdle, J. J. (1991). Genetic contributions to television viewing. *Psychological Science, 2*, 430–431.

Reese, H. W., & Overton, W. F. (1970). Models of development and theories of development. In L. R. Goulet & P. B. Baltes (Eds.), *Life-span developmental psychology: Research and theory* (pp. 115–145). New York: Academic Press.

Rogosa, D. R. (1988). Myths about longitudinal research. In K. W. Schaie, R. T. Campbell, W. Meredith, & S. C. Rawlings (Eds.), *Methodological issues in aging research* (pp. 171–209). New York: Springer.

Rubin, D. B. (1987). *Multiple imputation for nonresponse in surveys*. New York: Wiley.

Salmon, W. C. (1971). *Statistical explanation and statistical relevance*. Pittsburgh, PA: University of Pittsburgh Press.

Shoda, Y., Mischel, W., & Wright, J. C. (1994). Intraindividual stability in the organization and patterning of behavior: Incorporating psychological situations into idiographic analysis of personality. *Journal of Personality and Social Psychology, 67*, 674–687.

Skinner, B. F. (1950). Are theories of learning necessary? *Psychological Review, 57*, 193–216.

Steyer, R. (1987). Konsistenz und Spezifitaet: Definition zweier zentraler Begriffe der Differentiellen Psychologie und ein einfaches Modell zu ihrer Identifikation [Consistency and specificity: Definition of two crucial concepts of differential psychology and a simple model for their identification]. *Zeitschrift für Differentielle und Diagnostische Psychologie, 8*, 245–258.

Steyer, R., & Schmitt, M. J. (1990). The effects of aggregation across and within occasions on consistency, specificity, and reliability. *Methodika, 4*, 58–94.

Tesser, A. (1993). The importance of heritability in psychological research: The case of attitudes. *Psychological Review, 100*, 129–142.

Thurstone, L. L. (1938). *Primary mental abilities*. Chicago: University of Chicago Press.

Thurstone, L. L. (1957). *Multiple factor analysis*. Chicago: University of Chicago Press.

West, B. J. (1985). *An essay on the importance of being nonlinear*. Berlin: Springer-Verlag.

Widaman, K. (1985). Hierarchically nested covariance structure models for multitrait-multimethod data. *Applied Psychological Measurement, 9*, 1–26.

Wittmann, W. W. (1988a, August). *Brunswik symmetry and successfully predicting human behavior*. Paper presented at the 24th International Congress of Psychology, Sydney, Australia.

Wittmann, W. W. (1988b). Multivariate reliability theory: Principles of symmetry and successful validation strategies. In J. R. Nesselroade & R. B. Cattell (Eds.), *Handbook of multivariate experimental psychology* (2nd ed., pp. 505–560). New York: Plenum.

Wittmann, W. W. (1991). Meta-analysis and Brunswik symmetry. In G. Albrecht & H.-U. Otto (Eds.), *Social prevention and the social sciences: Theoretical controversies, research problems, and evaluation strategies* (pp. 381–393). Berlin: deGruyter.

Wold, H. O. A. (1975). Path models with latent variables: The NIPALS approach. In H. M. Blalock, A. Aganbegian, F. M. Borodkin, R. Boudon, & V. Capecchi (Eds.), *Quantitative sociology: International perspectives on mathematical and statistical model building* (pp. 307–357). New York: Academic Press.

3 The Validity of Neuropsychological Assessment Procedures

Michael D. Franzen
*Department of Psychiatry
and Allegheny Neuropsychiatric Institute
Allegheny General Hospital, Pittsburgh*

Peter Arnett
Washington State University

Validity is a term often applied to tests, but as frequently noted, validity is best applied to the inferences drawn from tests rather than applied to the tests themselves. We can speak of the validity of neuropsychological assessment procedures if we expand our conception to include the interpretation process. That still leaves us with the question of whether the uses of neuropsychological test scores are valid. The question of validity cannot be answered outside this context of the application of the information derived from the scores.

The problem is whether the neuropsychological test scores are useful in answering the question at hand. Part of that problem involves the qualitative issue of whether the test data can efficiently and accurately answer the question. Another part of the problem is the extent to which the utility of the test scores outweighs their cost. That is, can the prediction be made in some alternate way that involves other data that are more cheaply acquired? As a corollary of that question, we must then evaluate the extent to which the unique predictive power of the test data increases the overall predictive power of other data including behavioral observations, demographic information, and even other neuropsychological test data. This last question is sometimes referred to as *incremental validity*. In this chapter, we consider traditional forms of validity and discuss two newer forms—*ecological validity* and *descriptive validity*. The implications for validity concerns of different periods in the development of individuals is also discussed.

FORMS OF VALIDITY

Traditionally, the validity questions have been subdivided into smaller categories. We speak of *face, criterion* (concurrent and predictive), *factorial*, and *construct*, among other forms.

Face Validity

Face validity refers to the perceptions of the participant, and to a lesser extent, to the perceptions of the consumer of the test information (Franzen, 1989). The perceptions of the participant may influence his or her motivation to perform at optimal levels. Face validity can be a more important consideration in the assessment of very young or older persons. The argument regarding younger participants is that only if the task is interesting to them will they put forth their best effort. Similarly, older participants may not perform as well as younger participants on standardized tests because the purpose of the test and the relation of the test to the participants' everyday lives is not apparent.

Increasing the face validity of a test would help obviate these problems. This aspect of validity is partly determined by asking participants about their subjective impressions. These impressions can be used in the design and development stages of test construction. Face validity plays a lesser role in the decision by clinicians to use a certain instrument, because professional clinicians are more likely to depend on empirical evidence. However, a lack of face validity may prevent a clinician from investigating the use of a certain instrument in the first place.

Criterion Validity

Concurrent and *predictive validity* refer to similar processes, but they are separated by time. Both concurrent and predictive validity are aspects of criterion validity, in which the test score must provide information regarding some external variable. In concurrent validity, the test variable and the external variable are measured at the same time. For example, the score on a test of verbal memory may be compared to the ability to remember conversations. In predictive validity, the test score is obtained in advance of the criterion measure. As an example of predictive validity, the score on a test of verbal fluency at 7 years of age may be compared to performance on standardized achievement tests of reading skill at 11 years.

As another example of predictive validity, Aylward, Verhulst, and Colliver (1985) examined the use of a standardized neurological examination at 40 weeks conceptual age to predict performance on the Bayley Infant Development Scales at 9 and 18 months and the McCarthy Scales of

Children's Abilities at 36 months. These authors reported that normal performance on the neurological examination was associated with normal performance on the later tests (specificity) and that to a lesser extent, abnormal performance on the neurological examination was associated with abnormal performance on the later developmental evaluations (sensitivity). Sensitivity here is defined as the extent to which a score on a test is associated with a given criterion, and specificity is the extent to which that same score is not associated with something other than the criterion.

Factorial Validity

Although many early neuropsychological assessment devices were unifactorial—that is, they yielded only one score—this is clearly no longer the case. Tests such as the California Verbal Learning Test (Delis, Kramer, Kaplan, & Ober, 1987) yield a multitude of scores. Factorial validity refers to aspects of psychometric integrity of the combination or concatenation of individual items into scales. Factorial validity has relations to both internal consistency and, as is seen in the next subsection, construct validity (Franzen, 1989; Nunnally, 1967). The issue is whether the placement of items on a scale is justified by the interrelations among the items as well as the relation of the individual item to the scale. Additionally, we want to consider whether the division of scale scores is justified by the factor structure of the instrument. Although scales may originally be designed with reference to theory, their continued use requires empirical support.

An example of this concept can be found in the literature regarding the clinical assessment of memory. The factor structure of the Wechsler Memory Scale–Revised (WMS–R) has been investigated in multiple populations. The results of factor analyses conducted on the WMS–R generally indicate that although there are five summary indices available, there is usually a three-factor solution, namely either attention/concentration, verbal, and nonverbal memory (Bornstein & Chelune, 1988) or else attention/concentration, immediate recall, and delayed recall (Roth, Conboy, Reeder, & Boll, 1990). Interestingly, in the latter set of analyses, it appeared that when factor solutions were compared across three age groups, there were greater loadings of nonverbal tasks on verbal factors with increasing age. This last result indicates that the strategy used in a particular task may vary in different populations across the life span, implying that construct validity may be specific to a specific set of nontest variables as well as being related to the characteristics of the test itself.

Investigations of the factorial validity of the Wide Range Assessment of Memory and Learning (WRAML; Adams & Sheslow, 1990) have raised some questions about the subscales included in the indices. Reanalyses of the factor structure of the WRAML indicate that the subscales might be better positioned on different indices (Gioia, 1991). Subsequent correlational analyses indicate that two of the subtests on the Verbal Memory Index, namely Number/Letter Learning and Finger Windows, might have stronger relations to other measures of attention than to measures of learning (Haut, Haut, & Franzen, 1992). This information can then be used to construct new combinations of items into scales.

Construct Validity

In a broad sense, construct validity is the extent to which a test measures the construct purported to underlie the operationalization. Construct validity cannot be measured or evaluated by a single study. Instead, decisions about construct validity are made with reference to an accumulated body of empirical work. Studies investigating criterion validity and factorial validity may all contribute to the consideration of construct validity. Campbell and Fiske (1959) gave us the most elegant design for evaluating aspects of construct validity, namely the multitrait–multimethod matrix. The general idea here is that the instrument measuring the trait of interest must show stronger relations with scores obtained from other instruments measuring the same traits, but using different methods, than with other instruments measuring different traits using the same methods. In other words, there must be a demonstration of both convergent and discriminant validity as well as some attempt to partial out method variance.

O'Grady (1988) investigated the convergent and discriminant validity of Russell's Revision of the Wechsler Memory Scale by correlating the data of 228 participants on personality, intellectual functioning, and memory. He found that although the different scores for verbal and visual memory were relatively unaffected by noncognitive variables and were related to other memory measures, there was only moderate evidence to support discrimination between verbal and visual memory measures.

This issue is particularly important for clinical neuropsychology because every procedure measuring some function of the brain tends to correlate with another procedure measuring some other function of the brain. Although this phenomenon may seem to be at odds with the modularity concepts of cognitive neuropsychology (Ellis & Young, 1988), it is important to remember that the modularity of brain functions usually becomes apparent only during some disruption or impairment of normal function (McCarthy & Warrington, 1990). It is not sufficient to demonstrate that two measures of verbal memory correlate with each other; they should also not correlate as strongly with a measure of visual memory.

Incremental and Differential Validity

As noted previously, validity partly involves the extent to which a neuropsychological procedure can answer a question efficiently and accurately and whether this can be accomplished with a minimum of time and expense. Clinical neuropsychology has strong roots in the laboratory where the more information obtained, the better. As these procedures were implemented in the clinic, there developed a clinical lore regarding interpretation heuristics. These clinical interpretations were not always empirically established. Where there has been empirical investigation of the interpretative lore, the data have not always supported the interpretation.

Sherer, Parsons, Nixon, and Adams (1991) investigated some of the clinical lore regarding the use of the Speech Sounds Perception Test (SSPT) and the Seashore Rhythm Test (SRT) in the Halstead–Reitan battery. They obtained a sample of pseudoneurologic subjects (individuals with subjective complaints unsubstantiated by objective medical neurodiagnostic procedures) and neurologic subjects. Using the scores from the Halstead–Reitan, the investigators calculated two discriminant function analyses, one set of analyses with all of the test scores and one set with all of the test scores except the SSPT and SRT. The correct classification rates for the discriminant functions were 71.9% for all of the test scores and 72.8% for all of the test scores except the SSPT and SRT. Additionally, the authors evaluated whether the SSPT and SRT could be used to lateralize to the left or right hemisphere and found that this could not be done. Finally, investigating the hypothesis that the two tests tapped attention, they correlated the SRT and SSPT with the Attention index of the Wechsler Memory scale, partialling out the variance associated with each other. The resulting partial correlation coefficient values were $-.180$ and $-.197$. Thus, this investigation of incremental validity showed that information from one of the procedures does not provide unique information above that of the other.

EXTERNAL CRITERIA

One of the more common criteria of validity for neuropsychological assessment is *diagnostic accuracy*. In the past, the field has concentrated on diagnostic issues to the exclusion of descriptive issues. The diagnostic criteria have generally included either localization information or the identification of disease process. For example, clinical neuropsychological test results are sometimes used to identify whether a stroke has occurred, and if so, to determine the location of the infarct. Most of the studies conducted to examine this issue have consisted of examinations of mean differences in test scores among groups of participants with different disorders or different localizations.

This research approach has largely ignored the entire realm of classification accuracy. Granted, there has been some research involving this issue. For example, Kane (1986) reviewed the research conducted to compare the diagnostic accuracy of the Halstead–Reitan and Luria–Nebraska Neuropsychological Batteries. Previous research had detailed the psychometric relations between these two batteries (Golden et al., 1981; Kane, Parsons, & Goldstein, 1985; Shelly & Goldstein, 1982), but the next step was taken when the results of the two batteries were sent to clinicians and interpretative accuracies were compared (Kane, Sweet, Golden, Parsons, & Moses, 1981). These studies are in direct contrast to the usual practice of investigating group differences.

The more precise method of validating this information is to examine classification accuracy of various cutoff scores, examining the entire set of true and false positives and true and false negatives in an examination of sensitivity and specificity. As an extreme example, the Trailmaking Test Part B (Trails B) is very sensitive to frontal lobe impairment, but it is not especially specific to frontal lobe impairment. In a group of mixed localization patients, the frontal lobe patients will be "caught" by the use of the Trails B, giving a reasonable true positive rate, but there will also be a fairly large group of nonfrontal dysfunction patients in the false positives. As a result, the overall hit rate may not be so impressive.

The issue of hit rate invokes the notion of base rate, a usually ignored variable. It might be argued that base rate considerations apply only in those instances where actuarial diagnoses occur, and there is some weight to this argument. However, it is also true that the validation studies of neuropsychological assessment procedures typically utilize actuarial methodology. Few exceptions to this tendency exist, and most of these exceptions focus on the clinical decision-making process itself. Examining any manual for neuropsychological test instruments will provide the reader with cutoff scores for decisions about the existence of impairment. However, there is no discussion of how the base rate of impairment in the standardization sample affects the accuracy of detection. Furthermore, the manuals usually also have information regarding cutoff points that optimally separate different diagnostic groups, and here again base rate information would be very helpful.

Willis (1984) conducted an interesting reanalysis of five actuarial studies using the Halstead–Reitan Battery. In comparing the base rates to the hit rates, he found that in 9 out of 26 diagnostic decisions, the hit rates either did not differ from the base rates or were lower than the base rates! This last result indicates that the use of the base rate alone would have resulted in greater accuracy of diagnosis.

The methodology of the Willis study is an important addition to the neuropsychological literature especially because base rates may change across the life span. Knowing the base rate of Alzheimer's disease in 25-year-old men will change the diagnostic and interpretative significance of certain test results. For example, the presence of semantic paraphasia in a

25-year-old patient may be interpreted as indicative of left temporal lobe dysfunction, rather than as a sign of possible Alzheimer's disease.

Notions of base rate also include the determination of appropriate cutoff scores. If the base rate of different disorders changes across the life span, the cutoff should reflect these changes. To extend the example of Alzheimer's disease, if 20% of persons 65 to 75 years old have Alzheimer's disease and 30% of persons 75 to 85 years old have this disease, the cutoffs for a diagnostic test would be optimally set at the 80th percentile for the younger group and at the 70th percentile for the older group.

TWO NEWER FORMS OF VALIDITY

Ecological Validity

We stated earlier that the validity of neuropsychological assessment depends on the ability of the results to answer the assessment question accurately and efficiently. As the uses of assessment change, so do the validity concerns. Traditionally, clinical neuropsychological assessment was used largely to determine laterality, localization, and etiology, and the questions were largely diagnostic in nature. (There is currently a debate as to whether these three questions were the prevalent activity in the early stages of professional neuropsychology [Hartman, 1988, 1991; Loring, 1991; Reitan, 1989]. However, it is certainly true that the emphasis on laterality and localization is not as marked as it was previously.) Currently, neuropsychological assessment is increasingly being applied to the task of predicting extratest behavior. This task is highlighting interest in notions of ecological validity. Furthermore, the utilization of clinical neuropsychological data in rehabilitation settings has placed the behavior prediction aspects of neuropsychological assessment on a par with the diagnostic and treatment planning aspects.

Many authors have used the term *ecological validity* in different areas of psychology, but with little agreeement and even less specificity of definition. Recently, Franzen and Wilhelm (1996) offered a conceptual typology of ecological validity. They discussed two aspects of ecological validity, namely verisimilitude and veridicality. *Verisimilitude* refers to the degree of concordance between the topographical determinants of the behaviors elicited by a test and the topographical determinants of the behaviors to be predicted. *Veridicality* refers to the level of accuracy of predicting the behaviors in the free environment from the test results. There are similarities between verisimilitude and face validity. However, face validity refers to the perception of the test's intent, usually in the mind of the test participant. Verisimilitude refers to the conceptual argument that the test shares important features with the domain to be predicted, a judgment that would typically be acomplished by an expert. Veridicality has important similarities to criterion validity, although in these instances, the criterion is always some environmental behavior.

Both veridicality and verisimilitude are important in the evaluation of ecological validity, although they may not always be related. For example, test scores may be empirically related to certain behaviors even without topographical similarities. Alternatively, topographically similar behaviors may not necessarily be empirically related. Furthermore, as Chelune (1982) pointed out, the concerns of ecological validity require that the test scores be able to predict skills and not just deficits as has been the case in traditional neuropsychology.

In order to better understand the concepts of versimilitude and veridicality, it may be helpful to contrast them in terms of the levels of analysis associated with each and the types of information needed to judge test instruments on the basis of verisimilitude and veridicality. The behaviors to be predicted in an evaluation of veridicality in ecological validity can vary from the specific, such as the ability to drive an automobile, which, although a combination of complex behaviors, can be evaluated in a specific setting, to more molar outcomes, such as return to work, which entails a wider range of determining variables. In contrast, the evaluation of verisimilitude requires a consideration of the instrument with regard to the task demands of the test and the task demands of the setting to which prediction will occur (e.g., Do both tasks require a common form of visual spatial analysis?). A second consideration is whether the test taps the skills required in the same manner as the situation: Do both tasks have equivalent levels of distraction? Do they both allow equivalent compensatory mechanisms?

The evaluation of veridicality can take different forms. A weak test of veridicality can involve an empirical evaluation of the relation between the test in question and other tests that have been found to predict behavior in the free environment. Stronger tests of veridicality include comparison of the neuropsychological test results with the results of behavioral assessment, whether by self-report, report of informants, formal behavioral observations, or questionnaires.

The two aspects of ecological validity also have different levels of analysis once the data are obtained. Verisimilitude requires theoretical analysis: Can the test behaviors be theoretically related to the free environment behaviors? There is also conceptual analysis: Can a conceptual argument be made for a similarity between the test and the behavior of interest? Finally, there needs to be a rational analysis: Can an argument be made for including the test behavior as a component in the environmental behavior? The investigation of veridicality also involves a theoretical analysis: Is there theoretical justification for considering the relation between the test and the environmental behavior? Veridicality further requires an empirical analysis involving controlled observations to determine the qualitative and quantitative characteristics of the relation between the test and the behavior.

The concerns of ecological validity are particularly sensitive to developmental variables. The tasks involved in most memory tests are rarely called on in real life, except in the case of younger people where school-related tasks may require the memorization of what seem to be unrelated items. This becomes less true as the student becomes older and as the former student ages.

Zappala, Martini, Crook, and Amaducci (1989) reported the initial results of a memory test that possesses verisimilitude to everyday tasks. Instead of a paired verbal associates test with unrelated words, there is a first names–last names test. Instead of a digit span procedure, there is a telephone number memory test. Part of the reason for these changes is to increase the motivation of the older individual to perform at top capacity and thereby obtain a "truer" picture of the actual memory ability. However, by using such tasks, the procedures may possess greater veracity in predicting real-life memory performance.

Descriptive Validity

The main concern of descriptive validity is to evaluate whether the test accurately describes the processes involved in producing the measured behavior. Here we are talking about the psychological processes involved in producing the target test behavior. The physiological processes involved in a given neuropsychological task can be indexed by electrophysiological or metabolic (PET, rCBF) monitoring. Psychological–behavioral monitoring can provide only correlates of this physiological activity.

The question of descriptive validity needs to be examined separately from construct validity. Although construct validity is concerned with the extent of true measurement affected by the use of the instrument, it is only in regard to the proposed relations of the variable at hand with other, external variables. The classic and most elegant method of examining construct validity is the use of the multitrait–multimethod matrix. A test of vocabulary may possess adequate construct validity to the extent that it demonstrates the appropriate relations with both associated and independent external variables. However, the descriptive validity issue is concerned not with those relations but with the accurate demonstration of which of the processes is reflected in the obtained score. This distinction is similar to the recent discussion related to process assessment in clinical neuropsychology (Kaplan, 1990).

We can examine the implications of descriptive validity in greater detail by examining the assessment of memory across the life span. Although generally the use of memory strategies is thought to begin around 7 to 9 years of age and to increase across ages in children (Boyd, 1988; Kail, 1984), some evidence suggests that it may start earlier. Baker-Ward, Ornstein, and Holden (1984) reported that instructions to remember a subset of toys in a playroom resulted in less playing behavior and more direct naming of toys and staring at toys in a group of preschool children, although the behavioral use of strategy did not result in improved memory performance until the age of 6. This dissociation of process from achievement score may indicate a need to measure both separately.

The type of process and degree of utilization of process may change with age. Elaboration skills tend to increase across the first few years of life. Although 4-year-old children can use visual imagery to learn verbal paired associates, these children need to be prompted and cued to use this elaboration strategy (Bender & Levin, 1976). Children's facility at using this form of elaboration strategy increases until around age 13 (Pressley & Levin, 1977).

Changes in working memory associated with aging may be related to changes in discourse memory, at least for simpler texts (Stine & Wingfield, 1990). Any evaluation of discourse memory would therefore have to take into account the extent to which working memory was being utilized in the production of scores on discourse memory tests.

VALIDITY OF OTHER USES

Sometimes test data that are sensitive to certain variables may be used to answer other questions. For example, there has been an explosion of interest in techniques to detect malingering in neuropsychological assessment. Although the stated purpose of these instruments is to determine whether malingering has occurred, an examination of the instruments indicates that the test scores are probably best conceptualized as sensitive to nonoptimal effort in performance. That is, individuals giving minimal effort will score past the cutoffs. The diagnosis of malingering requires information that the behavior of test result manipulation is instrumental with clear and socially understandable motivations. Many of the malingering indices may be affected by low levels of attention to the task or random responding. Let us examine one of those methods, the forced choice memory test.

Forced choice memory tests were developed in tandem with other forced choice instruments such as Symptom Validity Testing for sensory deficits. The general rationale behind the procedures is that in cases of a binary decision, accuracy is unlikely to be lower than chance, which is approximately 50% correct. Of course by chance, a participant can answer less than 50% correct so the cutoffs are usually set at a point where chance responding can result in that score at a probability at the .05 level. Regardless of where the cutoffs are set, the actual information derived from the test scores is the probability of nonoptimal performance. The validity of these procedures is frequently assessed by judging the accuracy of the test in correctly identifying malingerers and true memory-impaired participants. So the underlying construct is not quite the same as the use to which the test results are put. Both questions are important, but in some instances classification may be relatively more important.

THREATS TO VALIDITY

Although internal validity and external validity are not technically forms of estimable validity, some individuals have found it useful to discuss the interpretation of test results in these terms. The division between internal and external validity parallels the existing and more well-known division of external and internal threats to the validity of a study using a particular research design. There are threats to the internal and external validity of clinical neuropsychological assessments (Franzen, 1989). Threats to internal validity are related to the conclusions drawn from the use of a neuropsychological test. Threats to external validity are related to limits on the generalizability of the test results.

Internal Validity

The threats to internal validity include history, which subsumes the uncontrolled effects of educational level, premorbid intellectual skills, aging, handedness, gender, and socioeconomic status. Some tests are designed to guard against these effects by offering norms separately for different levels of these variables. For example, the Benton tests offer separate norms for age and gender when empirical studies have indicated that there is an effect of these variables (Benton, Hamsher, Varney, & Spreen, 1983). The Luria–Nebraska uses a regression based correction factor that takes into account age and education (Golden, Purish, & Hammeke, 1985). Although interpretation of the Halstead–Reitan has traditionally ignored these variables, there is now normative information available for different levels of age, education, and gender (Heaton, Grant, & Matthews, 1991). Earlier research had demonstrated gender effects, but only for isolated tests (Chavez, Schwartz, & Brandon, 1982).

Other threats to internal validity come from the test interval. Particularly when a comprehensive evaluation is conducted, the time required for the complete evaluation may not be consistent with a day's work. Even in that majority of cases where the evaluation is finished in a single day, the participant may become fatigued across the course of the evaluation, or the level of motivation may change, compromising the validity of inferences drawn from tests administered later in the sequence.

As an example of the effects that might be due to aspects of the test session, the order of administration of some tests may have effects on the obtained scores (Franzen, Smith, Paul, & MacInnes, 1993). That is, experience with a certain procedure can either sensitize a participant to the principles underlying a test or provide a nonproductive cognitive set in the approach to the test. This phenomenon can be classified under the rubric of multiple procedures effects. This particular study examined the order effects of administering the Halstead Category Test and Wisconsin Card Sorting Test to clinical patients and found that there may be both facilitating effects and decrementing effects. The cautions engendered include specifying the order of administration or else separating administration times of tests that may share overlapping constructs.

Threats to internal validity may also be due to statistical artifacts in that the performance of the participant may be compared to inappropriate samples or to excessively homogeneous normative samples, resulting in faulty conclusions. Because of the possibility of cultural differences, test results from minorities should be compared to normative groups with the same cultural background, whenever possible. There may be testing effects in that some of the tests used may have been repeated without availability of alternate forms or knowledge regarding the possibility of practice effects.

Finally, at least for purposes of this discussion, there may be ceiling effects. Many clinical neuropsychological assessment instruments have their origins in behavioral neurology where the purpose was to uncover a behavioral deficit. The knowledge required was simply binary: impaired or intact. Such a strategy may result in procedures that are insufficiently challenging to uncover difficulties in previously high-functioning individuals or too simple to allow discrimination of subtle differences.

External Validity

Threats to external validity include interactive effects that can come about because inadequate attention is paid to the effects of medication, surgery, or other diagnostic procedures. That is, situational effects may exist that limit or modify the validity of conclusions drawn from test results. The influence of situational variables on neuropsychological performance has not been well investigated, because the effect of morphological or metabolic anomalies is usually assumed to be sufficiently robust to rule out the influence of other variables. However, there are parallels attesting to the importance of considering situation parameters in the psychophysiological literature.

J. I. Lacey (1967) first articulated the notion of situational stereotypy in the psychophysiological literature, demonstrating that individuals respond very differently physiologically depending on situational parameters. The presence of stereotypy is especially true in response to stress where two individuals could be shown to respond very differently if a number of modalities (e.g., behavioral, cortical, or electrodermal modalities) were indexed. For example, Individual A might respond to a particular stressful situation with behavioral activation, cortical arousal, and tonic heart rate increase. In contrast, Individual B might respond to the same stressor with behavioral inhibition, cortical inhibition, and tonic heart rate decrease. Furthermore, these individuals' patterns of arousal to the stressful stimuli are likely to be consistent if the stimuli are repeated in the future.

Related to the notion of situational stereotypy and of particular interest to clinical neuropsychology are findings such as those from a series of experiments by the Laceys (B. C. Lacey & J. I. Lacey, 1974, 1978; J. I. Lacey, 1967) and others demonstrating predictable psychophysiological changes in experimental situations requiring problem solving and sensorimotor skill. A consistent finding in the literature is that larger cardiac accelerations occur during the performance of difficult as opposed to simple sensorimotor tasks (Cacioppo & Sandman, 1978; B. C. Lacey & J. I. Lacey, 1974; Tursky, Schwartz, & Crider, 1970). Given that these kinds of tasks elicit predictable physiological responses, the extent to which a second stereotypic physiologic stress response interferes with the elicitation of the target response could impair the neuropsychological task performance. The extent to which a participant experiences a testing situation as stressful, combined with the participant's peculiar physiological response patterning to stress, could influence that participant's task performance.

Differences in physiological response patterns can be problematic in clinical situations where every effort is made to elicit the participant's optimal performance. The clinician makes efforts to reduce the anxiety level of the participant, and the effects of depression are taken into account when interpreting the test results. Currently, clinical judgment is used in these situations, but objective heuristics would be helpful. It is important to realize that both the affective response of the participant to the test situation and the characteristics of the response of the individual to specific emotional states may vary over the life span. For example, older participants who have been out of school for an extended period of time may find the test setting more intimidating. Additionally, there may be greater effects of emotional states on neuropsychological performance at both the early developmental stages and the later stages. Most of our information is derived from studies conducted on the middle stages and is therefore in need of examination in other age groups. The notion that an individual's response to the testing situation may include a physiological response that interferes with optimal performance may be one of the variables responsible for the discrepancy between test performance and open environment performance as discussed in the earlier section on ecological validity. For this reason, it is important that clinical neuropsychology develop a set of functional assessment tools possibly including assessment conducted in a naturalistic setting in order to help increase the validity of test interpretations.

Finally, there may be reactive effects of the transactions between the participant and the evaluator. This possibility is particularly true in those instances where maximum cooperation is required for reasonable interpretation. Having raised the issue of the importance of situational parameters on neuropsychological test performance, it must be acknowledged that it is difficult to control these situational parameters in such a way that each individual is experiencing a comparable situation. The difficulty arises because it is possible that two individuals may react to an objectively identical test situation (e.g., same room, same examiner, same tests) in different ways. For this reason, participant characteristics are very important. Level of depression and anxiety is of particular interest.

There is a large amount of clinical literature about the potential confound of depression on neuropsychological performance, especially in older participants. Older participants are supposedly more susceptible to the dampening effect of depression on memory, in a condition that is known as pseudodementia. Weingartner, Cohen, Murphy, Martello, and Gerdt (1981) delineated some of the quantitative and qualitative changes in the cognitive functioning of depressed participants, and Weingartner and Silberman (1982) discussed some of the theories that have been proposed to explain these changes. What is needed is a set of empirically derived guides for interpreting or correcting for the effect of depression, especially in older participants. Sweet, Newman, and Bell (1992) summarized some of the available knowledge, but it is clear that our knowledge of the relation among these important variables can be improved to allow greater validity of our interpretations of test data in this group of participants.

A smaller literature has developed regarding the importance of anxiety in influencing neuropsychological test performance. Tyler and Tucker (1982) demonstrated that participants high in trait anxiety performed worse than low-trait anxiety participants on nonverbal but not verbal tasks. Martin and Franzen (1989) found that state anxiety negatively influenced memory and mental control tasks, but not other neuropsychological functions. Eysenck (1985) proposed that in general, anxiety affects performance on more difficult cognitive tasks. Interestingly, as with the importance of situational variables on neuropsychological task performance and psychophysiological responding, there are parallels regarding anxiety in the psychophysiological literature. The finding of greater electrodermal response to the threat of punishment by highly anxious participants has been replicated consistently (Fowles, 1980).

From the psychopathy literature, a number of findings demonstrate the importance of anxiety not only in mediating group differences in neuropsychological test performance but also in mediating experimental task performance and psychophysiological response. Smith, Arnett, and Newman (1992) found that group differences between psychopaths and controls in neuropsychological task performance were mediated by level of trait anxiety. Additionally, Newman, Patterson, Howland, and Nichols (1990), Newman, Kosson, and Patterson (1992), and Arnett, Smith, and Newman (1991) all found that anxiety mediated the relation of psychopathy to performance on tasks employing reward and punishment incentives. Finally, Arnett, Howland, Smith, and Newman (1993) and Arnett et al. (1991) found that group differences between persons with mental disorders and controls in cardiovascular and electrodermal responses to reward and punishment for passive avoidance tasks were importantly mediated by anxiety.

Given the apparent importance of anxiety in mediating neuropsychological test performance, anxiety should be evaluated as part of any clinical neuropsychological examination. Additionally, the role of noncognitive states, such as anxiety in neuropsychological functions, should be examined. Current knowledge includes the general guide that highly anxious participants are likely to perform more poorly on more difficult tasks, but additional studies to examine the relation between noncognitive state and performance on specific neuropsychological tests will help answer the questions regarding both the external and internal validity of our test results.

FUTURE DIRECTIONS

Validity research in clinical neuropsychology has progressed a great deal since the original studies where validity required only that performance deficits be associated with specific lesions. However, the journey has just begun. Clinical neuropsychological assessment possesses its own unique problems, several of which are related to development across the life span. At the same time, much can be learned from examination of assessment research in other areas. Broadening the questions typically raised in validity research to include specific hypotheses in specific populations or at different levels of performance (e.g., using item response theory) will help more adequately define the error involved in clinical neuropsychological assessment.

The validity of clinical neuropsychological assessment techniques can be more rigorously addressed using the framework of traditional test theory as well as the framework of more innovative approaches. In addition to specifying and limiting the populations in which valid conclusions can be drawn using a certain assessment instrument, we should choose our validation criteria with consideration of the question to be answered. In other words, a broader and more thoughtful choice of external validation criteria is needed in the research conducted. Rather than assuming that noncognitive variables have minimal impact on neuropsychological performance, these variables should be studied explicitly.

It is puzzling that clinical neuropsychological assessment and psychophysiological assessment have not overlapped to a greater extent. Both assessment paradigms utilize the central nervous system as the mediating operator. There are some intriguing data suggesting that inclusion of psychophysiological data can augment the methods of the neuropsychological evaluation. Damasio, Tranel, and Damasio (1990) compared a small ($N = 5$) group of participants with bilateral lesions in the orbital and lower mesial frontal lobes with participants with lesions in other parts of the cortex and control participants. The measure of interest was electrodermal response to pictures with strong implied meanings (e.g., mutilation, nudity). The bifrontal lesion subjects were deficient in eliciting somatic markers in the form of electrodermal amplitude. This set of results may help explain why bifrontal lesion subjects may have difficulty in making social judgments even though their performance on standard neuropsychological tests may be adequate.

In general, a broader conceptualization of the components of validity and of the methods of evaluating these components will help advance the field. Typically, the components have been thought of as monolithic information; however, it is likely that the relations among variables will need to be investigated across the age span, a notion to which the previous discussions have only alluded. Finally, the newer categories of ecological validity and descriptive validity will increase our knowledge of test interpretation if future work provides empirical explication.

REFERENCES

Adams, W., & Sheslow, D. (1990). *Wide range assessment of memory and learning: Administration manual.* Wilmington, DE: Jastak.

Arnett, P. A., Howland, E. W., Smith, S. S., & Newman, J. P. (1993). Autonomic responsivity in psychopaths during passive avoidance. *Personality and Individual Differences, 14,* 173–184.

Arnett, P. A., Smith, S. S., & Newman. J. P. (1991, October). *Approach and avoidance in incarcerated psychopaths.* Paper presented at the meeting of the Society for Psychophysiological Research, Chicago.

Aylward, G. P., Verhulst, S. J., & Colliver, J. A. (1985). Development of a brief infant neurobehavioral optimality scale: Longitudinal sensitivity and specificity. *Developmental Neuropsychology, 1,* 265–276.

Baker-Ward, L., Ornstein, P. A., & Holden, D. J. (1984). The expression of memorization in early childhood. *Journal of Experimental Child Psychology, 37,* 555–575.

Bender, B. G., & Levin, J. R. (1976). Motor activity, anticipated motor activity, and young children's associative learning. *Child Development, 47,* 560–562.

Benton, A. L., Hamsher, K. deS., Varney, N. R., & Spreen, O. (1983). *Contributions to neuropsychological assessment: A clinical manual.* New York: Oxford University Press.

Bornstein, R. A., & Chelune, G. J. (1988). Factor structure of the Wechsler Memory Scale-Revised. *The Clinical Neuropsychologist, 4,* 141–150.

Boyd, T. A. (1988). Clinical assessment of memory in children: A developmental framework for practice. In M. G. Tramontana & S. R. Hooper (Eds.), *Assessment issues in child neuropsychology* (pp. 177–204). New York: Plenum.

Cacioppo, J. T., & Sandman, C. A. (1978). Physiological differentiation of sensory and cognitive tasks as a function of warning, processing demands, and unpleasantness. *Journal of Biological Psychology, 6,* 181–192.

Campbell, D. T., & Fiske, D. W. (1959). Convergent and discriminant validation by the multitrait-multimethod matrix. *Psychological Bulletin, 56,* 81–105.

Chavez, E. L., Schwartz, M. M., & Brandon, A. (1982). Effects of sex of subject and method of block presentation on the Tactual Performance Test. *Journal of Consulting and Clinical Psychology, 50,* 600–601.

Chelune, G. J. (1982). Toward a neuropsychological model of everyday functioning. *Psychotherapy in Private Practice, 3,* 39–44.

Damasio, A. R., Tranel, D., & Damasio, H. (1990). Individuals with sociopathic behavior caused by frontal damage fail to respond autonomically to social stimuli. *Behavioral Brain Research, 41,* 81–94.

Delis, D. C., Kramer, J. H., Kaplan, E., & Ober, B. A. (1987). *California Verbal Learning Test: Manual.* San Antonio, TX: Psychological Corporation.

Ellis, A. W., & Young, A. W. (1988). *Human cognitive neuropsychology.* Hillsdale, NJ: Lawrence Erlbaum Associates.

Eysenck, M. W. (1985). Anxiety and cognitive task performance. *Personality and Individual Differences, 6,* 579–586.

Fowles, D. C. (1980). The three arousal model: Implications of Gray's two-factor learning theory for heart rate, electrodermal activity and psychopathy. *Psychophysiology, 17,* 87–104.

Franzen, M. D. (1989). *Reliability and validity in neuropsychological assessment.* New York: Plenum.

Franzen, M. D., Smith, S. S., Paul, D., & MacInnes, W. D. (1993). Order effects in the administration of the Booklet Category Test and the Wisconsin Card Sorting Test. *Archives of Clinical Neuropsychology, 8,* 105–110.

Franzen, M. D., & Wilhelm, K. L. (1996). Conceptual foundations of ecological validity in neuropsychological assessment. In R. Sbordone & C. J. Long (Eds.), *Ecological validity in neuropsychology* (pp. 91–112). New York: Deutsch.

Gioia, G. A. (1991, February). *Re-analysis of the factor structure of the Wide Range Assessment of Memory and Learning: Implications for clinical interpretation.* Paper presented at the meeting of the International Neuropsychological Society, San Antonio, TX.

Golden, C. J., Kane, R., Sweet, J., Moses, J. A., Cardellino, J. P., Templeton, R., Vincente,

P., & Graber, B. (1981). Relationship of the Halstead–Reitan Neuropsychological Battery to the Luria–Nebraska Neuropsychological Battery. *Journal of Consulting and Clinical Psychology, 49*, 410–417.

Golden, C. J., Purish, A. D., & Hammeke, T. A. (1985). *Luria–Nebraska Neuropsychological Battery: Forms I and II.* Los Angeles: Western Psychological Services.

Hartman, D. E. (1988). Review of R. E. Tarter, D. H. Van Thiel, and K. L. Edwards, *Medical neuropsychology: The impact of disease on behavior. Archives of Clinical Neuropsychology, 3*, 299–301.

Hartman, D. E. (1991). Reply to Reitan: Unexamined premises and the evolution of clinical neuropsychology. *Archives of Clinical Neuropsychology, 6*, 147–165.

Haut, J. S., Haut, M. W., & Franzen, M. D. (1992, February). *Assessment of an attentional component of Wide Range Assessment of Memory and Learning (WRAML) subtests.* Paper presented at the meeting of the International Neuropsychological Society, San Diego, CA.

Heaton, R. K., Grant, I., & Matthews, C. G. (1991). *Comprehensive norms for the expanded Halstead–Reitan battery.* Odessa, FL: Psychological Assessment Resources.

Kail, R. (1984). *The development of memory in children* (2nd ed.). New York: Freeman.

Kane, R. L. (1986). Comparison of Halstead–Reitan and Luria–Nebraska Neuropsychological Batteries: Research findings. In T. Incagnoli, G. Goldstein, & C. J. Golden (Eds.), *Clinical applications of neuropsychological test batteries* (pp. 277–301). New York: Plenum.

Kane, R. L., Parsons, O. A., & Goldstein, G. (1985). Statistical relationships and discriminative accuracy of the Halstead–Reitan, Luria–Nebraska, and Wechsler I.Q. scores in the identification of brain damage. *Journal of Clinical and Experimental Neuropsychology, 7*, 211–223.

Kane, R. L., Sweet, J. J., Golden, C. J., Parsons, O. A., & Moses, J. A. (1981). Comparative diagnostic accuracy of the Halstead–Reitan and Luria–Nebraska Neuropsychological Batteries in a mixed psychiatric and brain-damaged population. *Journal of Consulting and Clinical Psychology, 49*, 484–485.

Kaplan, E. (1990). The process approach to neuropsychological assessment of psychiatric patients. *Journal of Neuropsychiatry, 2*, 72–87.

Lacey, B. C., & Lacey, J. I. (1974). Studies of heart rate and other bodily processes in sensorimotor behavior. In P. A. Obrist, A. H. Black, J. Brener, & L. V. DiCara (Eds.), *Cardiovascular psychophysiology* (pp. 32–59). Chicago: Aldine.

Lacey, B. C., & Lacey, J. I. (1978). Two-way communication between the heart and the brain: Significance of time within the cardiac cycle. *American Psychologist, 33*, 99–113.

Lacey, J. I. (1967). Somatic response patterning and stress: Some revisions of activation theory. In M. H. Appley & R. Trumbull (Eds.), *Psychological stress: Issues in research* (pp. 167–193). New York: Appleton.

Loring, D. W. (1991). A counterpoint to Reitan's note on the history of clinical neuropsychology. *Archives of Clinical Neuropsychology, 6*, 167–171.

Martin, N. J., & Franzen, M. D. (1989). The effect of anxiety on neuropsychological function. *International Journal of Clinical Neuropsychology, 9*, 1–8.

McCarthy, R. A., & Warrington, E. K. (1990). *Cognitive neuropsychology: A clinical introduction.* New York: Academic Press.

Newman, J. P., Kosson, D. S., & Patterson, C. M. (1992). Delay of gratification in psychopathic and nonpsychopathic offenders. *Journal of Abnormal Psychology, 101*, 630–636.

Newman, J. P., Patterson, C. M., Howland, E. W., & Nichols, S. L. (1990). Passive avoidance in psychopaths: The effects of reward. *Personality and Individual Differences, 11*, 1101–1114.

Nunnally, J. C. (1967). *Psychometric theory.* New York: McGraw-Hill.

O'Grady, K. (1988). Convergent and discriminant validity of Russell's Revised Wechlser

Memory Scale. *Personality and Individual Differences*, *9*, 321–327.

Pressley, M., & Levin, J. R. (1977). Task parameters affecting the efficacy of a visual imagery learning strategy in younger and older children. *Journal of Experimental Child Psychology*, *24*, 53–59.

Reitan, R. M. (1989). A note regarding some aspects of the history of clinical neuropsychology. *Archives of Clinical Neuropsychology*, *4*, 285–391.

Roth, D. L., Conboy, T. J., Reeder, K. P., & Boll, T. J. (1990). Confirmatory factor analyses of the Wechsler Memory Scale-Revised in a sample of head-injured patients. *Journal of Clinical and Experimental Neuropsychology*, *12*, 834–842.

Shelly, C., & Goldstein, G. (1982). Psychometric relations between the Luria–Nebraska and Halstead-Reitan Neuropsychological Test Batteries in a neuropsychiatric setting. *Clinical Neuropsychology*, *4*, 128–133.

Sherer, M., Parsons, O. A., Nixon, S. J., & Adams, R. L. (1991). Clinical validity of the Speech Sounds Perception Test and the Seashore Rhythm Test. *Journal of Clinical and Experimental Neuropsychology*, *13*, 741–751.

Smith, S. S., Arnett, P. A., & Newman, J. P. (1992). Neuropsychological differentiation of psychopathic and nonpsychopathic criminal offenders. *Personality and Individual Differences*, *13*, 1233–1243.

Stine, E. A. L., & Wingfield, A. (1990). How much do working memory deficits contribute to age differences in source memory? *European Journal of Cognitive Psychology*, *2*, 289–304.

Sweet, J. J., Newman, P., & Bell, B. (1992). Significance of depression in clinical neuropsychological assessment. *Clinical Psychology Review*, *12*, 21–45.

Tursky, B., Schwartz, G., & Crider, A. (1970). Differential patterns of heart rate and skin resistance during a digit transformation task. *Journal of Experimental Psychology*, *83*, 451–457.

Tyler, S. K., & Tucker, D. M. (1982). Anxiety and perceptual structure: Individual differences in neuropsychological function. *Journal of Abnormal Psychology*, *91*, 210–220.

Weingartner, H., Cohen, R. M., Murphy, D. L., Martello, J., & Gerdt, C. (1981). Cognitive processes in depression. *Archives of General Psychiatry*, *38*, 42–47.

Weingartner, H., & Silberman, E. (1982). Models of cognitive impairment: Cognitive changes in depression. *Psychopharmacology Review*, *18*, 27–42.

Willis, W. G. (1984). Reanalysis of an actuarial approach to neuropsychological diagnosis in consideration of base rates. *Journal of Consulting and Clinical Psychology*, *52*, 567–569.

Zappala, G., Martini, E., Crook, T., & Amaducci, L. (1989). Ecological memory assessment in normal aging: A preliminary report on an Italian population. *Clinics in Geriatric Medicine*, *5*(3), 583–594.

4

Correlates of Language Development: Electrophysiological and Behavioral Measures

Dennis L. Molfese
Victoria J. Molfese
Leslie A. Gill
Sharon Benshoff
Southern Illinois University at Carbondale

Since the 1970s, researchers and practitioners have been interested in the development of assessment tools for neonates that are predictive of cognitive status in later infancy and early childhood. The ideal measures would permit the assessment of abilities at birth, when virtually total populations of infants are readily accessible in hospitals, and would be easily administered, cost effective, and accurate in identifying those infants who are at risk for developmental delays. However, the ideal measures that satisfy all of these criteria have been difficult to identify. Most typical approaches to assessment have involved the use of a wide variety of newborn measures as predictors and a variety of performance measures as the criterion scores. The newborn and early infancy measures used as predictors have included measures of perinatal complications (e.g., the Obstetrical Complications Scale, Littman & Parmelee, 1978), neurological and behavioral assessments (e.g., the Brazelton Neonatal Assessment Scale, Brazelton, 1973; Prechtl Neurological Examination, Prechtl, 1968), electrophysiological measures of brain functioning (e.g., brainstem-auditory evoked responses, evoked brain potentials), and measures reflecting attention and tactile abilities. Criterion measures have included scores on scales such as the Bayley Scales of Infant Development (Bayley, 1969), the Denver Developmental Screening Test (Dunn, 1965), the Stanford–Binet Intelligence Scale (Thorndike, Hagen, & Sattler, 1986), and the McCarthy Scales of Children's Abilities (McCarthy, 1972).

In the majority of studies that have been published, the amount of variance accounted for by the predictor variables, alone or in combination, is low. Since 1990, there has been an increase in the variance accounted for and an increase in the number of studies reporting predictive relationships between neonatal measures and scores in later childhood. Still, the amount of variance accounted for is less than 60%. It appears that the variables studied thus far still do not accurately predict later abilities in reliable and meaningful ways. Findings from our laboratory over the past decade have shown that evoked potential response (AER) techniques can be used to provide dramatic improvements in the prediction of language and cognitive performance. Findings obtained in our laboratory document a strong relationship between AERs to speech-relevant stimuli recorded soon after birth and measures of later language and cognitive development. In our earliest reported study (D. L. Molfese & V. J. Molfese, 1985), 78% of the variance was accounted by five AER components in predicting McCarthy verbal scores of 3-year-olds ($F = 6.90, p < .005$), and 69% of the variance was accounted for in predicting Peabody vocabulary scores of 3-year-olds ($F = 4.43, p < .02$). Subsequent findings from our laboratory have verified and extended these initial results.

The review that follows divides the traditional studies into four groups: (a) prediction of childhood cognitive and language scores from perinatal measures (e.g., measures obtained before, during, or within a few days after birth), (b) predictions from measures obtained in later infancy, (c) predictions from auditory brainstem responses (ABER), and (d) predictions from AERs. The review concludes with a discussion of a longitudinal study currently underway in our laboratory, exploring changes in predictivity of language and cognitive outcome measures from birth to 5 years.

PREDICTIONS BASED ON PERINATAL MEASURES

Past studies have evaluated the relative values of perinatal and neonatal characteristics, postnatal status, scores on behavioral and neurological assessment scales, and social/demographic characteristics as predictors of general mental development in infancy. These studies generally show that infants with more neonatal risk conditions (e.g., prematurity, respiratory and neurological problems) do not perform as well as infants without complications (see Table 4.1). Efforts to predict outcomes throughout infancy from these neonatal measures generally account for 43% or less of the total variance. For example, V. J. Molfese and Thomson (1985) used a variety of perinatal risk scales with full-term infants to determine whether any could predict infant mental development and temperament scores. The best performance was produced by the Brazie perinatal scale, which was able to account for 11% of the variance of Bayley Mental Development Index scores at 6 months. Fox and Porges (1985) used heart rate measures and perinatal and postnatal measures with healthy and sick full-term and preterm infants and accounted for 13% of Bayley mental scores at 8 and 12 months. Ross (1985) reported that perinatal conditions for preterm and full-term infants accounted for 26% of the variance in Bayley mental scores at 12 months. Similar results in which perinatal and neonatal status measures accounted for 17% of the variance in visual information processing scores were found by Rose (1983) with full-term and preterm infants in a longitudinal study.

Other researchers have obtained somewhat greater success by combining perinatal, environmental, and social/demographic variables as predictors (see Table 4.1). For example, Pederson and colleagues (Pederson, Evans, Bento, Chance, & Fox, 1987; Pederson, Evans, Chance, Bento, & Fox, 1986) studied preterm infants and accounted for 17% of the Bayley mental score variance at 7 months when Minde Morbidity Scale scores, home environment, and socioeconomic status (SES) scores were combined. In a longitudinal study, Crisafi, Driscoll, Rey, and Adler (1987) combined measures of perinatal illness, SES, and infant sex in infants with very low birthweights and accounted for 32% of the Bayley mental score variance at 2 years and 21% of the variance in McCarthy perceptual scores. Vohr, Coll, and Oh (1988) found that gestational age, SES, and neurological scores accounted for up to 42% of the variance of 2-year-olds (representing premature and full-term samples) on receptive/expressive language tests. Hack and Breslau (1986) combined neonatal risks, newborn physical measures, neurological assessment, race, and SES in very low birthweight infants and accounted for 43% of the variance on the Stanford–Binet at 3 years. Yet, despite the encouraging signs that perinatal measures, especially when combined with social/demographic measures, can be used to predict cognitive and language measures obtained in later infancy and early childhood, many researchers (e.g., Cohen & Beckwith, 1979; Cohen & Parmelee, 1983; Reich, Holmes, Slaymaker, & Lauesen, 1984; Silva, McGee, & Williams, 1984) have found little or no predictive power in perinatal measures.

One possible reason for the low predictive power found when perinatal risk measures are used is that the measures used are summaries of risk points rather than individual risk items (V. J. Molfese, 1989). Most researchers use a standard perinatal risk assessment scale (e.g., Hobel, Hyvarinen, Okada, & Oh, 1973; Littman & Parmelee, 1978; Prechtl, 1968) that permits individual risk conditions to be assessed. These risk conditions reflect various complications that can arise in the prenatal, intrapartum, or postpartum periods. The individual risk conditions are then assigned a score representing either a "present" or an "absent" system or a specific risk value thought to represent how serious one risk condition is believed to be in affecting infant outcome compared to other risk conditions on the scale. Thus, point values of either one point per risk condition or up to 35 points

TABLE 4.1

Summary of Selected Studies Using Neonatal and Environmental Measures to Predict Early Cognitive Development

Author(s)	Sample	Predictors	Criteria	Results
Cohen & Beckwith (1979)	50 PT (< 38 weeks, < 2500g)	OCS, PNCS, BWT, GA, Hospitalization length, HOME	2-year Gesell, MDI, Receptive Language	Perinatal risks not predictive; Caretaking predictive of all criteria (R^2 = .33 to .54)
Cohen & Parmelee (1983)	126 PT (< 38 weeks, < 2501g)	BWT, GA, Hospitalization length, OCS, PNCS, Neurological Exam, Sensory Tests, 9-month Gesell, Ma Ed, Birth Order	2-year Gesell, MDI, Receptive Language, 5-year Stanford–Binet	Perinatal risks not predictive; Caregiving, Ma Ed correlated with Gesell scores; Ma Ed, visual attention, 9-month Gesell, and manipulation (R^2 = .31)
Crisafi, Driscoll, Rey, & Adler (1987)	144 VLBS (< 1500g)	BWT, GA, 1- & 5-min. Apgar, Sex, Asphyxia, SES, Race	2-year MDI, 3-year Merrill–Palmer, S–B at 4, 5, 6 years, WPPSI at 4, 5, 6 year, McCarthy 4, 5, 6 year	SES predicted 3–6 outcomes (R^2 = .20 to .27); Asphyxia, SES, Sex predicted MDI (R^2 = .32); Perinatal Risk and SES predicted McCarthy Percep. (R^2 = .21)
Fox & Porges (1985)	80 healthy and sick FT and PT	Heart Measures, GA, OCS, PNCS, RDS, Asphyxia, Ma Age	8- and 12-month MDI	Heart measures, GA, OCS, PNCS predicted 8- and 12-month MDI (R^2 = .13)
Hack & Breslau (1986)	139 VLBW (< 1500g)	BWT, Length, Head Circumference, Hobel Risk Scores, SES, Race, Neurological Scores	3-year S–B, Neurological Scores at 20 & 33 mo	Hobel Risk, BWT, Head Circumference, Neurological Scores, race, SES predicted 3-year S–B (R^2 = .43)
Kopp & Vaughn (1982)	76 PT	GA, SES, Ethnicity, 9-month Gesell, Attention Scores	2-year Gesell, MDI, Sensorimotor, Language Scores	Ethnicity, 9-month Gesell, Attention Scores predicted 2-year Gesell (R^2 = .42)
V. J. Molfese & Thomson (1985)	103 infants	5 Perinatal Risk Scales	6-month PCS, MDI, Carey Scores	Brazie scale predicted MDI (R^2 = .11)
O'Connor, Cohen, & Parmelee (1984)	9 FT and 19 PT (< 38 weeks, < 2500g)	GA, BWT, SES, Ethnicity, Ma Ed	18-month MDI, 5-year S–B	MDI predicted S–B (r^2 = .52)

Study	Sample	Measures	Outcome	Results
Pederson, Evans, Bento, et al. (1987)	50 PT (< 38 weeks)	Minde, GA, Apgar, BWT, SES, HOME, Parent Measures	7-month Denver, 12-month MDI and PDI	Minde, GA, Denver predicted MDI (R^2 = .37)
Pederson, Evans, Chance, et al. (1986)	135 LBW (< 2500g)	GA, BWT, Apgar, Medical Complications, Hospitalization, SES, Maternal Measures	6-month MDI	Quality of Mothering (R^2 = .14) and intervention (R^2 = .18) predicted MDI
Reich et al. (1984)	17 PT (< 37 weeks), 36 healthy and sick FT	GA, OCS, PNCS, Brazelton Scores, Infant Sex	3-year S-B	Perinatal risk not predictive
Rose (1983)	40 FT and 40 PT	BWT, GA, OCS, PNCS	Visual Info. Process at 6- and 12-months	BWT and GA correlates of 6- and 12-month performance
Rose, Feldman, McCarton, & Wolfson (1988)	50 PT and 43 FT	BWT, GA, Length, OCS, PNCS, Apgar Scores, Hospitalizations, Respirator	7-month Info Processing Scores	GA and OCS predicted General Recognition scores (R^2 = .17)
Ross (1985)	46 PT (< 1501g), 46 FT	Apgar Scores, GA, BWT, Sepsis, Ventilation, Specific Physiological Measures, SES	12-month MDI and PDI	Apgar Scores, ICH, Hypoglyc., GA, Sepsis, BWT, PH and NEC predicted MDI (R^2 = .26)
Sostek et al. (1987)	113 PT (< 34 weeks)	IVH, BWT, SES	1-year & 2-year MDI, PDI, Neurological Scores	1-year, Neurological Scores, 1-year MDI predicted 2-year MDI (R^2 = .62)
Silva et al. (1984)	1037 tested 3, 5, and 7 year	Perinatal Risks, GA, BWT, Apgar, Delivery, Neonatal Comp., SES	3-year Language Measures, 5-year S-B and Language Measures, 7-year ITPA & WISC	Perinatal Risks predicted outcomes at 3, 5, & 7 year (R^2 = 3, 2, 1, respectively)
Vohr et al. (1988)	50 LBW (< 1500g) 18 FT	BWT, GA, SGA vs AGA, Perinatal Risks, 8-months Neurological Status, SES, Ma Age	2-year MDI, 2-year Language Measures	GA, SES, Neurological Scores predicted language (R^2 = .42)

Note: Abbreviations: PT — preterm, FT — fullterm, BWT — birthweight, LBW — low birthweight, VLBW — very low birthweight, GA — gestational age, AGA — appropriate for gestational age, SGA — small for gestational age, OSC — Obstetric Complications Scale, PNCS — Postnatal Complications Scale, PCS — Pediatric Complications Scale, RDS — respiratory distress syndrome, IVH — intraventricular hemorrhage, MDI — Mental Development Index, PDI — Psychomotor Development Index, S-B — Stanford-Binet, Ma Ed — maternal education, Ma Age — maternal age.

per risk condition can be given. The individual risk points are then summed for a total risk score. These total risk scores are commonly used as predictors. However, Siegel (1982a, 1982b) showed that the use of individual risk items results in greater predictive power. Siegel's risk index contains perinatal complications and SES characteristics, and separate scales have been developed for preterm and full-term infants. Siegel reported accounting for up to 42% of the variance in predicting scores on the Stanford–Binet, Reynell Language Scales, and the McCarthy scales in a longitudinal study of preschool children using her risk index. Because the use of individual perinatal risk items results in a large number of variables being used to predict outcomes, and this has the potential of violating the cases to measures ratios recommended for reliability in statistical analyses, it makes sense that certain perinatal risk conditions would have greater influence in infant outcomes when considered individually than when diluted with other variables. The use of individual perinatal risk measures rather than summed perinatal risk scores has been found to produce improved results in predictive studies (V. J. Molfese, DiLalla, & Lovelace, 1995).

PREDICTIONS BASED ON INFANT MEASURES

In considering the predictive value of neonatal measures, some researchers have argued that these early measures may be too unstable to use as long-term predictors and measures obtained in later infancy might be better, possibly more stable predictors. Several researchers have examined the relationship between measures obtained in the infancy period and cognitive and language scores in late infancy and the early preschool period. However, the predictive power obtained in these studies, although stronger than those obtained in the studies reported previously, still leaves 40% or more of the variance unaccounted for (see Table 4.1). For example, Kopp and Vaughn (1982) studied preterm infants and found that 42% of the variance in the scores of male children on the Gesell at 2 years could be accounted for by a combination of gestational age, 9-month Gesell scores, attention measures, and ethnicity. Sostek, Smith, Katz, and Grant (1987) found with a sample of preterm infants that 1-year Bayley mental and physical (Physical Development Index) scores and neurological assessment scores accounted for 62% of the Bayley mental scores at 2 years. Cohen and Parmelee (1983) found 31% of the variance on Stanford–Binet scores could be accounted for from a combination of education, visual and manipulative schema scores, and 9-month Gesell scores in a preterm sample. O'Connor, Cohen, and Parmelee (1984) found that the Bayley mental scores at 18 months alone accounted for 52% of the variance on the Stanford–Binet at 5 years in a sample of preterm and full-term children.

Especially encouraging results have been found when individual perinatal risk items, SES, HOME environment measures, and first-year mental status scores have been used to predict outcomes. Siegel (1982b) and Smith, Flick, Ferriss, and Sellmann (1972) compared classification accuracy obtained with 6- and 7-year-old children when perinatal measures and social measures were used as predictors and when first-year Bayley scores were added to the equations. Siegel found that classification accuracy improved from 71% to 89% when the first-year measures were added in predicting performance on the McCarthy General Cognitive Index in a preterm, very low birthweight sample. Smith et al. found that classification accuracy improved from 89% and 77% to 94% and 93% for normal and risk groups, respectively, when 8-month Bayley scores were added to the equation along with individual perinatal risk items, demographic variables, and maternal IQ. A confirmation of these findings was reported by V. J. Molfese et al. (1993) in a study with high- and low-risk 3- and 4-year-old children. In this study, classification accuracy was improved by up to 9% (with classification accuracy reaching 83%) when 12-month Bayley mental scores were added to the equation along with individual perinatal risk items, SES, and HOME (Caldwell & Bradley, 1978) scores. Interestingly, all three of these studies found greater improvements in the low-risk groups than in the high-risk group.

A growing number of studies reported in recent years are longitudinal. Longitudinal studies optimally provide ideal conditions for observing changes in the influence of variables on developmental outcomes over time. Some of these studies have supported the Transactional Model (Sameroff & Chandler, 1975), which postulates an interrelationship between the infant and its environment. A variation in the model (proposed by V. J. Molfese, Holcomb, & Helwig, 1994) postulates that perinatal variables influence the infant during the neonatal and early infancy periods more strongly than environmental variables. After infancy, social/demographic and environmental variables begin to exert stronger influences on development, eventually outweighing many perinatal variables. Recent studies reporting outcomes during the preschool years provide support for this view of the Transactional Model. Wilson (1985) found that the influence of perinatal risk measures stabilized by 18 months, with correlations in the low .20s thereafter. The influence of maternal education and SES increased after 18 months, with correlations in the .40s. Yeates, MacPhee, Campbell, and Ramey (1983) reported on the increasing influence of HOME scores from 2 to 4 years and the increasing ability of HOME scores and maternal IQ to predict Stanford–Binet scores from 2 to 4 years. The amount of variance accounted for by these variables rose from 11% to 29%. Rose and Wallace

(1985a, 1985b) reported on the early influence of perinatal risk measures, which account for 9% of the Bayley mental scores variance at 2 years. Parental education, which shows its strongest influence at 3 and 4 years, accounted for up to 66% of the variance at those ages. Visual novelty scores remained relatively constant, accounting for about 25% of the variance. A recent study by V. J. Molfese et al. (1994) used path analysis to examine the influence of perinatal risk, pediatric health, which was assumed to reflect lingering effects of perinatal risks, and SES on measures of cognitive development at 1 and 2 years and on cognitive and language measures at 3 years. The results showed that total perinatal risk scores were related only to cognitive measures obtained in the first year, but pediatric health was a weak correlate at 2 and 3 years. In contrast, SES was a weak correlate at 1 year but a stronger correlate at 2 and 3 years. These results appear to support that notion that perinatal risk (and pediatric health) conditions are predictive of outcomes in early infancy but weaken as correlates at later ages, with SES becoming a stronger correlate with age.

PREDICTIONS USING AUDITORY BRAINSTEM EVOKED RESPONSE MEASURE

Some researchers have examined the use of brainstem evoked responses (BSER) to predict developmental outcomes. In general, the results have not appeared promising as indicated by the brief review provided later. BSERs show little success in predicting long-term developmental outcomes.

The BSER consists of seven peaks that occur during the first 10 to 15 ms of the brain's response to an auditory or visual stimulus (e.g., a click or a photic flash). Each peak lasts for approximately 1 ms and the maximum amplitude is approximately $\frac{1}{2}$ microvolt. Barden and Peltzman (1980) used this technique with newborn infants, including 12 with no risk factors and 15 with 3 or more perinatal risk factors. No significant difference in the latency of Wave V, where the difference was expected, was found among subjects when grouped according to birthweight and according to 5-min Apgar scores. Correlations of Wave V with other perinatal risks were also not significant. Cox, Hack, and Metz (1984) studied a population of 50 very low birthweight infants. BSER indicated that 9 infants had abnormal responses at birth, but only 1 of the 9 was still abnormal at 4 months. BSER results were found to be correlated with individual perinatal risk conditions. Murray, Dolby, Nation, and Thomas (1981) studied 60 high-risk and 28 low-risk neonates. The latency difference between Waves I and V were found to be correlated with specific perinatal events and with postnatal assessment on the Brazelton scale. Murray (1988) later studied 65 high-risk and 28 low-risk infants at birth and 9 months. The accuracy rate overall was 45% (5 of 11 correctly identified at birth) when newborn BSER abnormalities were used to predict the presence of varying levels of neurobehavioral handicaps at 9 months. When used to provide information on neuromaturational delay, the accuracy rate overall was 12% (2 of 16 correctly identified at birth). Eldredge and Salamy (1988) used BSER to study 15 neonates at risk for neurological problems and 15 normal infants. Although a neurological screening test was able to distinguish between the two subject groups, the BSER test could not. Also there were no significant correlations between BSER and the number of perinatal risk factors.

Given the number of false positives and negatives and the inconsistencies in the abilities of BSER to distinguish between risk and no risk subjects, the BSER procedure does not appear to be effective when used as a general assessment tool for screening neonates.

PREDICTIONS USING EVOKED POTENTIAL BRAIN RESPONSES

The auditory evoked response (AER) has been used extensively to study language and cognitive processes (see D. L. Molfese, 1983, for a review of this literature). The AER is a synchronized portion of the ongoing EEG pattern that is detectable at the scalp and occurs immediately in response to some stimulus (Callaway, Tueting, & Koslow, 1978; Rockstroh, Elbert, Birbaumer, & Lutzenberger, 1982). The AER has been demonstrated to reflect both general and specific aspects of the evoking stimulus and the person's perceptions and decisions regarding it (D. L. Molfese, 1983; D. L. Molfese & Betz, 1988; D. L. Molfese & V. J. Molfese, 1979a, 1979b, 1980, 1985; Nelson & Salapatek, 1986; Ruchkin, Sutton, Munson, & Macar, 1981).

Studies conducted since the 1970s to predict later development based on neonatal evoked potential (EP) measures have varied in their effectiveness. In general, studies with restricted analyses to a single early peak or peak latency (usually the N1 component) have achieved some success in short-term prediction but failed to reveal a long-term relationship. Other studies of additional portions of the waveform have shown that AERs have long-term predictive value in assessing later language skills. Butler and Engel (1969) reported the first success in noting correlations between the neonatal evoked potential latencies and later measures related to intelligence. They recorded visual evoked potentials from 433 newborn infants in response to a series of photic flashes. Although the correlations were significant between motor behaviors and photic latency, the effects were small and accounted for little of the variance (Mental: $r = .33, p < .01$;

Fine Motor: $r = .24, p < .01$; Gross Motor: $r = .23, p < .01$). Jensen and Engel (1971) also reported correlations between neonatal photic latencies and later motor skills when they divided the photic latency response into three regions. Engel and Fay (1972) found that infants with faster visual evoked response N1 latencies (less than 146 ms) performed better at 3 years on an initial and final consonant articulation task than slow reactors, although no differences were noted on the Stanford–Binet at 4 years. In subsequent studies with older populations of children, Engel and Henderson (1973) and Henderson and Engel (1974) failed to find a relationship between neonatal visual evoked responses and a variety of later IQ and achievement scores. However, different electrode sites were used in their study than in those employed by earlier investigators (Ertl, 1969). Henderson and Engel (1974) assessed whether the neonatal visual evoked responses could predict total IQ and subtest scores, sensorimotor, perceptual–motor, and achievement test scores at 7 years. The photic latency data from 809 infants did not correlate 7 years later with their performance on a variety of IQ tests and subtests.

Thus, several studies have reported some early relationships between one component of the visual evoked response, usually the latency or length of the interval between stimulus onset and the N1 peak, and subsequent motor, cognitive-motor, or language-related abilities up to 3 years. However, further research that compared early neonatal evoked responses with later intelligence score measures failed to demonstrate a relationship. Although such conclusions may appear discouraging, more recent studies suggest that relationships might in fact exist (D. L. Molfese, 1989; D. L. Molfese & V. J. Molfese, 1985, 1986; D. L. Molfese & Searock, 1986). The differences in success among such studies may reflect a number of differences in both methodology and experimental design:

1. Molfese and his associates analyzed the entire evoked potential waveform, and Ertl and others confined their analysis to a single initial peak. Analysis of all data collected instead of only a subset should increase the likelihood of finding a relationship between early brain responses and later development, if such relationships do in fact exist.

2. The frequency range of the evoked potential studied by Molfese includes a lower range of frequencies (below 2 Hz) than those employed by earlier investigators. Given that the brain wave frequencies characterizing the evoked potentials of young infants are concentrated in the frequency range below 3 Hz, such a strategy should utilize more of the neonate's brain wave activity.

3. The studies reported by Molfese employ language-related, speech sounds as stimuli. Since predictors of successful performance are generally better if they measure predicted skills, the inclusion of more language-

relevant stimuli should increase the likelihood for predicting later language performance.

EVOKED POTENTIAL STUDIES USING CHANGES IN THE ENTIRE WAVEFORM TO PREDICT LATER DEVELOPMENT

Molfese and Molfese, in addition to investigating changes in developmental patterns of lateralization across the life span, have isolated and identified electrophysiological correlates of various speech perception cues across and within a number of developmental periods (D. L. Molfese & V. J. Molfese, 1979a, 1985, 1988). The implications of these lateralized patterns of response for later language development is an important issue. Are these patterns of responses related to later language development for individual children, or do they reflect some basic pattern of auditory processing in the brain that has little relation to language development? Given Lenneberg's (1967) notion that lateralization is a biological sign of language, could such early patterns of lateralized discrimination of speech sounds predict later language outcomes? Theoreticians have speculated that the absence of hemispheric differences in a child indicates that the child is at risk for certain cognitive or language disabilities (Travis, 1931). Although the data generally have not supported such a position, predictions concerning later performance could be enhanced when hemispheric differences are considered in light of specific processing capacities.

In this regard, D. L. Molfese and V. J. Molfese (1985, 1986) attempted to establish the predictive validity for a variety of factors in predicting long-term outcomes in language development from measures taken shortly after birth and during the first year of life. In their first study (D. L. Molfese and V. J. Molfese, 1985), 16 infants were studied longitudinally from birth through 3 years. Information was collected on gender, birthweight, length, gestational age, and scores on the Obstetric Complications Scale (Littman & Parmelee, 1978), the Brazelton Neonatal Assessment Scale (Als, Tronick, Lester, & Brazelton, 1977; Brazelton, 1973), the Bayley Scales of Infant Development (Bayley, 1969), the Peabody Picture Vocabulary Test (Dunn, 1965), and the McCarthy Scales of Children's Abilities (McCarthy, 1972). Parental ages, incomes, educational levels, and occupations were also obtained. In addition, AERs were recorded in response to speech stimuli from the left and right temporal areas (T3 and T4) at birth and again at 6-month intervals until the child's third birthday. The speech stimuli were chosen because they produced reliable general hemispheric difference effects as well as bilateral and lateralized discrimination effects. Eight other stimulus tokens were added to facilitate tests of generalizeability across different consonant and vowel contrasts. Such stimuli appeared to be ideally suited for determining whether general hemispheric differences per se or specific lateralized discrimination abilities were the best predictors of later language skills.

Analyses of the AER data indicated that electrophysiological measures recorded at birth could identify children who performed better or worse on language tasks 3 years later. One component of the auditory AER that occurred between 88 and 240 ms reliably discriminated among children whose McCarthy Verbal Index scores were above 50 (the High group) and those who scored lower (the Low group). Only AERs recorded over the left hemisphere of the High group systematically discriminated among the different consonant speech sounds. The right-hemisphere responses of this group, in contrast, discriminated among the different nonspeech stimuli. However, the Low group displayed no such lateralized discrimination for either the speech or the nonspeech sounds. A second portion of the AER with a late peak latency of 664 ms also discriminated between the High and Low groups. Unlike the earlier peak, however, this component occurred over both hemispheres and, consequently, reflected bilateral activity. This second component did not behave in exactly the same manner as the first. Although the second component discriminated among speech and non-speech stimuli, discrimination between consonant sounds depended on which vowel followed the consonant. A third component of the AER (peak latency = 450 ms) that varied only across hemispheres failed to discriminate between the two groups.

Thus, hemispheric differences per se could not discriminate at birth among infants who would have better or poorer language skills 3 years later. Furthermore, given that the AER components that discriminated between the two groups were sensitive to certain speech and nonspeech contrasts but not to others, the AERs appear to reflect the infant's sensitivity to specific language-related cues rather than overall readiness of the brain to respond to any general stimulus in its environment.

A stepwise multiple regression model of these data was developed using the Peabody and McCarthy Verbal Index scores as the dependent variables and the AER components obtained at birth that best discriminated the different consonant sounds as the independent variables. This model accounted for 78% of the total variance in predicting McCarthy scores from the brain responses and 69% of the variance in predicting Peabody scores (D. L. Molfese & V. J. Molfese, 1988). Clearly, early AER discrimination of speech-related stimuli is strongly related to later language skills.

D. L. Molfese and Searock (1986) later noted that this relationship between early AER activity and later language skills also exists at 1 year. AERs were recorded from 16 infants within 2 weeks of their first birthday. A series of three vowel sounds with speech formant structure and three nonspeech tokens containing 1 Hz-wide formants that matched the mean frequencies of the speech sounds were presented to these infants, and their AERs were recorded in response to each sound. Two regions of the AERs, one centered between 300 and 400 ms and another centered around 200 ms following stimulus onset, discriminated among the 1-year-old infants who 2 years later would perform better or worse on the McCarthy language tasks. Infants who were able to discriminate among more vowel sounds performed better on the language tasks at 3 years.

Subsequently, D. L. Molfese (1989) recorded the AERs at birth from scalp electrodes placed over frontal, temporal, and parietal scalp areas over the left and right hemispheres. The speech and nonspeech sounds that served as stimuli were a subset of those employed by D. L. Molfese and V. J. Molfese (1985) and consisted of the speech syllables (bi, gi) and the nonspeech analogues for these two consonant–vowel sounds. These four sounds had been found to be the best predictors in the earlier study. This sample of 30 infants had McCarthy verbal scores at 3 years that ranged from 32 to 69 (mean = 53, SD = 9.41). The mean for the infants who scored 50 or below on the McCarthy test was 45 (SD = 4.97, range = 32–50), and the mean for the infants who scored above 50 was 61 (SD = 4.95, range = 54–69). Overall, both groups of children possessed largely average language scores. A discriminant function procedure was applied. The time points of the averaged AERs were used to discriminate the language scores obtained when the children were 3 years. The stepwise analysis, with an F-to-enter of 3.0, selected 17 points in order of their effectiveness in classifying each of the 720 original averaged AERs into one of the two groups. These points clustered in four regions of the AER — the first between 20 and 140 ms, the second between 230 and 270 ms, the third between 410 and 490 ms, and the fourth between 600 and 700 ms. The likelihood of correctly classifying a brain response as belonging to a Low or High language performance child was 50%, but the actual classification accuracy was significantly higher than chance. For the Low and High groups, respectively, the classification was accurate 69.7% and 68.6% of the time. A z-test of proportions indicated that the actual classification was significantly better than chance for each group (z = 9.98, 10.57, p < .001). Applying a rule that at least 54% of an individual's AERs must be classified into the Low group before that infant would be classified as having a lower-than-average language performance, Molfese noted that, out of 30 infants, only 1 infant from the Low group and 1 from the High group would be misclassified.

One region of the AER waveforms that distinguish among the brain waves of infants who will later develop differently in language skills is illustrated in Fig. 4.1. The top two figures are from the data published by D. L. Molfese and V. J. Molfese (1985). The waveform on the left is the averaged AER for the 8 neonates who at 3 years obtained a verbal subtest

Low McCarthy Scores   High McCarthy Scores

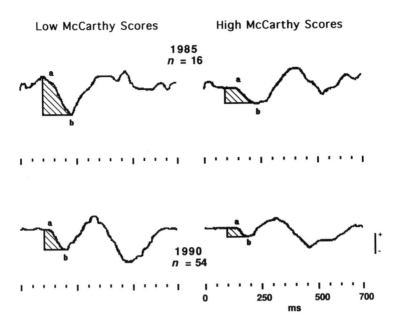

FIG. 4.1.   Newborn auditory evoked responses to high and low language performing children.

score on the McCarthy of 20.5 (*SD* = 12.6) and that on the right is the average waveform for the 8 infants who obtained an average score of 77.25 (*SD* = 15.5). The amplitude of the region responsible for this discrimination is between the positive peak labeled *a* and the leading edge of the following negative wave labeled *b*, which occurred between 88 and 240 ms. The group differences were marked. The amplitude or vertical distance between a and b for the positive peak is larger for the Low than the High group.

One interpretation of these results is that early discrimination abilities relate directly to later language development. The children who performed better on language tasks at age 3 discriminated better at birth among consonant sounds alone and consonant sounds in combination with different vowel sounds (D. L. Molfese, 1989; D. L. Molfese & V. J. Molfese, 1985). Such a pattern of responding suggests that more linguistically advanced children are already at an advantage at birth because their nervous systems can make finer discriminations along a variety of dimensions. As D. L. Molfese (1989) suggested: "Perhaps the earlier an infant can discriminate between speech sounds in its environment, the more likely that infant will be able to use such information to discriminate word sound differences" (p. 55). Such early discrimination abilities may later play a major role in the infant's early word learning as it attempts to relate one sound pattern to a specific object and a different sound pattern to a second object.

These data provide further support for the position that early physiological indices are predictive of long-term developmental trends. One especially striking aspect of these data concerns the range of language abilities that are differentiated 3 years after the newborn brain responses were recorded. Although the language skills in the D. L. Molfese and V. J. Molfese (1988) study ranged from relatively poor receptive and productive skills to well above average skills, the amount of variance was not as large as has been reported in other studies that have included children with significant perinatal risk conditions. In spite of this degree of relative similarity across children, the brain responses are able to distinguish children who perform differently on the language tasks.

LONGITUDINAL STUDY OF ELECTROPHYSIOLOGICAL CORRELATES OF LANGUAGE DEVELOPMENT

Currently underway in our laboratory is a second longitudinal study designed to determine whether the results of our previous longitudinal study can be replicated and extended using a larger sample of normal and at-risk children. The longitudinal study began with the testing of 387 newborn infants using AER procedures and the abstracting of medical information needed to quantify a battery of 290 perinatal risk variables. Risk variables from the battery were used to explore different predictive models involving various configurations of these variables. Subsequently, 196 infants were tested at their first birthdate and 186 in Year 2, 3, and 4. Testing of 5-year-old children is in progress with 147 tested to date and 39 more to be tested. The highest attrition rate (49%) occurred in Year 1 because families moved, were unreachable after repeated attempts, or lost interest. The remaining participant population was stable with only the loss of 10 additional children after Year 1. Within the sample are 60 infants considered at risk because of perinatal and early neonatal complications. Participant data are shown in Table 4.2.

Testing of the children has occurred yearly, with evoked potential testing and behavioral assessments occurring at each age. Shown in Table 4.3 are the assessments used at each age.

Four independent analysis procedures were used: (a) the principal components analysis of the digitized time points from averaged AERs followed by an analysis of variance of factor scores from the principal components analysis as the dependent measures; (b) a discriminant function analysis using the jackknife procedure in which the dependent variables were the digitized time points of the averaged AERs obtained in the present

TABLE 4.2
Descriptive Statistics in Children in Longitudinal Study

		Normal Participants		At-Risk Participants	
		M	SD	M	SD
Birthweight		3415.38	690.88	2649.30	1030.72
Gestational Age		39.39	2.38	36.48	4.23
One-Min Apgar		7.47	1.75	6.0	2.5
Five-Min Apgar		8.75	1.02	7.7	1.89
Postnatal Complications Score		54	1.57	3.07	2.31
Perinatal Risks		6.18	3.39	10.33	4.19
Maternal Age		27.71	5.25	26.32	5.35
Maternal Employment		Yes = 87	No = 41		
Paternal Employment		Yes = 110	No = 8		
		Full Sample			
	M	SD		M	SD
PSC – One Year	1.67	1.41			
PSC – Two Years	1.62	1.35			
PCS – Three Years	1.51	1.23			
HOME Total	45.54	4.39	HOME–Academic Stimulation	4.22	.83
HOME Learning Materials	8.76	1.72	HOME–Modeling	3.38	1.18
HOME Communicative Competence	6.24	.81	HOME–Variety in Experience	7.01	1.04
HOME Environment	6.69	.78	HOME–Acceptance of Child	3.61	.96
HOME-Nurturance	5.75	1.15			
Bayley – 1	115.37	17.21	Bayley – 2	109.16	19.31
Stanford–Binet – 2	103.81	7.49	Stanford–Binet – 3	104.62	10.09
Stanford–Binet – 4	105.55	11.71	Stanford–Binet – 5	101.87	9.69
McCarthy Verbal – 3	53.66	9.02	Peabody – Three	100.02	16.09

study; (c) a control analysis that utilized a Monte-Carlo like procedure in which the input order of the AERs to the principal components analysis was randomized (this step provides additional information concerning the likelihood of Type I error); and (d) a regression analysis that used language performance scores noted at 3 years as the dependent variables and the various measures of the AERs recorded at birth (e.g., factor scores, amplitude, latency, area), perinatal variables, HOME, and demographic measures as the independent variables. To date, the results of the current longitudinal study are comparable to the results of the initial longitudinal study. We have briefly outlined some of our findings to date concerning the principal components analysis/analysis of variance procedures and the discriminant function procedures that we have employed to isolate and identify neonatal AER components that predict long-term outcomes.

TABLE 4.3
Behavioral Assessments Administered in Longitudinal Study

Age 4
    Stanford–Binet Intelligence Scale (4th Edition)
    McCarthy Scales of Children's Abilities (VSI only)
    Parent Demographic Information Sheet
    Pediatric Complications Scale
Ages 5 and 6
    Stanford–Binet Intelligence Scale (4th Edition)
    Parent Demographic Information Sheet
    Pediatric Complications Scale
    School Achievement Test results
Age 7
    Weschler Intelligence Scale for Children–III
    50 Utterance Language Sample
    Parent Demographic Information Sheet
    Pediatric Complications Scale
    School Achievement Test results
Age 7
    Weschler Intelligence Scale for Children–III
    Wide-Range Achievement Test
    Word Attack
    Parent Demographic Information Sheet
    Pediatric Complications Scale
    School Achievement Test results

PCA/ANOVA

Initial Findings.   Principal components analysis procedures were used with AER time points as the variables and AER averages as the cases. Seven factors, accounting for 79.93% of variance, were retained using the Cattell Scree Test criterion. The seven factors characterized the different regions of the averaged AERs that varied most across the entire set of brain responses. The factor scores from one portion of the AERs between 88 and 240 ms as reflected by Factor 3 were included as dependent variables in an ANOVA that included a single between-participants measure based on a median split separating the brain responses of newborn infants who later scored above 50 (High MCVSI) on the McCarthy verbal scale index at 3 years from those scoring below 50 (Low MCVSI). Repeated measures characterized the remaining variables: two consonant sounds (/b/, /g/), the two formant structures (speech, nonspeech), the three vowel sounds (/i, æ, ɔ/), and the two electrode positions (left- and right-hemisphere temporal sites). The factor scores for Factor 3 varied systematically as a function of group membership as reflected by a Group × Formant × Hemisphere interaction, $F(1, 14) = 8.65, p < .01$. Scheffe tests indicated that for children in the High MCVSI group, the AER region between 88 and 240 ms discriminated between the /b/ and /g/ speech stimuli only at the left hemisphere site, $F(1, 14) = 8.95$, $p < .01$. The right hemisphere AER for the High MCVSI children discriminated the nonspeech /b/ and /g/ consonants, $F(1, 14) = 4.40$, $p < .04$. No comparable effects were found for Low MCVSI children.

Present Findings. Analyses conducted to date for a set of 54 children also identified an early portion of the AER recorded over the left hemisphere of newborn infants that discriminates among children who 3 years later differ in their language performance. As before, this region discriminates among consonant sounds. Scheffe tests of a Group × Consonant × Hemisphere interaction, $F(1, 52) = 12.12$, $p < .001$, indicated that AERs recorded from the left hemisphere differed in response to the /b/ and /g/ consonant sounds, $F(1, 52) = 8.37$, $p < .0057$, for only the High language performance group. An analysis just completed with 120 children and modeled after D. L. Molfese and V. J. Molfese (1985) also revealed a Group × Consonant × Hemisphere interaction, $F(1, 118) = 6.00$, $p < .0158$ at this same latency in the brainwave. As before, Scheffe tests indicated that for children in the High MCVSI group, the AER region up to 230 ms discriminated between the /b/ and /g/ speech stimuli only at the left hemisphere site, $F(1, 118) = 7.11$, $p < .009$. No comparable effect was found for the Low MCVSI children. This effect overlaps both temporally and functionally with the original effects reported by D. L. Molfese and V. J. Molfese (1985). Once all the 3-year data are obtained for our entire sample, these analyses will be repeated with the full sample of 186 children. However, given that these results have held up across different subsamples of this population with up to 120 children and the important fact that the region of the AER waveform that discriminates between the two groups is identical to that reported in the original study (D. L. Molfese & V. J. Molfese, 1985), we anticipate that comparable findings will be obtained with the entire population. One additional point is that the current population of children have a somewhat narrower range of language and cognitive scores than the original population. In spite of this difference, the analyses of newborn AERs continue to indicate strong differences between the Low and High language performers 3 years later.

Discriminant Function

Initial Findings. Linear discriminant function procedures were developed for the averaged AERs based on the digitized time points for each waveform. This step used the amplitude values of the averaged AERs as the input data to discriminate participant groups and conditions. Results were cross-validated using the jackknifed procedure. There were 16 classes to be discriminated—the 2 participant groups, the 2 consonant sounds, the 2 formant bandwidths, and the 2 electrode sites. The stepwise discriminant function analysis selected two points (96 ms, U-statistic = .90, $p < .01$ and 224 ms, U-statistic = .82, $p < .01$) based on effectiveness in classifying each original averaged AERs into 16 conditions. Chance classification was 6.25%. For High MCVSI children, classification was successful for the left-hemisphere site for normal formant /b/ (62.5%, $z = 64.4, p < .01$) and normal formant /g/ (29.2% correct, $z = 26.3, p < .01$). The right-hemisphere site correctly classified AERs for sinewave formant /b/ (29.2% correct, $z = 26.3, p < .01$) and sinewave formant /g/ (20.8% correct, $z = 16.7, p < .01$). Significant levels of classification for Low MCVSI children occurred for only normal formant /g/ AERs recorded from the right temporal site (16.7% correct, $z = 12.0, p < .010$). When jackknifed classification was used, the classification accuracy for the High MCVSI was 58.3%, 29.2%, 29.2%, and 26.7%, respectively (all at $p < .01$). Classification accuracy for the Low MCVSI dropped to chance levels. The discriminant function analysis correctly classified the same stimuli and participant groups found to be important for the PCA/ANOVA analyses. In addition, data points selected by discriminant function analysis were within the region dominated by the factor identified in the PCA. This level of high agreement across the two procedures was interpreted as a further indicator of the reliability of the effects.

Present Findings. These discriminant analyses procedures are continuing. Preliminary indications are that when AERs from 79 neonates are classified by their actual electrode site of origin, the evoking stimulus, and the language performance group from which they were recorded, classification accuracies of 100% can be reached. For example, in one analysis of the 79 infants, the verbal performance score on the Stanford–Binet intelligence test at 3 years was used to identify and separate three groups of scores—those one standard deviation (117) above the mean of 105.4, those one standard deviation (94) below the mean, and the intermediate group with scores between these two groups. These groups included 22, 19, and 38 infants, respectively. The AERs from this sample of 79 neonates included those obtained in response to nine different auditory stimuli recorded over 6 scalp electrode sites. As in the D. L. Molfese and V. J. Molfese (1985) study, the AERs were recorded at 10 ms intervals over a 700 ms period following the onset of the acoustic stimuli. Electrodes were placed at left and right temporal sites, T_3 and T_4 (Jasper, 1958), as well as at left and right frontal (F_l, F_r) and parietal (P_l, P_r) locations midway between the external meatus and F_z and P_z, respectively. The electrodes were referred to linked ear references. These 4,266 AERs were normalized using a z-score transformation and then input to a principal components analysis procedure that employed a varimax rotation. Six factors accounting for 85.5% of the total variance were then selected and rotated. The resulting factor scores for each electrode site and stimulus event were then used as variables in a discriminant function procedure to distinguish the three language performance groups at 3 years. As indicated in Table 4.4, all seventy-nine 3-year-old children were correctly assigned to their language performance group based on their newborn AERs ($x^2 = 127.3$, $p < .0001$).

SUMMARY AND IMPLICATIONS

The studies described in this chapter illustrate a number of research issues of importance to the task of developing a predictive assessment tool for use with neonates and young infants. First, the perinatal variables have been shown to have some use in prediction of cognitive and language scores, particularly early in infancy. The simple correlations, multiple correlations, and attempts to classify subjects have shown that perinatal measures used alone have some power. Yet the amount of variance accounted for by perinatal measures alone is at best 43% and is not high enough to make confident predictions of the implications that these early measures have for later functioning. When perinatal risk measures are combined with social and demographic measures or used as individual predictors, the picture improves somewhat in that more studies report multiple correlations over 40%, yet the total amount of variance accounted for does not improve much beyond 60%. We have argued, and continue to argue here, that the problem is less one of little predictability for measures obtained in the neonatal period than one of selecting more sensitive measures. AER measures of neonatal participants have yielded high correlations with language scores in the preschool period. The discriminant function data reported previously that demonstrate 100% classification accuracy serve to reinforce this point.

TABLE 4.4
Classification Results

			Predicted Group Membership		
	Actual Group	No. of Cases	1	2	3
Group	1	22	22	0	0
			100%	0%	0%
Group	2	38	0	38	0
			0%	100%	0%
Group	3	19	0	0	19
			0%	0%	100%

Note: Percentage of "grouped" cases correctly classified: 100%.

Second, although many studies are cross sectional, some issues such as the prediction of long-term development for individuals need to be addressed in longitudinal studies. Unfortunately, reports from longitudinal studies frequently do not contain information on the influence over time of the same variables on the measures under study. Further, many studies are focused on discriminating between groups (e.g., premature/low birthweight vs. full-term) rather than using analyses that permit assessment of predictivity. A few studies, described previously do provide information on the influence of variables over time. These studies, plus the current research reported from our laboratory, offer unique opportunities to observe and document the relative roles that perinatal, physiological, social/demographic, and environmental variables play in influencing development over the infancy and preschool years.

Third, advantages of a longitudinal approach to the study of cognitive and language abilities can be realized only if the measures are appropriate across the age range covered. Unlike some measures, which depend on the maturity of the infant's behavioral response, AER methods can be used with infants, children, and adults to provide measures of brain processing of stimuli from many modalities. Further, the AER methods have shown promise as providing a basis by which accurate predictions of language and cognitive status can be made even when the scales used for status assessments must change as the children mature.

ACKNOWLEDGMENT

Support for this work was provided in part by a grant to the first two authors from the National Institutes of Health (R01 HD17860).

REFERENCES

Als, H., Tronick, E., Lester, B., & Brazelton, T. (1977). The Brazelton Neonatal Behavioral Assessment Scale. *Journal of Abnormal Child Psychology, 5*, 215–231.

Barden T., & Peltzman, P. (1980). Newborn brain stem auditory evoked responses and perinatal clinical event. *American Journal of Obstetric Gynecology, 136*, 912–919.

Bayley, N. (1969). *Bayley Scales of Infant Development: Birth to two years.* New York: Psychological Corporation.

Brazelton, T. (1973). Neonatal Behavior Assessment Scale. *Clinics in Developmental Medicine* (No. 50). Philadelphia: Lippincott.

Butler, B., & Engel, R. (1969). Mental and motor scores at 8 months in relation to neonatal photic responses. *Developmental Medicine and Child Neurology, 11*, 77–82.

Caldwell, B., & Bradley, R. (1978). *Manual of the Home Observation for Measurement of Environment.* Unpublished manuscript, University of Arkansas, Little Rock.

Callaway, C., Tueting, P., & Koslow, S. (1978). *Event-related brain potentials and behavior.*

New York: Academic Press.

Cohen, S., & Beckwith, L. (1979). Preterm infant interactions with the caregiver in the first year of life and competence at age two. *Child Development, 50,* 767–777.

Cohen, S., & Parmelee, A. (1983). Prediction of five-year Stanford–Binet scores in preterm infants. *Child Development, 54,* 1242–1253.

Cox, L., Hack, M., & Metz, D. (1984). Auditory brain stem response abnormalities in the very low birthweight infant: Incidence and risk factors. *Ear and Hearing, 5,* 47–51.

Crisafi, M., Driscoll, J., Rey, H., & Adler, A. (1987, April). *A longitudinal study of intellectual performance of very low birthweight infants in the preschool years.* Paper presented at the meeting of the Society for Research in Child Development, Baltimore.

Dunn, D. (1965). *Peabody Picture Vocabulary Test.* Circle Pines, MN: American Guidance Service.

Eldridge, L., & Salamy, A. (1988). Neurobehavioral and neurophysiological assessment of healthy and "at risk" full-term infants. *Child Development, 59,* 186–192.

Engel, R., & Fay, W. (1972). Visual evoked responses at birth, verbal scores at three years, and IQ at four years. *Developmental Medicine and Child Neurology, 14,* 283–289.

Engel, R., & Henderson, N. (1973). Visual evoked responses and IQ scores at school age. *Developmental Medicine and Child Neurology, 15,* 136–145.

Ertl, J. (1969). Brain response correlates of psychometric intelligence. *Nature, 223,* 421.

Fox, N., & Porges, S. (1985). The relation between neonatal heart period patterns and developmental outcome. *Child Development, 56,* 28–37.

Hack, M., & Breslau, N. (1986). Very low birth weight infants: Effects of brain growth during infancy on intelligence quotients at 3 years of age. *Pediatrics, 77,* 196–202.

Henderson, N., & Engel, R. (1974). Neonatal visual evoked potentials as predictors of psychoeducational testing at age seven. *Developmental Psychology, 10,* 269–276.

Hobel, C., Hyvarinen, M., Okada, D., & Oh, W. (1973). Prenatal and intrapartum high-risk screening: I. Prediction of the high-risk neonate. *American Journal of Obstetrics and Gynecology, 117,* 1–9.

Jasper, H. (1958). The ten–twenty electrode system of the International Federation of Societies for Electroencephalography: Appendix to report of the committee on methods and clinical examination of electroencephalography. *Journal of Electroencephalography and Clinical Neurophysiology, 10,* 371–375.

Jensen, D. R., & Engel, R. (1971). Statistical procedures for relating dichotomous responses to maturation and EEG measurements. *Journal of Electroencephalography and Clinical Neurophysiology, 30,* 437–443.

Kopp, C., & Vaughn, B. (1982). Sustained attention during exploratory manipulation as a predictor of cognitive competence in preterm infants. *Child Development, 53,* 174–182.

Lenneberg, E. (1967). *Biological foundations of language.* New York: Wiley.

Littman, B., & Parmelee, A. (1978). Medical correlation of infant development. *Pediatrics, 61,* 470–474.

McCarthy, D. (1972). *Manual for the McCarthy Scales of Children's Abilities.* New York: Psychological Corporation.

Molfese, D. L. (1983). Event related potentials and language processes. In A. Gaillard & W. Ritter (Eds.). *Tutorials in AER research — Endogenous components* (pp. 345–368). Amsterdam: Elsevier.

Molfese, D. L. (1989). The use of auditory evoked responses recorded from newborns to predict later language skills. In N. Paul (Ed.), *Research in infant assessment* (Vol. 25, No. 6). White Plains, NY: March of Dimes.

Molfese, D. L., & Betz, J. (1988). Electrophysiological indices of the early development of lateralization of language and cognition, and their implication for predicting later development. In D. L. Molfese & S. J. Segalowitz (Eds.), *Brain lateralization in children: Developmental implications* (pp. 171–190). New York: Guilford.

Molfese, D. L., & Molfese, V. J. (1979a). Hemisphere and stimulus differences as reflected in the cortical responses of newborn infants to speech stimuli. *Developmental Psychology, 15*, 505–511.

Molfese, D. L., & Molfese, V. J. (1979b). Infant speech perception: Learned or innate? In H. Whitaker & H. Whitaker (Eds.), *Advances in neurolinguistics* (Vol. 4, pp. 225–240). New York: Academic Press.

Molfese, D. L., & Molfese, V. J. (1980). Cortical responses of preterm infants to phonetic and nonphonetic speech stimuli. *Developmental Psychology, 16*, 574–581.

Molfese, D. L., & Molfese, V. J. (1985). Electrophysiological indices of auditory discrimination in newborn infants: The bases for predicting later language development. *Infant Behavior and Development, 8*, 197–211.

Molfese, D. L., & Molfese, V. J. (1986). Psychophysical indices of early cognitive processes and their relationship to language. In J. E. Obrzut & G. W. Hynd (Eds.), *Child neuropsychology: Theory and research* (Vol. 1, pp. 95–115). New York: Academic Press.

Molfese, D. L., & Molfese, V. J. (1988). Right hemisphere responses from preschool children to temporal cues contained in speech and nonspeech materials: Electrophysiological correlates. *Brain and Language, 33*, 245–259.

Molfese, D. L., & Searock, K. (1986). The use of auditory evoked responses at one year of age to predict language skills at 3 years. *Australian Journal of Communication Disorders, 14*, 35–46.

Molfese, V. J. (1989). *Perinatal risk and infant development: Assessment and prediction.* New York: Guilford.

Molfese, V. J., DiLalla, L., & Lovelace, L. (1995). Perinatal, home environment, and infant measures as successful predictors of preschool cognitive and verbal abilities. *International Journal of Behavioral Development, 18*, 1–19.

Molfese, V. J., Holcomb, L., & Helwig, S. (1994). Biomedical and environmental influences on verbal abilities in children one to three years. *International Journal of Behavioral Development, 17*, 271–287.

Molfese, V. J., & Thomson, B. (1985). Optimality versus complications: Assessing predictive values of perinatal scales. *Child Development, 56*, 810–823.

Murray, A. (1988). Newborn auditory brainstem evoked responses (ABRs): Longitudinal correlates in the first year. *Child Development, 59*, 1542–1554.

Murray, A., Dolby, R., Nation, R., & Thomas, D. (1981). Effects of epidermal anesthesia on newborn and their mothers. *Child Development, 52*, 71–82.

Nelson, C., & Salapatek, P. (1986). Electrophysiological correlates of infant recognition memory. *Child Development, 57*, 1483–1497.

O'Connor, M., Cohen, S., & Parmelee, A. (1984). Infant auditory discrimination in preterm infants as a predictor of five-year intelligence. *Developmental Psychology, 20*, 159–165.

Pederson, D., Evans, B., Bento, S., Chance, G., & Fox, A. (1987, April). *Invulnerable high risk preterm infants.* Poster presented at the Society for Research in Child Development, Baltimore.

Pederson, D., Evans, B., Chance, G., Bento, S., & Fox, A. (1986, September). *Stress resistant low birthweight infants.* Poster presented at the International Association for Infant Mental Health Conference, Chicago.

Prechtl, H. (1968). Neurological findings in newborn infants after pre and perinatal complications. In J. Jonis, H. Vissern, & J. Trodstran (Eds.), *Aspects of prematurity and dysmaturity: Nutricia symposium* (pp. 305–332). Springfield, IL: Thomas.

Reich, J., Holmes, D., Slaymaker, F., & Lauesen, B. (1984). *Infant assessments as predictors of 3-year IQ.* Paper presented at International Conference on Infant Studies, New York.

Rockstroh, B., Elbert, T., Birbaumer, N., & Lutzenberger, W. (1982). *Slow brain potentials and behavior.* Baltimore: Urban-Schwarzenberg.

Rose, S. (1983). Differential rates of visual information processing in full-term and preterm infants. *Child Development, 54*, 1189–1198.

Rose, S., Feldman, J., McCarton, C., & Wolfson, J. (1988). Information processing in seven-month-old infants as a function of risk status. *Child Development, 59*, 589–603.

Rose, S., & Wallace, I. (1985a). Cross-modal and intramodal transfer as predictors of mental development in full-term and preterm infants. *Developmental Psychology, 21*, 949–962.

Rose, S., & Wallace, I. (1985b). Visual recognition memory: A predictor of later cognitive functioning in preterms. *Child Development, 56*, 843–852.

Ross, G. (1985). Use of the Bayley Scales to characterize abilities of premature infants. *Child Development, 56*, 835–842.

Ruchkin, D., Sutton, S., Munson, R., & Macar, F. (1981). P300 and feedback provided by the absence of the stimuli. *Psychophysiology, 18*, 271–282.

Sameroff, A., & Chandler, M. (1975). Reproductive risk and the continuum of caretaking casualty. In F. D. Horowitz (Ed.), *Review of child development research* (Vol. 4, pp. 115–151). Chicago: University of Chicago Press.

Siegel, L. (1982a). Reproductive, perinatal and environmental factors as predictors of the cognitive and language developments of preterm and full term infants. *Child Development, 53*, 963–973.

Siegel, L. (1982b). Reproductive, perinatal and environmental variables as predictors of development of preterm (< 1500 grams) and full term infants at 5 years. *Seminars and Perinatology, 6*, 274–279.

Silva, P., McGee, R., & Williams, S. (1984). A seven year follow-up study of the cognitive development of children who experienced common perinatal problems. *Australian Pediatric Journal, 20*, 23–28.

Smith, A., Flick, G., Ferriss, G., & Sellmann, A. (1972). Prediction of developmental outcomes at seven years from prenatal, perinatal and postnatal events. *Child Development, 43*, 495–507.

Sostek, A., Smith, Y., Katz, K., & Grant, E. (1987). Developmental outcome of preterm infants with intraventricular hemorrhage at one and two years of age. *Child Development, 58*, 779–786.

Thorndike, R., Hagen, E., & Sattler, J. (1986). *Guide for administering and scoring the fourth edition Stanford–Binet Intelligence Scale.* Chicago: Riverside.

Travis, L. E. (1931). *Speech pathology.* New York: Appleton-Century.

Vohr, B., Coll, C., & Oh, W. (1988). Language development of low-birthweight infants at two years. *Developmental Medicine and Child Neurology, 30*, 608–615.

Wilson, R. (1985). Risk and resilience in early mental development. *Developmental Psychology, 21*, 795–805.

Yeates, K., MacPhee, D., Campbell, F., & Ramey, C. (1983). Maternal IQ and home environment as determinants of early childhood intellectual competence: A developmental analysis. *Developmental Psychology, 19*, 731–739.

5 Electrophysiological Correlates of Memory Development in the First Year of Life

Charles A. Nelson
University of Minnesota

Despite the tremendous gains that have been made recently in examining the relation between brain and memory in the adult human and monkey, relatively little progress has been made in studying the ontogeny of this relation (for some exceptions, see Bachevalier, 1990, 1992; Diamond, 1990; Nelson, 1995). This is unfortunate, for two reasons. First, the study of development is important in and of itself. Second, the study of development has important implications for understanding adult functioning. Assuming the first premise is self-evident, let me elaborate on the second. The argument has been made that studying memory impairment in the human adult and inducing memory deficits in the monkey may provide methods of converging operations on the study of normal memory (e.g., Mishkin & Appenzeller, 1987; Squire, 1986, 1987). In both cases, it is assumed that when a particular brain structure has been manipulated (as a result of disease or an induced lesion), changes that occur in the resulting function can provide insight into the importance of the manipulated structure. A developmental approach, on the other hand, provides for the ability to study how the elements of a memory system are assembled at the outset and to assess each element's contribution to that system. Such a prospective view has the singular advantage of being able to monitor in "real time" how the mature organism was formed, thus simplifying the task of analyzing how the components of the system interact.

Given all we have to gain by studying development, the question arises as to why so little is known about the neural foundations underlying early memory. The most obvious answer has been the sheer difficulty of studying an organism that is incapable of talking, responding motorically, or sitting still and attending for more than a few seconds. Thus, although adequate tools exist for studying brain function in the intact human adult (e.g., positron emission tomography [PET]; functional magnetic resonance imaging [fMRI]), most of these tools place demands on the participant that are unrealistic for use with the human infant; some, of course, are also invasive. Accordingly, the armamentarium of the human developmental cognitive neuroscientist is exceedingly meager relative to that of those who study the adult or the nonhuman subject.

One tool used increasingly with infants, children, and adults that is exempt from these constraints is the recording of event-related potentials (ERPs). ERPs represent transient voltage oscillations in the brain that occur in response to a discrete event (for discussion of the physiological basis of ERPs, see Allison, 1984; Regan, 1989; Vaughan & Kurtzberg, 1992). The electrical activity generated by these oscillations is thought to originate in a relatively narrow population of neurons that propagates to the scalp through extracellular space (see Kandal, Schwartz, & Jessell, 1991, for a discussion of volume conduction). There are three attributes of ERP methodology that are particularly relevant to the study of infants. First, the recording of ERPs is entirely noninvasive; in our case, for example, we fix electrodes to the scalp using adhesive foam and headbands, which results in minimal if any discomfort (for discussion of ERP methodology with infants, see Nelson, 1994). Second, ERPs can be recorded in a matter of minutes. This satisfies the defacto requirement in all studies with infants that the participant need not be capable of sustained and prolonged periods of attention. Finally, ERPs do not require a verbal or motor response. All three attributes, of course, make the recording of ERPs an ideal methodology to be used not just with infants but across the life span as well; for example, this procedure lends itself to testing neurologically compromised children or adults in whom verbal or motor skills may be impaired.

Having established that it is theoretically possible to study the neural correlates of brain function in the human infant, let me now cast the work I present in this chapter in a broader cognitive neuroscience context. As mentioned previously, my interest is in studying the relation between brain and memory. This general topic is currently receiving a great deal of attention by those who study adult humans and monkeys. For example, it is now fairly well established that memory is not a unitary trait, but rather, may be broken down into memory systems or memory types (e.g., Mishkin & Appenzeller, 1987; Nadel, 1992; Schacter, 1987; Squire, 1987, 1992; Tulving, 1985) The memory system with which I am interested concerns explicit or declarative memory. Explicit memory refers to memory that can be brought to mind as an image or proposition; it is memory that can be declared or about which one is consciously aware. It is perhaps our prototype of memory and includes many subtypes, including at the broadest levels our ability to recall and recognize events experienced previously.

The neural substrate for explicit memory appears to be the medial temporal lobe. Work from a number of laboratories (Squire & Mishkin, among others) has recently pointed to the hippocampus and surrounding tissue (entorhinal, perirhinal, and parahippocampal cortices in particular) as playing prominent roles (cf. Mishkin & Appenzeller, 1987; Squire, 1992, 1994; Squire & Zola-Morgan, 1991). As already mentioned, these conclusions have been based on work with neuropsychological populations of human adults (e.g., patient H.M.; cf. Scolville & Milner, 1957) and on ablation studies with monkeys (cf. Mishkin, Malamut, & Bachevalier, 1984).

The findings summarized thus far have proven valuable in developing a model of memory development, although the methods used in this work have helped little in formulating a research program to be used with infants. As stated earlier, I am interested in looking at the relation between brain and memory in the human infant. This presents two, somewhat unique challenges. First, how is one to decide what is explicit memory in an organism that cannot state verbally or through some other unambiguous means what it is that he or she "remembers"? Second, how does one examine temporal lobe functioning in a normal, healthy infant?

In attempt to address these issues, I have modeled my work after adult electrophysiological studies (for review, see Donchin, 1984; Regan, 1989). Here event-related potentials are recorded as participants engage in a memory task, usually a task of explicit memory. A series of ERP components is typically invoked, some reflecting the attentional demands of the task and others the memory demands. Within the latter class of ERPs, one component receiving a disproportionate amount of attention is the P300 response (see Fabiani, Gratton, Karis, & Donchin, 1987). The P300 is a positive deflection in the ERP waveform that has a latency of somewhere between 300 and 600 ms and is maximal at the central parietal electrode location (Pz). Although a consensus has not yet emerged, the P300 is thought by a number of investigators to reflect some memory process, very possibly context updating, or the updating of working memory (e.g., Donchin, 1981; Donchin & Coles, 1988). Figure 5.1 illustrates a fairly classic P300 response, recorded in our laboratory from normal adults.

Given the (purported) link between memory and the P300, a concerted effort has been made to identify the neural generator or generators responsible for invoking this component. A consensus has not been reached here either, although it is fair to say the hippocampus may make a prominent contribution (e.g., Halgren, 1988; Halgren et al., 1980; McCarthy, Darcey, Wood, Williamson, & Spencer, 1987; Smith et al., 1990;

Adults

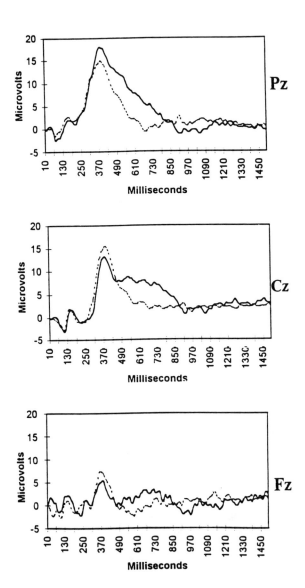

FIG. 5.1. We presented participants with a frequently occurring (80% probability) nontarget (ignore) stimulus (dashed line) and an infrequently occurring (20% probability) target (attend) stimulus (solid line). The data displayed represent the average of individual participant averages (i.e., a grand average). The P300 is represented by the prominent positive (upward deflection) component peaking between 300 and 500 ms. Note that this peak is: (a) largest to the target than nontarget event, (b) greatest in amplitude at the midline parietal electrode (Pz), and (c) decreases in amplitude as one moves toward more anterior midline scalp locations (Cz, Fz). From Thomas & Nelson (1996). Copyright 1996 by Elsevier Science. Adapted with permission.

Wood et al., 1984). This, of course, should not be surprising if we consider the type of memory evaluated in many P300 paradigms to reflect a form of explicit memory.[1]

The argument I have proposed thus far, then, goes as follows: The P300 component of the ERP appears to index a memory process, perhaps the updating of working memory, and may (depending on the task demands) be generated by structures that lie in the temporal lobe, possibly the hippocampus. The question before us, then, is whether this logic can be used to study the relation between brain and memory in the infant. To do so requires some additional groundwork.

There is currently a rather large behavioral literature concerned with infant memory (for reviews, see Fagan, 1990; Moscovitch, 1984; Nelson, 1995, in press; Olson & Sherman, 1983; Rovee-Collier, 1990). It has been well documented, for example, that infants just a few months old are capable of encoding one stimulus into memory and distinguishing this stimulus from previously unseen or novel stimuli. If this is recast in more Hebbian terms, one could argue that, having developed a neuronal template for the familiar stimulus, infants compare all subsequently presented stimuli against this template. If these stimuli match, they are considered familiar, and the infants do not devote much attention to them. If they do not match, however, the stimuli are perceived as novel, and the template is revised or updated. This updating process is expressed by longer looking to the novel stimulus. Interestingly, it is a process very much like this that has been proposed to underlie the adult P300 response; that is, the P300 reflects the electrophysiological manifestation of updating some neuronal template.

Little is known about the neural mechanisms or neural substrate underlying infants' novelty preferences, although a few observations are worth noting. First, Gunderson and colleagues demonstrated that infant monkeys tested in a Fantz-like paired comparison paradigm also demonstrate evidence of novelty preferences (e.g., Gunderson, Grant-Webster, & Fagan, 1987; Gunderson & Swartz, 1985, 1986). Such novelty preferences appear to develop by the 15th day or so of life, at least in the Rhesus Macaque, which roughly corresponds to 1.5 to 2 months in the human infant. Second, Bachevalier and colleagues reported that adult monkeys and infant monkeys older than 15 days did not demonstrate novelty preferences if they have undergone bilateral removal of the amygdala and hippocampus (e.g., Bachevalier, 1990; Bachevalier, Brickson, & Hagger, 1993). This suggests,

---

[1]It needs to be stressed that not all P300 studies are designed to examine memory qua memory (e.g., Johnson, 1988); some, for example, are more concerned with the detection of a target event that occurs against a background of nontarget events. The point being made here pertains to studies specifically designed to examine memory using the P300 as a dependent measure (e.g., Fabiani et al., 1990; Karis et al., 1984).

of course, that these temporal lobe structures are responsible for performance in this paradigm; these data also suggest that these structures become operational in the first weeks and months of life.

Putting these pieces together, it appears reasonable to propose the following. First, the cognitive processes mediating novelty preferences may be similar to the memory updating hypothesis proposed to underlie the generation of the P300 response. Second, the kind of memory studied by paired-comparison (and perhaps also habituation) paradigms may be mediated by the temporal lobe (see Nelson, 1995, for elaboration on this point). Third, if we assume that the process of memory updating in the adult and/or novelty preferences in the infant is mediated by the temporal lobe, then we should see evidence of this at the scalp, as revealed by event-related potentials. This is certainly the case with adults; whether it is also the case with infants is the subject of the remainder of this chapter. It should be added, however, that what is seen at the scalp in infants may differ substantially from what is seen at the scalp in adults. Specifically, it would be unlikely to see an adult-like P300 in the infant, given the vast differences between infant and adult brains (for discussion, see Nelson, 1994; but also see McIssac & Polich, 1992). However, whether infants demonstrate evidence of a P300 qua P300 is less relevant than whether they demonstrate patterns of ERP activity that reflect a similar underlying process.

INFANT ERP RESEARCH ON RECOGNITION MEMORY

In most of the studies we have conducted to date, we have combined the adult oddball paradigm (Fabiani et al., 1987) with the infant habituation paradigm (Bornstein, 1985). In the oddball paradigm, we present participants with an interlace of stimuli, some of which occur less often than others. Participants keep track of some event, generally an infrequently presented event; additional instructions might be to keep a running count of how often such events are presented. It is these rare target events that typically invoke the P300 response.

As might be imagined, giving such instructions to the infant is unfruitful. We have therefore modified the paradigm to achieve what I think is a similar end. We familiarize infants to a stimulus to the point that we think it is well encoded into memory; this allows them to compare all subsequently presented stimuli (i.e., not previously seen) to this familiar stimulus. Because these stimuli are presented for just a few hundred milliseconds, one at a time, and are separated by several seconds from each other, it is assumed that any such comparison takes place on some representational scratch pad, rather than in some perceptual store.

Over the years, we have fairly consistently observed four characteristics of the infant ERP waveform. The first is a fairly well-defined negative peak with a maximum amplitude over central and frontal scalp locations (corresponding to Cz and Fz in the 10/20 classification; see Jasper, 1958), whose latency declines from approximately 1000 to 1200 ms in the newborn to about 500 ms at 1 year. Figure 5.2 illustrates the change in latency of this negative peak from 6 to 12 months.

This negative peak is a robust component, is easily identifiable in both the single and averaged trial data, and has been observed by other investigators (e.g., Karrer & Ackles, 1987). However, because this component is highly reproducible, appears not to be manipulated by task conditions, and is invoked even when the same stimulus is presented repeatedly, we have come to believe that this negative peak reflects an attentional response. Whether this response is exogenous (externally driven) or endogenous (internally driven) cannot at present be determined, although it does share some similarities to the match–mismatch negativity (MMn) observed by Näätanen

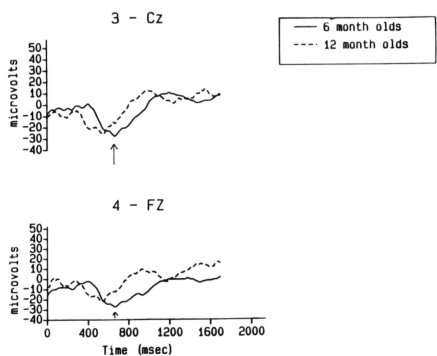

FIG. 5.2. This figure displays the prominent negative peak described in the text, thought to reflect an obligatory attentional response. The ERP pattern displayed in this figure was invoked by presenting infants with the same face 20 times. This peak (seen as a downward deflection) occurs at approximately 750 ms at 6 months (solid line) and 500 ms at 12 months.

and his colleagues in auditory selective attention studies (e.g., Näätanen, 1990).

Following this negative peak, infants' ERPs generally move in one of three directions (see Fig. 5.3).

First, if the stimulus has been fully encoded into memory, such that no decay or interference occurs when it is compared against either the same or different events, the waveform returns to baseline following this earlier negativity (this can be seen in the thin, solid line in Fig. 5.3). However, if the stimulus has been only partially encoded and does require updating or periodic revision, the waveform will shift positive and give rise to a late positive slow wave. This positive slow wave is maximal at central and frontal scalp and is illustrated by the dashed line in Fig. 5.3. Finally, if the

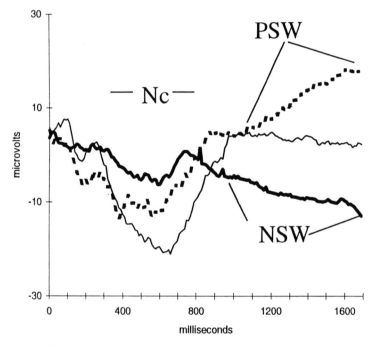

FIG. 5.3. This figure depicts the major components that have been observed in the infant ERP waveform. The negative component thought to reflect an obligatory aspect of attention can be seen most clearly in the thin, solid line, peaking between 400 and 800 ms after stimulus onset. As depicted by this same curve (thin, solid line), this negative peak resolves to baseline. This baseline response is thought to reflect a fully encoded stimulus. In contrast, if the stimulus is partially encoded into memory, but must be updated, the negative peak shifts positive and becomes a positive slow wave. This is illustrated by the dashed line. Finally, if the infant attends to the stimulus but merely detect its presence against a background of recurring other events, the negative peak shifts further negative, manifesting itself in a negative slow wave. This is reflected by the thick, solid line.

infant is confronted with a stimulus that has not been encoded, and thus updating is not possible because there is no template to update, the waveform appears to shift or remain negative following the earlier negative peak. This negativity is also maximal at central and frontal scalp. This negative slow wave, which can be seen in the thick, solid line in Fig. 5.3, has been interpreted as reflecting novelty detection but not memory updating. A qualifier is in order, however: We do not think of this response as an orienting response (OR). The OR may be reflected by the negative peak. Rather, we think this response is only invoked by presenting novel stimuli against a background of familiar or partially familiar stimuli. Thus, it is a comparative process. Although speculative, we base this argument on the observation that we do not see this negative slow wave when the same stimulus is repeatedly presented, even when we examine the first few trials of its occurrence.

Having discussed this glossary of components, let me now review some of the specific studies we have done to derive at these conclusions. Let me begin with the simplest case. We familiarize infants to some stimulus that was previously unfamiliar. The question now becomes, what happens to this general waveform when the task requires recognition memory; for example, when we now present the infants with the so-called familiar stimulus juxtaposed or interspersed with a previously unfamiliar or novel stimulus?

The data illustrated in Fig. 5.4 come from a study in which cross-modal recognition memory was examined (Nelson, Henschel, & Collins, 1993). Here 8-month-old infants may feel, but not see, a certain object. Immediately following this familiarization period, we present them with alternating pictures of this familiar object and a picture of a novel object, each presented on 50% of the trials. The return to baseline invoked by the picture of the familiar event (the dashed line in Fig. 5.4, leads Cz and Fz in particular) suggested that this event had been well consolidated and buffered against decay or interference. In contrast, the positive slow wave invoked by the novel event (the solid line in Fig. 5.4) suggested that this stimulus had likely been seen enough to encode partially (i.e., it had been seen 30 times) but unlike the familiar stimulus, had been encoded incompletely, thus invoking updating.

The cross-modal study just described was the last of a lengthy series of studies we have conducted to examine recognition memory across the first year of life. In order to describe the full range of ERP deflections we have observed and the functional significance we have attributed to these deflections, it would be useful to describe this project in fuller detail.

In the first of these studies (Nelson & Salapatek, 1986), we familiarized 6-month-old infants to one stimulus (a face) and then presented them with an interlace of this (familiar) face and a previously unseen novel face.

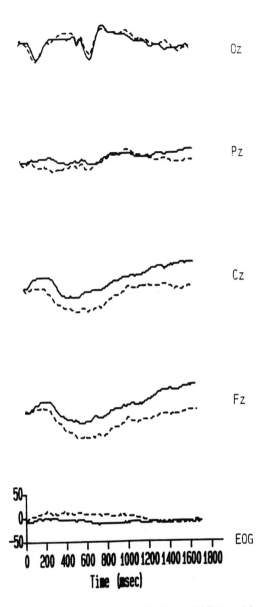

FIG. 5.4. Grand average data for the novel stimulus (solid line) and familiar stimulus (dashed line) in the cross-modal study discussed in the text. The data displayed are from Condition 4 from Nelson et al. (1993), in which infants were haptically familiarized to one stimulus, then shown alternating pictures of the familiar stimulus (dashed line) and a novel stimulus (solid line). The positive slow wave (observed most prominently at the Fz lead) was thought to reflect the infants' updating for a partially encoded stimulus. From Nelson et al. (1993). Copyright 1993 by American Psychological Association. Adapted with permission.

In Experiment 1, the novel stimulus was presented on a random 20% of the trials, with the familiar stimulus presented on the remaining 80% of the trials. In Experiment 2, these two events were presented with equal probability.

Without going into detail, it was reported that the 20% rare event invoked a late positive slow wave beginning about 800 ms into the epoch; this slow wave was not present, however, when the familiar and novel events were presented with equal probability. Although admittedly this 50%:50% ratio would seem to have the potential to facilitate the encoding of the novel event (i.e., it would be seen more often than if it had been presented only 20% of the time), it would be to the detriment of remembering the familiar event; that is, while infants were struggling to encode the novel event, their memory of the familiar event would be decaying. This should result in both events being perceived as relatively but equally unfamiliar, yielding similar patterns of ERP activity. These results are in contrast to those I just mentioned with 8-month-old infants (i.e., where the 8-month-olds demonstrated a positive slow wave to a 50% novel stimulus) and describes a developmental pattern that is discussed more fully in a subsequent section.

There is, of course, a different interpretation of the findings. This is that the positive slow wave invoked by the rare event occurred because infants were sensitive to the probability information; that is, they responded to the novel event not because it was recognized as novel per se but because it was presented so infrequently. This latter interpretation assumes that infants are sensitive to probability information, along with (or instead of) novelty information.

To examine this issue, a series of experiments was undertaken with 4-, 6-, and 8-month-old infants (Nelson & Collins, 1991, 1992). In this work, we presented infants with two faces equally often, for 10 trials each. The aim was to familiarize infants to two events, not one. We then presented infants with three classes of events. On 60% of the trials, one of the faces seen during familiarization was presented. This was designated the Frequent-Familiar event. On a random 20% of the trials the other familiarization face was presented; this was designated the Infrequent-Familiar face. Finally, on each of the remaining 20% of the trials (12 in all), a different face was presented; this was designated the Infrequent-Novel event. If infants had fully encoded both events during familiarization, then we might expect them to respond equivalently to these same two faces presented during test; that is, both should evince a return to baseline. Alternatively, infants might enter the test phase with these events fully encoded, but when one of these events is presented infrequently, some decay in memory would result, and thus infants would be forced to update their memory. This should result in a positive slow wave for the infrequently presented familiar event. As for the Infrequent-Novel event, one of two scenarios seemed possible. If infants had begun to encode (albeit incompletely) each of these events or perhaps formed a template that represented all novel events, then this class of stimuli might invoke a positive slow wave. On the other hand, given that each face was presented only one time and given the behavioral literature suggesting that categorization abilities are relatively poor in infants less than 10 or so months, a more likely scenario is that none of these faces would be encoded, and infants would (simply) detect the presence of these events against a background of familiar and/or partially familiar events. In this case, the Infrequent-Novel event should invoke a negative slow wave.

Let me begin with the familiarization data. At all three ages, infants' ERPs to the two faces presented during the familiarization period were identical (Fig. 5.5 and 5.6 display the data for the 6- and 8-month-old infants, respectively). These data were interpreted to suggest that both faces were treated as equivalent and were fully encoded.

Turning now to the test trial data, at 4 months, infants' ERPs were indistinguishable to the three classes of events, suggesting that infants were unable to tell them apart. At 6 months, infants' responses to the Frequent-Familiar face evinced a return to baseline (dashed line). In contrast, their response to the Infrequent-Familiar face took the form of a positive slow wave (thick, solid line), whereas their response to the Infrequent-Novel face took the form of a negative slow wave (thin, solid line; see lead Cz in particular). These data are displayed in Fig. 5.7.

The pattern of findings at 8 months was slightly different. As had been the case at 6 months, the Frequent-Familiar face evinced a return to baseline (dashed line), and the Infrequent-Novel face evinced a negative slow wave (thin, solid line). However, unlike the pattern to emerge at 6 months, at 8 months, the Infrequent-Familiar face also returned to baseline (thick, solid line) and was indistinguishable from the Frequent-Familiar face. These data can be seen in Fig. 5.8.

We have interpreted these differences as pointing to an improvement in memory from 4 to 8 months. At 4 months, infants appeared unable to do the task at all, possibly because there were simply too many stimuli to remember. At both 6 and 8 months, infants were able to retain in memory a familiarized face subsequently seen relatively frequently — that is, on 60% of the trials. However, for 6 month olds, an otherwise-familiar face begins to decay in memory when presented infrequently (20% of the trials) and against a background of many novel faces, and thus requires updating; this updating is indexed by the positive slow wave discussed earlier. The return to baseline evinced by this same Infrequent-Familiar stimulus at 8 months suggested that no decay in memory had occurred, and thus no updating was required. Finally, at neither age were infants able to encode into memory any of the Infrequent-Novel faces; rather, they merely detected the presence

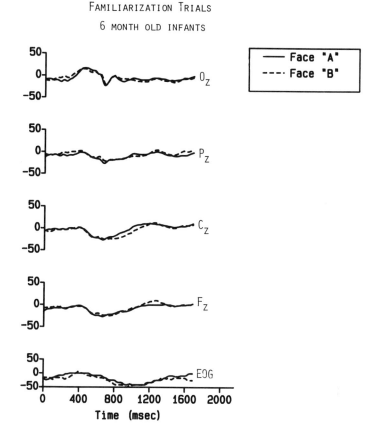

FIG. 5.5. Grand average data from the familiarization trials from 6-month-old infants tested in Nelson & Collins (1991). The data displayed are those derived from the response to the two faces seen during the familiarization trials. Stimulus onset occurred at time zero, and stimulus offset occurred 500 ms later. Positive is up. From Nelson & Collins (1991). Copyright 1991 by American Psychological Association. Adapted with permission.

of these faces against a background of familiar faces. This process of novelty detection was evident by the negative slow wave invoked by these faces at both 6 and 8 months.

At least two questions follow from this pattern of findings. First, how early in life do these positive and negative slow waves manifest themselves? Second, what is the pattern of development after 8 months of age?

With respect to the latter question, although we see negative slow wave activity at 4 months, it has proved somewhat more difficult to observe positive slow wave activity at this age. In our early studies, in which we familiarized infants to one stimulus for a certain number of trials prior to

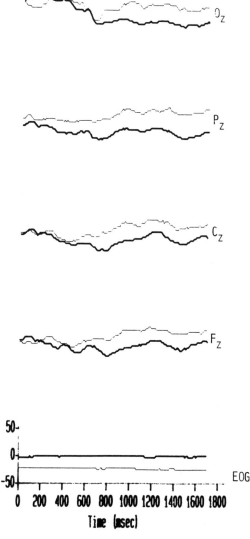

FIG. 5.6.   Grand Grand average data from the familiarization trials from 8-month-old infants tested in Nelson & Collins (1992). In all other respects, Fig. 5.6 is identical to Fig. 5.5. Positive is up. From Nelson & Collins (1992). Copyright 1992 by Academic Press. Adapted with permission.

test (e.g., 20), we did not observe slow wave activity in infants under 6 months (see Nelson, 1994, for details). However, more recently our laboratory (Pascalis, de Haan, Nelson, & de Schonen, 1996) modified this procedure, based on the assumption that perhaps this method of familiarization was insufficient to promote full encoding. In this more recent work,

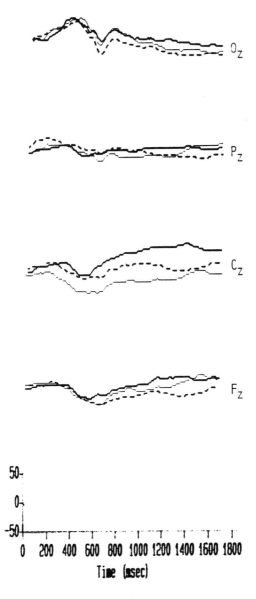

FIG. 5.7. Grand average data for the test trials from 6-month-olds tested in Nelson & Collins (1991). The data from the Frequent-Familiar (dashed line), Infrequent-Familiar (thick, solid line), and Infrequent-Novel (thin, solid line) stimuli are displayed. The major differences among these conditions occurred primarily at Cz, between 750 and 1400 ms after stimulus onset. Stimulus onset occurred at time zero, and stimulus offset occurred 500 ms later. Positive is up. From Nelson and Collins (1991). Copyright 1991 by American Psychological Association. Adapted with permission.

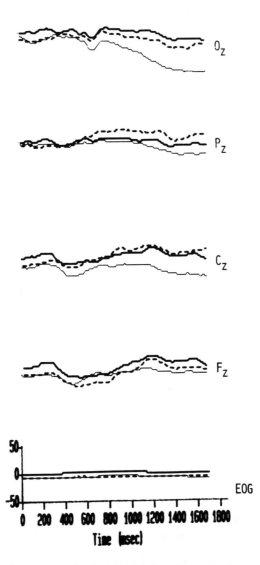

FIG. 5.8. Grand average data for the test trials from 8-month-olds tested in Nelson & Collins (1992). The data from the Frequent-Familiar (dashed line), Infrequent-Familiar (thick, solid line), and Infrequent-Novel (thin, solid line) stimuli are displayed. The major differences among these conditions occurred primarily at Cz, between 750 and 1400 ms after stimulus onset. Stimulus onset occurred at time zero, and stimulus offset occurred 500 ms later. Positive is up. From Nelson & Collins (1992). Copyright 1992 by Academic Press. Adapted with permission.

we habituated (using an infant-controlled procedure) 3-month-old infants to a single face until criterion was met (because we permitted infants to look for as long as they wished, ERPs were not recorded, only looking times). A 2-minute delay followed habituation, after which we presented infants with the familiar face and a novel face, with equal probability. Under these conditions, we observed the characteristic baseline response to the familiar event (indicative of complete encoding and thus recognition) and a positive slow wave to the novel face. Recall this is the pattern initially observed in 6-month-old infants by Nelson and Salapatek (1986). These results, then, suggest that if infants are given ample opportunity to encode the familiar face, even after a delay period, they are able to (a) distinguish a novel from a familiar face and (b) display evidence of recognition in a manner comparable to what has been observed in older infants.

Let me now turn to the first question. One might easily presuppose that the function of detecting novel events would ontogenetically precede the encoding into memory of such events. For example, if we assume that infants are not born with "innate" knowledge of events, then all events must first be perceived as novel. The novelty of events would quickly diminish, however, and be replaced by memory of these events (thus relegating them to familiar or at least partially familiar). When presented with a familiar event and a novel event, infants should be drawn to the novel event; that is, attention should be shifted from the familiar to the novel event. This is exactly what is thought to underlie the novelty response observed in behavioral studies.

If this scenario is true, the question arises as to when in development the negative slow wave we have come to associate with novelty detection emerges. One might predict, for example, that this response should emerge before the positive slow wave we have associated with memory. To address this issue, a series of studies was conducted with newborn infants (see deRegnier & Nelson, 1992).

Because of the relative superiority of the auditory system relative to the visual system at birth, auditory stimuli were used in this work. The data that are discussed are based on eight, full-term, healthy infants, most of whom were tested on their first day of life. Using a small ear insert, we presented infants with 40 presentations of a 200 ms duration 500 Hz pure tone. This was followed by presenting 120 test trials, 80% of which were the familiar tone, and a random 20% of which were a novel tone (1000 Hz). The Interstimulus Interval (ISI) varied randomly between 2900 and 3400 ms. ERPs were recorded from four midline leads (Oz, Pz, Cz, Fz) for 2600 ms.

After rejecting data that were contaminated by eye or other artifacts, the familiar and novel trials were averaged separately; grand averages were then composed from these averages. As seen in Fig. 5.9, no differences were evident when the familiar events were compared to the novel events.

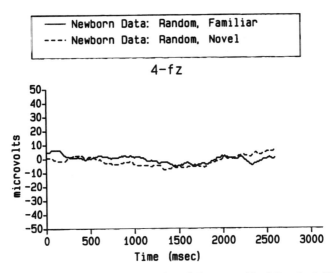

FIG. 5.9. Grand average data from 8 newborn infants tested in deRegnier & Nelson (1992). The solid line represents data from a random sample of familiar stimuli, whereas the dashed line represents the response to the novel stimulus. Stimulus onset (a pure tone) occurred at time zero, and stimulus offset occurred 200 ms later. Positive is up.

The failure of the novel stimulus to invoke any perturbation in the waveform suggested that these infants had simply not encoded or perhaps, even detected these stimuli. Although one might argue that memory at or near the time of birth is fragile at best (for discussion of memory in the newborn period, see Slater, 1995), the ability to engage and sustain attention does exist at this age, and thus we were surprised not to see any negative slow wave activity. To this end, we reviewed the heart rate work on attention reported by John Richards (e.g., Richards, 1989). For example, Richards reported that attentional state can vary by as much as 10–20 s after the introduction of a stimulus. Accordingly, we speculated that perhaps infants' attentional state had not stabilized during the initial series of trials, and thus neither the familiar nor novel stimuli received adequate study. To examine this hypothesis, we predicted that a familiar stimulus that was at least fifth in a sequence of familiar events would provide a better and more stable metric of familiarity than familiar events presented before the fifth event in the sequence. The rationale for this speculation was that it would not be until the fifth trial that at least 15 s had elapsed from the start of the sequence. We tested this model by computing an average of familiar stimuli that were at least fifth in the sequence. This average was then statistically compared against an average of novel stimuli that occurred after three or fewer familiar stimuli (designated "early" novel events), and against an average of novel stimuli that occurred five or more trials after a familiar stimulus (designated "late" novel events). The expectation, of course, was that late novel events (i.e., those occurring five or more trials into the sequence) would be more likely to be detected as novel than early novel events (i.e., those occurring three or fewer trials before a familiar event), primarily because of how well they would have stood out against a background of highly familiar "familiar" stimuli.

The results of this analysis are illustrated in Fig. 5.10. As seen, the ERPs invoked by the late novel stimulus differed from that invoked by the "late" familiar stimulus; specifically, the ERP invoked by this late familiar stimulus (solid line) evinced a return to baseline, whereas the ERP invoked by the late novel stimulus (dashed line) evinced a negative slow wave. These results were only evident at Fz and are illustrated in Fig. 5.10.

There were no statistically significant differences between the early novel events and these late familiar events, although as seen in Fig. 5.11, there were differences between the early novel events and the late novel events, with the latter showing a more pronounced negativity.

These data are, of course, preliminary, although this does not preclude their interpretation. First, the presence of the negative slow wave invoked by the late novel events suggested that infants had detected the presence of these events against the background of familiar events. However, the absence of a positive slow wave indicated that the infants had failed to encode, even partially, these same novel events, despite having heard them more than 20 times. Finally, the absence of either positive or negative slow

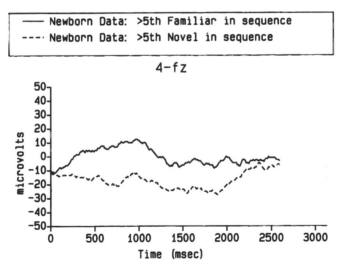

FIG. 5.10. Grand average data from 8 newborn infants tested in deRegnier & Nelson (1992). The solid line represents data from a sample of familiar stimuli that occurred at least fifth in the sequence of familiar stimuli (referred to in the text as late familiar), whereas the dashed line represents the response to novel stimuli that occurred after the late familiar stimuli (referred to in the text as late novel). Stimulus onset occurred at time zero, and stimulus offset occurred 200 ms later. Positive is up.

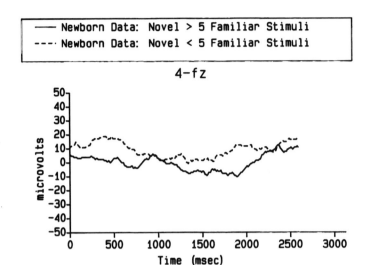

FIG. 5.11.   Grand average data from 8 newborn infants tested in deRegnier & Nelson (1992). The solid line represents data from the novel stimuli that occurred after at least five familiar stimuli had been presented (referred to in the text as "late" novel), whereas the dashed line represents the response to novel stimuli that occurred before the fifth in a sequence of familiar stimuli (referred to in the text as "early" novel). Stimulus onset occurred at time zero, and stimulus offset occurred 200 ms later. Positive is up.

wave activity among the late familiar events and even among the total class of familiar events suggests that these events were fully encoded into memory.

These speculations notwithstanding, several qualifiers are in order. First, it is not clear whether these findings are due to infants responding differently to the late novel stimulus or to the late familiar stimulus (e.g., was it the case that infants only noticed the novel events because of how well encoded the familiar events were, or were the novel events noticed because of the relatively greater number of familiar events that intervened between presentations?); clearly more analyses need to be conducted. More importantly, it is not clear whether we are correct in assuming that the functional significance attributed to the positive and negative slow wave activity for older infants applies to newborn infants. Both proposals therefore require further evaluation.

Summary

Before turning to a discussion of the possible neural sources involved in memory and that may be responsible for the ERPs described herein, let me first summarize the findings that have been reviewed thus far.

First, I would propose that the process of simply attending to a stimulus, regardless of the local context in which this stimulus is presented (i.e., be it a single stimulus or multiple stimuli that surround it in time), results in a well-defined negative peak. The latency of this peak declines with increasing age (see Fig. 5.2), although its scalp topography remains distributed over central and frontal scalp. Although we have not systematically tested infants with stimuli presented in different modalities, there is some suggestion from our work with auditory and visual stimuli that this negative peak may be nonmodality specific.

In contrast to the previously described negative peak, a second deflection of the ERP we have observed is a negative slow wave that follows the earlier negative peak. This slow wave appears to index the process of detecting novel events embedded against a background of familiar events. This negative slow wave, like the negative peak, is also maximal at central and frontal scalp, a distribution that may not change, at least across the first year of life. This process of novelty detection is a prerequisite to a later developing memory system, and as such we should not be surprised by the data reported herein, indicating that this process may be present at birth.

In terms of recognition memory, we have consistently observed positive slow wave activity indicative of some memory process by 6 months of life. This is not to say that such slow wave activity might not be observed in younger infants; as described previously (Pascalis et al., 1996), there is evidence that infants as young as 3 months may demonstrate such a pattern under appropriate conditions. It should be noted, however, that should we be correct that this positive slow wave reflects memory, and is dependent on neural structures that lie in the temporal lobe, our data would be consistent with: (a) infant behavioral data that speak to the superior memory of the 6- versus 4-month-old infant, (b) anatomical data that suggest increasing maturity of the hippocampus in the second half of the first year of life (e.g., Humphrey, 1966; Kretschmann, Kammradt, Krauthausen, Sauer, & Wingert, 1986; O'Neil, Friedman, Bachevalier, & Ungerleider, 1986; Paldino & Purpura, 1979; see Nelson, 1995, for review), and (c) the functional maturity of the infant hippocampus (e.g., Bachevalier, Hagger, & Mishkin, 1991; Bachevalier & Mishkin, 1992).

The findings reviewed thus far have provided much need information about the neural transactions that occur during stimulus encoding and subsequent recognition. What remains unclear, however, are the neural structure or structures responsible for generating the observed ERPs and mediating memory performance. In the section that follows, some attempt is made to address both issues.

THE QUESTION OF NEURAL GENERATORS

It should be apparent that knowing where in the brain certain operations are performed would complement our description of what these operations are.

Identifying the physical source or sources of such operations, however, may prove to be even more challenging than describing the operations themselves.

In my estimation there are two ways to address the issue of where in the brain memory takes place and where ERPs representing memory are generated. One approach, adopted from the adult cognitive neuropsychology literature, concerns the study of individuals known to have suffered a well-circumscribed and documentable neural insult. The second involves the use of current dipole analysis to determine mathematically the origin of the scalp-recorded ERPs. Each approach is discussed in turn.

The Study of Neurologically Impaired Populations

The classic neuropsychological approach to determining structure–function relations is to test individuals suffering from discrete forms of brain damage with tasks assumed to reflect specific cognitive abilities and then examine the outcome on these tasks depending on the type of brain damage incurred (for an overview of this approach, see McCarthy & Warrington, 1990). Frontal lobe patients, for example, typically perform poorly on tasks of executive function and planning; temporal lobe patients perform poorly on tasks of explicit memory; and patients with damage to the caudate or other striatal areas perform poorly on tasks of procedural memory.

In the context of our interest in memory and the temporal lobe, it seemed apparent that we should test infants with temporal lobe pathology. However, because this general, cognitive neuropsychological approach is relatively new to the field of infancy (for an example of such work with preschoolers, see work on spatial analysis and function by Stiles and colleagues; e.g., Stiles & Thal, 1993), it seemed judicious to pilot such work with adults first. In this manner, we would be able to work out the details of the methods and determine the efficacy of the approach. This, in turn, would be followed by modifying the methods and then extrapolating them to infants. In this context, I first talk about our adult work and then discuss our pilot studies with infants.

Memory, Temporal Lobe Pathology, and ERPs

Adults.   My colleagues and I have been studying adolescents and adults who suffer from a form of epilepsy that results from seizures that originate in the temporal lobe (historically referred to as temporal lobe epilepsy and more recently [and correctly] referred to as *complex partial seizures*). What is unique about the individuals in our studies is that they are all refractory to medication, and thus, their seizures are uncontrolled. Accordingly, their last recourse for normal functioning is to have the temporal lobe in question surgically removed, a so-called temporal lobectomy. Because all such individuals have seizures that are confined to one temporal lobe, the resection is limited to one side. The resection is, however, fairly dramatic and can include as much as 6–7 cm in length, beginning from the tip of the temporal pole.

This is a very unique population to study, for several reasons. First, because the epilepsy is confined to a relatively narrow region of the brain, most individuals possess normal to above average intellectual function. Similarly, by virtue of the localized nature of the seizures themselves (e.g., medial temporal lobe structures such as the hippocampus), most individuals appear to suffer from rather specific impairments, generally impairments in memory. Finally, by testing such individuals before and after surgery, one is able to determine the independent contributions of one or both temporal lobes to memory function and to the electrophysiological manifestation of memory function.

In an initial study, we tested 10 individuals suffering from seizures originating in the left temporal lobe, 10 whose seizures originated in the right temporal lobe, and a normal control group (for details, see Nelson, Collins, & Torres, 1990, 1991). We tested all individuals before surgery. We presented participants with the word *bat* and a set of Chinese characters, with the instructions to attend to one stimulus or the other (both stimuli served as target and as nontarget stimuli; target stimuli were presented on a random 20% of the trials, whereas nontarget stimuli were presented on 80% of the trials). These stimuli were presented to the left and right visual fields (LVF, RVF) separately, thereby permitting us to isolate the processing of these stimuli to one hemisphere.

As can be seen in Fig. 5.12 and 5.13, the control participants demonstrated prominent P300 activity regardless of the visual field; their behavioral performance in the task (which involved pushing a button whenever a target stimulus occurred and keeping a running count of the number of target stimuli presented) was virtually perfect. In contrast, although both patient groups displayed excellent behavioral performance, they demonstrated much smaller P300 amplitudes. This pattern was more true for the left group than the right group; indeed, many of these individuals demonstrated quite abnormal patterns of P300 activity, with nearly half not demonstrating a P300 at all (the individual participant data are not displayed; for details, see Nelson et al., 1991).

These results suggested to us that our electrophysiological index of memory, the P300, was sensitive to temporal lobe pathology, memory impairment, or both. In light of our preoperative findings, we were curious as to what would happen to this response after surgery.

To examine this question, individuals tested before surgery participated in a test again after surgery, under exactly the same conditions. Thus far,

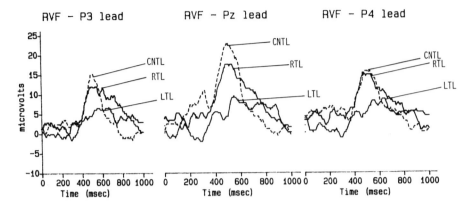

FIG. 5.12. Grand average data from a group of healthy, control adult participants (dashed line), a group of patients whose seizures originated in the right temporal lobe (RTL), and a group of patients in whom seizures originated in the left temporal lobe (LTL). In this study participants received the word *bat* and a set of Chinese characters. The data displayed in Fig. 5.12 are those obtained with right visual field stimulation (RVF) and were derived by subtracting the response to the target word *bat* from the response to the nontarget stimulus of Chinese characters (i.e., a difference wave). Positive is up. From Nelson et al. (1991). Copyright 1991 by American Medical Association. Adapted with permission.

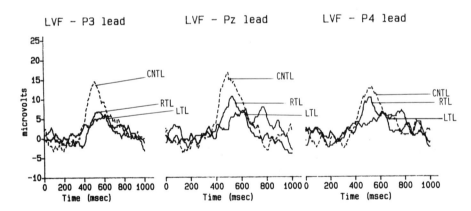

FIG. 5.13. Grand average data from a group of healthy, control adult participants (dashed line), a group of patients in whom seizures originated in the right temporal lobe (RTL), and a group of patients in whom seizures originated in the left temporal lobe (LTL). The data displayed in Fig. 5.13 are those obtained with left visual field stimulation (LVF); in all other respects Fig. 5.13 is identical to Fig. 5.12. Positive is up. From Nelson et al. (1991). Copyright 1991 by American Medical Association. Adapted with permission.

our postoperative testing has been limited to 9 patients (and of these 9, 6 had seizures originating in the right temporal lobe, and 3 had seizures originating in the left temporal lobe). As seen in Fig. 5.14, patients demonstrated P300s that are reduced after surgery relative to before surgery.

These data strengthen the conclusions reached after testing our preoperative sample: The P300 reflects a memory process that is dependent on temporal lobe structures and as such provides a sensitive index as to the damage to these structures. We are hoping to explore the relation between the extent of damage to the temporal lobe (based on surgical pathology reports or volumetric MRI) and the amplitude of the P300, with the expectation that the greater the damage, the smaller the response.

Although the results described thus far are encouraging in the link we have been able to make among the temporal lobe, memory, and ERPs, the task employed in this work made relatively few demands on memory. Accordingly, we were interested in what happens to the P300 when memory load increases. Our expectation, of course, was that this link would be

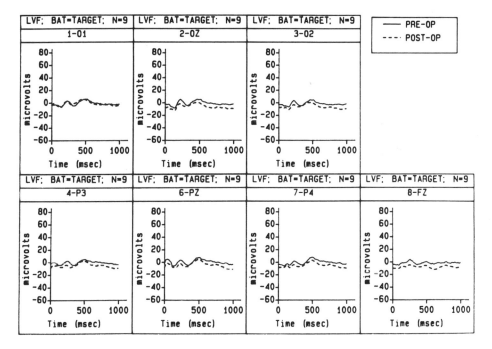

FIG. 5.14.   Grand average data from a group of individuals ($N = 9$) suffering from seizures originating in the temporal lobe (left and right seizure groups combined). The data were obtained as described in Fig. 5.12. The solid line represents these individuals' preoperative response, whereas the dashed line represents their postoperative response. The P300 can be seen most clearly at the Pz lead (latency = 500 ms). Positive is up.

forged even further. In an attempt to examine this question, we (Wegesin & Nelson, 1994) began to test temporal lobectomy patients in a more demanding paradigm. Here participants saw words flashed on a screen for 1000 ms, one word at a time. Participants were to pay close attention to these words, as a subset of them would repeat one time. Also when they saw a word for the second time, they were to push a button. We did not inform them that the lag between the first and second presentation could vary by 1, 4, or 16 intervening items. Our expectation was that both control participants ($n = 14$) and patients ($n = 13$ left temporal lobectomy candidates and 16 right temporal lobectomy candidates) would demonstrate similar P300 responses at a lag of 1, as the demand on memory was relatively slight. However, it would be at lags of 4 and 16 that patients' performance would depart from that of controls.

Figure 5.15 illustrates the data from this study. As seen in the left panel, P300 activity is most evident at lags of 1 (thick, dashed line) and 4 (thin, solid line), with a marked decline in amplitude at lag 16 (thin, dashed line); no P300 is invoked to the items that do not repeat (thick, solid line). These

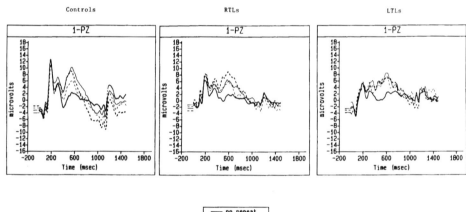

FIG. 5.15. Grand average data (Pz lead) from the continuous recognition memory paradigm described in the text. The data displayed in the left-most panel are from 14 normal control participants, those in the middle from 16 right temporal lobectomy candidates, and those on the right from 13 left temporal lobectomy candidates. As discussed in the text, we presented participants with words flashed on a screen, a subset of which repeated one time. The thick, solid line represents the response to the words that did not repeat (NR); the thick, dashed line represents the response to the words that repeated with an interitem lag of 1; the thin, solid line represents the response to words that repeated with an interitem lag of 4; and the thin, dashed line represents the response to words that repeated with an interitem lag of 16. The P300 can be seen most clearly for the control participants (left panel), with a peak of approximately 600 ms. Positive is up.

data, in part, parallel the behavioral data, where participants' accuracy scores decline across lags (e.g., accuracy at lags of 1, 4, and 16 were, respectively, 93%, 87%, and 90%).

The situation with patients is different, however. As seen in Fig. 5.15, the right temporal lobectomy patients (center panel) evince a P300 to the lag of 1 events (although it is smaller than that of the controls), with a marked reduction at lags of 4 and 16. In contrast, the left temporal lobectomy patients demonstrated very small P300s to stimuli at all lags. Behaviorally the patients' data resembled that of the controls, with a gradual reduction in accuracy with increasing lag (accuracy for the right temporal lobectomy group was 88%, 73%, and 68% for lags of 1, 4, and 16, respectively; for the left group, these figures were 84%, 76%, and 70%). Collectively, then, although patients and controls behaved similarly, their electrophysiological data differed. Unlike controls, patients' P300 responses demonstrated steep reductions after a lag of 1, suggesting deficits of the medial temporal lobe structures that were (presumably) mediating the P300.

Although we have not yet seen any of these patients after surgery, we would expect to see a further reduction in their P300 and perhaps a further decline in their memory performance.

Summary

The work conducted thus far with adults seems to confirm our expectations that the P300 is a sensitive index of the integrity of the temporal lobe structures that underlie explicit memory. Across two different tasks we have seen evidence that: (a) the P300 in temporal lobectomy candidates is reduced relative to controls, and (b) the amplitude of this response is manipulated by the demands placed on memory, and in turn, the degree of temporal lobe pathology. As such, we seem to have established the utility of using the ERP to examine structure–function relations.

As I alluded to earlier, I have discussed this work to illustrate how one might forge a link between brain function and brain structure by studying unique clinical populations. In the next section, I describe our early efforts to examine this link in the infant.

Infants.   A straightforward generalization of our adult work to infants is not possible, for several reasons. First, and most obvious, infants do not read. Second, infants do not suffer from complex partial seizures, and thus, we cannot study a group of infants comparable to the children and adults we have studied. The first caveat can be avoided by designing a different task. The second caveat presents a somewhat more interesting challenge. As previously stated, infants do not, as a rule, suffer from complex partial seizures, nor do they typically incur localized infarcts in the temporal lobe.

However, we have reason to believe that other neurological events can result in such localized lesions. The basis for this model is discussed below.

A number of investigators has observed that adults who have suffered an ischemic or hypoxic episode appear to suffer memory impairments afterwards (e.g., Petito, Feldman, Pulsinelli, & Plum, 1987; Volpe & Hirst, 1983). In some elegant work published a number of years ago by Squire, Zola-Morgan, and colleagues (Zola-Morgan, Squire, & Amaral, 1986), it was demonstrated that the hippocampus in one such individual was bilaterally damaged; indeed, this damage seemed restricted to the CA1 field. This work has since been confirmed by others, thus laying the foundation for proposing that infants might also suffer from a memory impairment if they, too, suffer from a temporal lobe infarct brought about by hypoxia or ischemia. Unfortunately, it is extremely difficult to find full-term infants who suffered mild to moderate degrees of hypoxemia or ischemia. (The rationale for avoiding infants who suffered severe insults was that the corresponding brain damage would not be restricted to the temporal lobes.) Accordingly, in our initial work, we focused on a heterogenous group of 4-month-old infants who suffered from various perinatal complications, although a commonality was neurological compromise due to immature or damaged lungs or hypoxic-ischemic encephalopathy (deRegnier, Georgieff, & Nelson, in press). The rationale for testing this population was based on the observation that children who had incurred moderate degrees of hypoxia at birth suffered from a variety of learning problems as preschoolers and later, at school, despite scoring in the normal range for IQ (e.g., Robertson & Finer, 1985; Robertson, Finer, & Grace, 1989). Accordingly, our prediction was that such infants, both as a group and as individuals, would demonstrate differences in their ERP responses to familiar and novel events, relative to healthy control infants.

We tested infants in a fairly simple ERP paradigm. After familiarizing them with a picture of a geometric object, we then presented them with a picture of the familiar object alternating with a picture of the novel. As seen in Fig. 5.16, the healthy, control infants tested evinced a negative slow wave to the novel stimulus (dashed line in Fig. 5.16), most prominently at the Oz lead, and a return to baseline. In contrast, as seen in Fig. 5.17, the neonatal intensive care unit (NICU) infants evinced a positive slow wave to this same stimulus (dashed line in Fig. 5.17), most prominently observed at the Pz lead.

These results are noteworthy, for two reasons. First, the normative, negative slow wave observed in the control group was not observed in the NICU group. Moreover, the NICU group evinced a positive slow wave to the novel stimulus. Although positive slow wave responses to novel events have been observed in older infants, the fact that (a) the control infants in the present study did not evince this response, and (b) this response was not

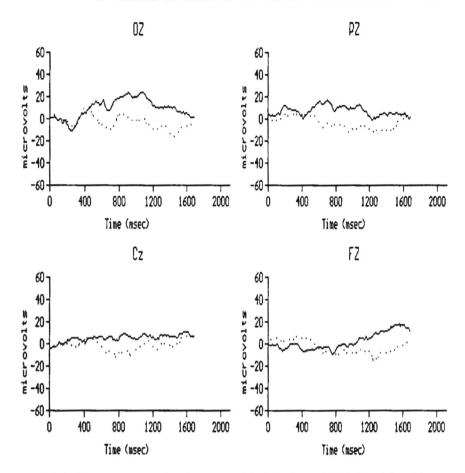

FIG. 5.16.   Grand average data for a group of healthy, 4-month-old infants. The solid line represents the response to the familiar stimulus, whereas the dashed line represents the response to the novel stimulus. Positive is up. From deRegnier et al. (in press). Copyright by Wiley. Adapted with permission.

observed over frontal locations (as it has been in older infants) suggests that this was not a normative response. As a result, it appears that our ERP measures were sensitive to distinguishing differences between these two groups of infants.

Summary

Our research with oxygen-deprived infants and other infants with perinatal complications, although far from complete, was raised to illustrate one approach to examining the question of structure–function relations. Because clinical work such as this can only provide a partial answer to the

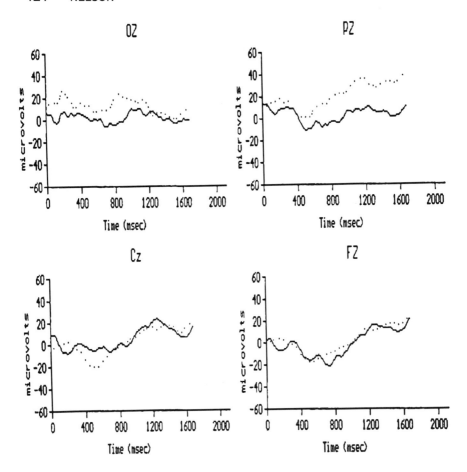

FIG. 5.17.   Grand average data for a heterogenous group of 4-month-old Neonatal Intensive Care Unit survivors. The solid line represents the response to the familiar stimulus, whereas the dashed line represents the response to the novel stimulus. Positive is up. From deRegnier et al. (in press). Copyright by Wiley. Adapted with permission.

question of neural generators (e.g., such studies are always limited in their generalizability to normative populations), it is necessary to examine this issue from another perspective, one that can hopefully utilize healthy participants. To this end, we are currently exploring the use of current dipole analysis to examine the issue of neural generators. It is this final topic that is discussed next.

Current Dipole Analysis: A Mathematical/Physical Approach to Structure–Function Relations

Any given ERP component is typically thought to derive from some neuronal aggregate that fires synchronously in response to the processing demands of a task. The activity derived from this aggregate then propagates to the scalp and eventually gives rise to the ERP recorded at the scalp surface. Unfortunately, the conventional scalp-recorded ERP is potentially comprised of multiple and overlapping components (due, in part, to amplitude and latency variability), and as a result, it has been difficult to infer the neural generator or generators that may underlie any given ERP response. There are a number of factors that might potentially contribute to the lack of a one-to-one correspondence between what is observed at the scalp and what is generated in neural tissue itself. For example, the signals generated in the brain need to pass through cerebral-spinal fluid (CSF), muscle, skin, and so on, each of which has the potential to distort and/or attenuate the signal. To complicate matters further, other considerations that might determine the ability to infer underlying sources include the shape of the skull; variations in skull thickness; the location, size, and shape of the ventricles; and whether the parenchyma itself is normal or pathological (e.g., the presence of gliosis or necrosis might attenuate signals). The final factors in localizing sources include the orientation of the dipole generating the response and the depth of the dipole (for elaboration of these issues, see Wong, 1991). When coupled with the physical factors just described, the challenge of working from a surface-recorded ERP to its underlying neural source would seem considerable.

As insurmountable as this problem would appear, great progress has been made on resolving some of these issues. As Scherg (1990) discusses, by using anatomical and physiological information about the brain, one may construct an electric model of the head, place equivalent dipole sources within all hypothetically determined structures known or presumed to be involved in performing a given task, and then attempt to explain the ERP over spatial and temporal coordinates. The procedures we are currently exploring to achieve these goals includes both Current Source Density Analysis (CSDA) and Brain Electric Source Analysis (BESA). BESA, like other current dipole approaches, seeks to resolve the issue of overlapping components by providing information about the number of equivalent dipole generators activated, their temporal courses of activation, and their locations and orientations. The only functional requirement is that the number of recording electrodes exceed the number of active sources; for all practical purposes, it has been suggested that there be (at least) twice as many electrodes as there are sources.

BESA is essentially a descriptive tool that is enhanced by knowledge of underlying anatomy and physiology. To this end, it is critical that studies be designed to capitalize on this information. In our work, for example, we are assuming that we are studying a type of memory that is performed by temporal lobe structures. Accordingly, we optimize our recording situation by concentrating our electrode array over targeted scalp areas, for example, lateral temporal and vertex electrodes (e.g., T5, T6, C3, C4 in the international 10/20 system).

Thus far, we have had limited opportunity to utilize CSDA or BESA in our studies. Nevertheless, we are optimistic that when used conservatively and in conjunction with other converging information (e.g., clinical populations of infants on whom other neuroimaging information is available, such as MRI), we may eventually reach the point where we can not only describe the neural operations underlying memory but can also identify their neural origin.

CONCLUSIONS

In the first part of this chapter, I attempted to describe the electrophysiological properties of attending to a stimulus, encoding a stimulus, and updating memory for a partially encoded stimulus. It was proposed that simply attending to a stimulus (regardless of whether the stimulus is novel or familiar) is manifested by a well-defined negative peak whose latency is approximately 1,000 or so ms at birth, 500–700 ms by 6 months, and approximately 400 ms by 1 year. The presence of this negative peak early in life coincides with the infant behavioral literature, in which the ability to attend to a stimulus has clearly been demonstrated at or close to the time of birth (cf. Berg & Berg, 1987; Olson & Sherman, 1983). If the infant has fully encoded the stimulus (or stimuli) being presented, this negative peak is followed by a return to baseline. Although not yet empirically evaluated, the behavioral manifestation of this baseline ERP response might be the infant's relative lack of interest in a familiar stimulus that has been seen repeatedly or over an extended period of time. In contrast, if the infant has only partially or incompletely encoded the stimulus, and thus the stimulus requires periodic updating or revision, the ERP waveform will shift positive and remain positive (i.e., a positive slow wave) for several hundred ms following the earlier negative peak. The behavioral expression of this positive slow wave may be the familiarity preference seen in paired-comparison procedures. (As discussed by Rose, 1983, such a preference has been attributed to the failure of the infant to encode completely the familiar event, which results in the infant continuing to attend to this event.) Finally, if the stimulus confronting the infant is one that has not been encoded but instead is simply detected as occurring against a background of other familiar or partially familiar stimuli, the ERP will shift further negative following the earlier negative peak and may remain negative for several hundred ms. This negative slow wave has been proposed to reflect the detection of novel events but not the encoding of such events into memory. The behavioral analog to this negative slow wave may be a novelty preference if the novel stimulus is presented along with a highly familiar stimulus.[2]

This taxonomy of infant ERPs has proven useful in describing what actually goes on in the brain during the time an infant is initially presented with an unfamiliar stimulus, has partially processed this stimulus, and finally, has completely encoded this stimulus. It was asserted in the second half of this chapter that the information derived from our ERP procedures thus far would be complemented by determining where in the brain these operations originate. To this end, I presented our adult temporal lobectomy data and our infant hypoxemia data as one approach to the question of neural generators. It was asserted further that this approach would be complemented if one also attempted to determine mathematically the source or sources responsible for a given ERP. To this end I described current dipole analysis and our exploration of one variant on this method, BESA.

The research program described in this chapter is still very new, and considerable work remains to be done. For example, the previous speculations notwithstanding, we have still not grounded our ERP measures in behavior (or vice versa). As described elsewhere (Nelson, 1994), this may prove a formidable challenge, if for no other reason than the difficulty of identifying a behavioral response that can be time locked to an ERP. This challenge notwithstanding, I think our understanding of behavior would be greatly improved if we also understood the underlying physiology, and for this reason, it is critical that combined electrophysiological and behavioral studies be conducted. A second, more practical application of the work described herein is to extend our ERP measures to a variety of neurologically compromised populations. At the theoretical level, doing so may help facilitate our understanding of structure–function relations; at the clinical level, doing so may help us to understand the functional expression of neuropathology that much better.

In conclusion, the research reviewed herein represents a first attempt to examine the neural bases of memory. Because few would argue with the premise that the brain is the source of all behavior, a more complete understanding of such bases would greatly improve not only our understanding of the brain, but also as importantly, behavior.

ACKNOWLEDGMENTS

The studies described in this chapter have been made possible by various sources, including grants from the NIH (HD23389; NS32976) and NIMH

---

[2]As discussed by Nelson and Collins (1991), it should be noted that in behavioral studies it is difficult to determine if infants prefer a novel stimulus because it is novel per se, or because it is seen infrequently—relative, of course, to a frequently occurring familiar stimulus.

(MH46860). I wish to express my gratitude to the members of my developmental cognitive neuroscience laboratory, who have facilitated this work in numerous ways.

REFERENCES

Allison, T. (1984). Recording and interpreting event-related potentials. In E. Donchin (Ed.), *Cognitive psychophysiology: Event-related potentials and the study of cognition* (pp. 1–36). Hillsdale, NJ: Lawrence Erlbaum Associates.

Bachevalier, J. (1990). Ontogenetic development of habit and memory formation in primates. In A. Diamond (Ed.), *Development and neural bases of higher cognitive functions* (pp. 457–484). New York: New York Academy of Sciences Press.

Bachevalier, J. (1992). Cortical versus limbic immaturity: Relationship to infantile amnesia. In M. R. Gunnar & C. A. Nelson (Eds.), *Minnesota Symposia on Child Psychology: Developmental neuroscience* (Vol. 24, pp. 129–153). Hillsdale, NJ: Lawrence Erlbaum Associates.

Bachevalier, J., Brickson, M., & Hagger, C. (1993). Limbic-dependent recognition memory in monkeys develops early in infancy. *NeuroReport, 4,* 77–80.

Bachevalier, J., Hagger, C., & Mishkin, M. (1991). Functional maturation of the occipito-temporal pathway in infant rhesus monkeys. In N. A. Lassen, D. H. Ingvar, M. E. Raichle, & L. Friberg (Eds.), *Brain work and mental activity* (pp. 231–240). Copenhagen: Munksgaard.

Bachevalier, J., & Mishkin, M. (1992). *Dissociation of the effects of neonatal inferior temporal cortical versus limbic lesions on visual recognition in 10-month-old rhesus monkeys.* Manuscript submitted for publication.

Berg, W. K., & Berg, K. M. (1987). Psychophysiological development in infancy: State, startle, and attention. In J. D. Osofsky (Ed.), *Handbook of infant development* (2nd ed., pp. 238–317). New York: Wiley.

Bornstein, M. H. (1985). Habituation as a measure of visual information processing in human infants: Summary, systematization, and synthesis. In G. Gottlieb & N.A. Krasnegor (Eds.), *The measurement of audition and vision in the first year of postnatal life: A methodological overview* (pp. 253–300). Norwood, NJ: Ablex.

deRegnier, R. A., Georgieff, M. K., & Nelson, C. A. (in press). Cognitive event-related brain potentials in four-month-old infants at risk for neurodevelopmental impairments. *Developmental Psychobiology.*

deRegnier, R. A., & Nelson, C. A. (1992). *Auditory event-related potentials in newborn infants: The effects of stimulus sequence on discriminative responses.* Manuscript in preparation.

Diamond, A. (1990). The development and neural bases of memory functions as indexed by the AB and delayed response tasks in human infants and infant monkeys. In A. Diamond (Ed.), *Development and neural bases of higher cognitive functions* (pp. 267–317). New York: New York Academy of Sciences Press.

Donchin, E. (1981). Surprise! . . . Surprise? *Psychophysiology, 18,* 493–513.

Donchin, E. (1984). *Cognitive psychophysiology.* Hillsdale, NJ: Lawrence Erlbaum Associates.

Donchin, E., & Coles, M. G. H. (1988). Is the P300 component a manifestation of context updating? *Brain and Behavioral Sciences, 11,* 357–374.

Fabiani, M., Gratton, G., Karis, D., & Donchin, E. (1987). The definition, identification, and reliability of measurement of the P300 component of the event-related potential. In P. K. Ackles, J. R. Jennings, & M. G. H. Coles (Eds.), *Advances in psychophysiology* (Vol. 2, pp. 1–78). Greenwich, CT: JAI.

Fabiani, M., Karis, D., & Donchin, E. (1990). Effects of mnemonic strategy manipulation in a Von Restorff paradigm. *Electroencephalography and Clinical Neurophysiology, 75,* 22–35.

Fagan, J. F., III. (1990). The paired-comparison paradigm and infant intelligence. In A. Diamond (Ed.), *Development and neural bases of higher cognitive functions* (pp. 337–364). New York: New York Academy of Sciences Press.

Gunderson, V. M., Grant-Webster, K. S., & Fagan, J. F. (1987). Visual recognition memory in high- and low-risk infant pigtailed macaques (Macaca Nemestrina). *Developmental Psychology, 23,* 671–675.

Gunderson, V. M., & Swartz, K. B. (1985). Visual recognition in infant pigtailed macaques after a 24-hour delay. *American Journal of Primatology, 8,* 259–264.

Gunderson, V. M., & Swartz, K. B. (1986). The effects of familiarization time on visual recognition memory in infant pigtailed macaques (Macaca Nemestrina). *Developmental Psychology, 22,* 477–480.

Halgren, E. (1988). The P3: A view from the brain. *Brain and Behavioral Sciences, 11,* 383–385.

Halgren, E., Squires, N. K., Wilson, C. L., Rohrbaugh, J. W., Babb, T. L., & Crandall, P. H. (1980). Endogenous potentials generated in the human hippocampal formation by infrequent events. *Science, 210,* 803–805.

Humphrey, T. (1966). The development of the human hippocampal formation correlated with some aspects of its phylogenetic history. In S. Hassler (Ed.), *Evolution of the forebrain* (pp. 104–116). Stuttgart: Thieme.

Jasper, H. H. (1958). The ten–twenty electrode system of the international federation. *Electroencephalography and Clinical Neurophysiology, 10,* 371–375.

Johnson, R., Jr. (1988). The amplitude of the P300 component of the event-related potential: Review and synthesis. In P. K. Ackles, J. R. Jennings, & M. G. H. Coles (Eds.), *Advances in psychophysiology* (Vol. 3, pp. 69–137). Greenwich, CT: JAI.

Kandal, E. R., Schwartz, J. H., & Jessell, T. M. (1991). *Principles of neural science* (3rd ed.). New York: Elsevier.

Karis, D., Fabiani, M., & Donchin, E. (1984). "P300" and memory: Individual differences in the von Restorff effect. *Cognitive Psychology, 16,* 177–216.

Karrer, R., & Ackles, P. K. (1987). Visual event-related potentials of infants during a modified oddball procedure. *Electroencephalography and Clinical Neurophysiology (Supplement), 40,* 603–608.

Kretschmann, J.-J., Kammradt, G., Krauthausen, I., Sauer, B., & Wingert, F. (1986). Growth of the hippocampal formation in man. *Bibliotheca Anatomica, 28,* 27–52.

McCarthy, G., Darcey, T. M., Wood, C. C., Williamson, P. D., & Spencer, D. D. (1987). Asymmetries in scalp and intracranial endogenous ERPs in patients with complex partial epilepsy. In J. Engel, Jr., G. A. Ojemann, H. O. Lüders, & P. D. Williamson (Eds.), *Fundamental mechanisms of human brain function* (pp. 51–59). New York: Raven.

McCarthy, R. A., & Warrington, E. K. (1990). *Cognitive neuropsychology: A clinical introduction.* New York: Academic Press.

McIssac, H., & Polich. J.P. (1992). Comparison of infant and adult P300 from auditory stimuli. *Journal of Experimental Child Psychology, 53,* 115–128.

Mishkin, M., & Appenzeller, T. (1987). The anatomy of memory. *Scientific American, 256,* 2–11.

Mishkin, M., Malamut, B., & Bachevalier, J. (1984). Memories and habits: Two neural systems. In G. Lynch, J. L. McGaugh, & N. M. Weinberger (Eds.), *Neurobiology of learning and memory* (pp. 65–77). New York: Guilford.

Moscovitch, M. (1984). *Infant memory: Its relation to normal and pathological memory in humans and other animals.* New York: Plenum.

Näätanen, R. (1990). The role of attention in auditory information processing as revealed by event-related potentials and other brain measures of cognitive function. *Brain and Behavioral Sciences, 13,* 201–288.

Nadel, L. (1992). Multiple memory systems: What and why. *Journal of Cognitive Neuroscience, 4,* 179–188.

Nelson, C. A. (1994). Neural correlates of recognition memory in the first postnatal year of life. In G. Dawson & K. Fischer (Eds.), *Human development and the developing brain* (pp. 269–313). New York: Guilford.

Nelson, C. A. (1995). The ontogeny of human memory: A cognitive neuroscience perspective. *Developmental Psychology, 31,* 723–738.

Nelson, C. A. (in press). The neurobiological bases of early memory development. In N. Cowan (Ed.), *The development of memory in childhood.* London: University of London College Press.

Nelson, C. A., & Collins, P. F. (1991). Event-related potential and looking time analysis of infants' responses to familiar and novel events: Implications for visual recognition memory. *Developmental Psychology, 27,* 50–58.

Nelson, C. A., & Collins, P. F. (1992). Neural and behavioral correlates of recognition memory in 4- and 8-month-old infants. *Brain and Cognition, 19,* 105–121.

Nelson, C. A., Collins, P., & Torres, F. (1990). The lateralization of language comprehension using event-related potentials. *Brain and Cognition, 14,* 92–112.

Nelson, C. A., Collins, P. F., & Torres, F. (1991). P300 brain activity in patients preceding temporal lobectomy. *Archives of Neurology, 48,* 141–148.

Nelson, C. A., Henschel, M., & Collins, P. F. (1993). Neural correlates of cross-modal recognition memory in 8-month-old infants. *Developmental Psychology, 29,* 411–420.

Nelson, C. A., & Salapatek, P. (1986). Electrophysiological correlates of infant memory. *Child Development, 57,* 1483–1497.

Olson, G. M., & Sherman, T. (1983). Attention, learning, and memory in infants. In P. H. Mussen (Series Ed.) & M. M. Haith & J. J. Campos (Vol. Eds.), *Handbook of child psychology* (Vol. 2, pp. 1001–1080). New York: Wiley.

O'Neil, J. B., Friedman, D. P., Bachevalier, J., & Ungerleider, L. G. (1986). Distribution of muscarinic receptors in the brain of a newborn rhesus monkey. *Society for Neuroscience Abstracts, 12,* 809.

Paldino, A. M., & Purpura, D. P. (1979). Branching patterns of hippocampal neurons of human fetus during dentritic differentiation. *Experimental Neurology, 64,* 620.

Pascalis, O., de Haan, M., Nelson, C. A., & de Schonen, S. (1996). *Long term recognition memory assessed by visual comparison in 3- and 6-month-old infants.* Manuscript submitted for publication.

Petito, C. K., Feldman, E., Pulsinelli, W. A., & Plum, F. (1987). Delayed hippocampal damage in humans following cardiorespiratory arrest. *Neurology, 37,* 1281–1286.

Regan, D. (1989). *Human brain electrophysiology.* Amsterdam: Elsevier.

Richards, J. E. (1989). Development and stability in visual sustained attention in 14-, 20-, and 26-week-old infants. *Psychophysiology, 26,* 422–430.

Robertson, C., & Finer, N. (1985). Term infants with hypoxic-ischemic encephalopathy: Outcome at 3–5 years. *Developmental Medicine and Child Neurology, 27,* 473–484.

Robertson, C., Finer, N., & Grace, M. (1989). School performance of survivors of neonatal encephalopathy associated with birth asphyxia at term. *Journal of Pediatrics, 114,* 753–760.

Rose, S. A. (1983). Differential rates of visual information processing in full-term and preterm infants. *Child Development, 54,* 1189–1198.

Rovee-Collier, C. (1990). The "memory system" of prelinguistic infants. In A. Diamond (Ed.), *Development and neural bases of higher cognitive functions* (pp. 517–542). New York: New York Academy of Sciences Press.

Schacter, D. L. (1987). Implicit memory: History and current status. *Journal of Experimental*

Psychology: Learning, Memory, and Cognition, 13, 501–518.

Scherg, M. (1990). Fundamentals of dipole source potential analysis. In F. Grandori, M. Hoke, & G. L. Romani (Eds.), *Auditory evoked magnetic fields and electric potentials. Advances in audiology* (Vol. 6, pp. 40–69). Basel: Karger.

Scolville, W. B., & Milner, B. (1957). Loss of recent memory after bilateral hippocampal lesions. *Journal of Neurology, Neurosurgery, and Psychiatry, 20,* 11–21.

Slater, A. (1995). Visual perception and memory at birth. *Advances in infancy research* (Vol. 9, pp. 107–162). Hillsdale, NJ: Lawrence Erlbaum Associates.

Smith, M. E., Halgren, E., Sokolik, M., Baudena, P., Musolino, A., Liegeois-Chauvel, C., & Chauvel, P. (1990). The intracranial topography of the P3 event-related potential elicited during auditory oddball. *Electroencephalography and Clinical Neurophysiology, 76,* 235–248.

Squire, L. R. (1986). Mechanisms of memory. *Science, 232,* 1612–1619.

Squire, L. R. (1987). *Memory and brain.* New York: Oxford University Press.

Squire, L. R. (1992). Declarative and nondeclarative memory: Multiple brain systems supporting learning and memory. *Journal of Cognitive Neuroscience, 4,* 232–243.

Squire, L. R. (1994). Declarative and nondeclarative memory: Multiple brain systems supporting learning and memory. In D. L. Schacter & E. Tulving (Eds.), *Memory systems 1994* (pp. 203–231). Cambridge, MA: MIT Press.

Squire, L. R., & Zola-Morgan, S. (1991). The medial temporal lobe memory system. *Science, 253,* 1380–1386.

Stiles, J., & Thal, D. (1993). Linguistic and spatial cognitive development following early focal brain injury: Patterns of deficit and recovery. In M. Johnson (Ed.), *Brain development and cognition: A reader* (pp. 643–664). Oxford, England: Blackwell.

Thomas, K. M., & Nelson, C. A. (1996). Age-related changes in the electrophysiological response to visual stimulus novelty: A topographical approach. *Electroencephalography and Clinical Neurophysiology, 98,* 294–308.

Tulving, E. (1985). How many memory systems are there? *American Psychologist, 40,* 385–398.

Vaughan, H. G., & Kurtzberg, D. (1992). Electrophysiological indices of human brain maturation and cognitive development. In M. R. Gunnar & C. A. Nelson (Eds.), *Developmental behavioral neuroscience. The Minnesota Symposia on Child Psychology* (Vol. 24, pp. 1–36). Hillsdale, NJ: Lawrence Erlbaum Associates.

Volpe, B. T., & Hirst, W. (1983). The characterization of an amnesic syndrome following hypoxic-ischemic injury. *Archives of Neurology, 40,* 436–440.

Wegesin, D. J., & Nelson, C. A. (1994, March). *Recognition memory and visual P300 brain activity in seizure patients preceding temporal lobe resection.* Poster presented at the inaugural meeting of the Cognitive Neuroscience Society, San Francisco, CA.

Wong, P. K. H. (1991). *Introduction to brain topography.* New York: Plenum.

Wood, C. C., McCarthy, G., Squires, N. K., Vaughan, H. G., Woods, D. L., & McCallum, W. C. (1984). Anatomical and physiological substrates of event related potentials: Two case studies. *Annals of the New York Academy of Sciences, 425,* 681–721.

Zola-Morgan, S., Squire, L. R., & Amaral, D. G. (1986). Human amnesia and the medial temporal region: Enduring memory impairment following a bilateral lesion limited to field CA1 of the hippocampus. *The Journal of Neuroscience, 6,* 2950–2967.

6

Neurological Risk Factors and Soft Signs in Early Neuropsychological Development

David E. Tupper
Hennepin County Medical Center, Minneapolis

It is well known that children and adults who suffer brain dysfunction demonstrate psychological or neurological characteristics that reflect in some manner the nature of their neural insults. Although the inferences made about brain dysfunction in cases of severe brain injuries are rather direct, minor degrees of brain pathology may be less likely to produce consistent and clear patterns of neurobehavioral abnormality and therefore may require more inferences than most clinicians would normally like to make. Neurological soft signs may not always be accompanied by disorders of the central nervous system and do not have a specific relationship to any particular disorder. The topic of soft signs of neurological dysfunction has been a controversial one that touches on brain-behavior issues that are difficult to address directly (Taylor, 1983; Tupper, 1987).

This chapter reviews much of the research relating soft indicators of neurobehavioral functioning to early developmental risk factors. First, the conceptual and methodological issues concerning soft signs are reviewed. The relationship among soft signs, clinical disorders, and early neurological risk factors is then addressed with particular attention paid to the few follow-up studies that have been performed. Finally, an attempt is made to relate the information gained from studying soft signs and early risk factors to broader neuropsychological mechanisms in development. Appropriate critical hypotheses about soft signs are reviewed in this context.

SOFT SIGNS AND MINOR NEUROLOGICAL DYSFUNCTION

Numerous investigators, especially in the 1930s and 1940s, made the assumption that brain damage or dysfunction was a unitary quantity that was either present or absent in a given individual. Although this myth has been debunked by the multiplicity of neuropsychological investigations in children completed in recent years, assessment of minor variations in performance poses difficulties for both clinicians and researchers in our present state of knowledge. There has been little direct evidence, and few well-designed studies, available to show strong support for the assumed, perhaps simplistic, connection between minor cerebral damage and border-line test performances.

Nevertheless, it is clinically apparent that there is a relatively large group of children who show minor deviations from the norm on neuropsychological or neurological measures and who show no other signs of definite brain dysfunction, yet they demonstrate disorders suspected to be of neurological origin. Similarly, many children suffering prenatal or perinatal trauma or complications, especially those potentially affecting the nervous system, are presumed to be at risk for minor neurological dysfunction or other behavioral disturbances later in their life.

In the neurodevelopmental assessment of children with minor behavioral disturbances, suspected neurological dysfunction, or children with learning disabilities and without obvious neurological impairment, there is sometimes uncertainty or variability in the determination of traditional pathognomonic or hard neurological signs, that is, those invariably associated with neurological disturbance. The resulting findings, called soft (neurological) signs, are usually not found with the same frequency or severity with which the pathognomonic signs can be associated with definite brain damage, although the soft sign findings are clearly apparent. These soft signs include such signs as associated movements, motor incoordination, right–left confusion, and so forth (see examples in Table 6.1). Most soft signs are traditionally related to sensorimotor functions (Deuel & Robinson, 1987).

One of the major hypotheses regarding soft signs remains to be definitively demonstrated, namely, whether or not soft signs are direct reflections of subtle neurological deficit. The reasons for this state of affairs are many, including the difficulties in making inferences about brain function from specific tests, the wide-ranging disorders associated with soft signs, the poor quality of past research investigating so-called minimal brain dysfunction (MBD), the numerous psychometric concerns regarding the evaluation of soft signs, the lack of consensus regarding particular soft signs, and in particular, the absence of an agreed-upon classification or taxonomy of soft signs.

TABLE 6.1
Examples of Soft Signs

Associated Movements: Concurrent movement in a body part not required for the motor
   task being performed
Choreiform Movements: Quick, jerky movements of body parts with no obvious purpose
(Dys)diadochokinesis: Difficulty in performing rapid alternating movements (in a limb or
   body part)
(A)stereognosis: Problems recognizing the size, shape, or identity of objects by touch or
   feel
Mirror Movements: Associated movements occurring on the contralateral side of the
   body; they are usually identical concurrent movements of a limb or fingers
Others: Clumsiness, (Dys)graphesthesia, Motor Impersistence, Nystagmus, Reflex
   Asymmetries

Psychometric Concerns

There are a variety of conceptual, psychometric, terminological, and measurement concerns relating to soft signs. Issues related to terminology have been problematic, in that a sign may be called soft because it is not reproducible, is clinically minor, is nonpersisting, or gradually improves with development. Ingram (1973) stated that soft signs are "diagnostic of soft thinking" (p. 529) although he was talking about the thinking of the investigators rather than the essence of the signs themselves. A variety of terms have been proposed for soft signs, including *soft neurological signs* (soft signs, neurological soft signs), *minor neurological signs, equivocal signs,* and *nonfocal neurological signs.* Each of these terms emphasizes a different aspect of the sign and has been preferred by different investigators.

Classification and measurement concerns are many and include issues about the organization of soft signs into subgroups (see later), concerns about the reliability and internal validity of soft signs, methodological issues about studies of hypothesized minimal brain dysfunction, and issues related to the sensitivity and specificity of soft signs in determining neurological or behavioral dysfunction (Shafer, Shaffer, O'Connor, & Stokman, 1983). Most soft-sign examinations have not provided adequate demonstration of psychometric stability (see Table 6.2 for a listing of common examinations). Details about these examinations are reviewed by Franzen and Berg (1989) and Tupper (1986) in the context of clinical neuropsychological screening for brain dysfunction.

Some of the major methodological concerns in soft-sign measurement have been discussed by Shafer et al. (1983) and Neeper and Greenwood (1987) and relate to the reliability, agreement, and stability of soft signs. Interrater agreement of soft signs has ranged from 57% to 80%, which Shafer et al. (1983) indicated is "adequate," although clearly reliability and

TABLE 6.2
Representative Soft-Sign Examinations

Examination	Reference
Examination of the Child with Minor Neurological Dysfunction	Touwen, 1979
Isle of Wight Neurological Items	Rutter, Graham, & Yule, 1970
National Collaborative Perinatal Project (NCPP) Neurological Items	Nichols & Chen, 1981
Neurological Dysfunctions of Children (NDOC)	Kuhns, 1979
Neurological Examination for Subtle Signs– Revised (NESS-R)	Denckla, 1985
Nonfocal Neurological Sign Examination	Hertzig, 1981; Hertzig & Shapiro, 1987
Pediatric Early Elementary Examination (PEEX)	Levine, Meltzer, Busch, Palfrey, & Sullivan, 1983
Physical and Neurological Examination for Soft Signs (PANESS)	Guy, 1976; Tupper, 1987
Quick Neurological Screening Test, revised edition (QNST)	Mutti, Sterling, & Spalding, 1978
Special Neurological Examination	Peters, Davis, Goolsby, Clements, & Hicks, 1973; Peters, Romine, & Dykman, 1975

agreement can be improved. Shapiro, Burkes, Petti, and Ranz (1978) measured soft signs three times in a week and noted no practice effects and good consistency of soft sign items. Denckla (1978) and Peters, Romine, and Dykman (1975), with regard to the stability of soft-sign measures, reported consistency over time and little intraobserver variability. On the other hand, Foster, Margolin, Alexander, Benitez, and Carr (1978) noted practice effects in repeated testing. Hertzig (1982) found good temporal stability and consistency of soft signs, but Shafer et al. (1983), in reviewing data from soft-sign examinations in the National Collaborative Perinatal Project (NCPP) study, noted the extreme variation in soft-sign prevalence across institutions and emphasized the need for examiner training, as examiner bias can clearly affect reliability and interrater agreement. Many studies report no reliability data, and issues related to the developmental nature of the signs and the appropriate unit of measurement for assessing reliability (the individual item or summary scores) have obscured understanding.

Additional measurement concerns include the lack of normative—especially age-related—data for specific soft-sign items, as well as the variability in the appropriate scaling of the items. For example, some soft-sign examinations (e.g., Neurological Dysfunctions of Children [NDOC]) use all-or-none items, whereas many others use items measured on a continuous scale. Denckla (1978) and Shafer et al. (1983) argued for soft-sign items to be measured on a continuous scale, as these authors believed that neuro-developmental assessment should utilize solid normative data and psycho-metrically sound items.

The confounding effects of a variety of subject variables on soft signs has been particularly troublesome, especially when considering the hypothesis of minor neurological dysfunction. Confounds such as IQ, attention, medication effects, and selection bias have been described (e.g., Schonfeld, Shaffer, & Barmack, 1989). The presence of a focal neurological deficit, for instance, can notably affect construct validation for a soft-sign examina-tion. Many studies have not defined exclusion criteria for focal abnormal-ities, although some investigators have dealt with the issue directly. Hertzig, Bortner, and Birch (1969), for example, had separate focal and nonfocal groups in their investigation of neurological signs in children with brain damage in an educational context, and Hertzig and her colleagues have been very interested in specific nonfocal signs that they feel are related to early developmental abnormalities (Hertzig, 1981; Hertzig & Shapiro, 1987).

Diagnostic heterogeneity as a confound in a great many early studies has led to considerable confusion. Frequently, minimal brain dysfunction (MBD) was used as an omnibus diagnostic category for neurological or neuropsychological investigation even though this "wastebasket" term has little specificity, and most times the diagnosis was actually made on behavioral, not neurological grounds (Benton, 1973). A wide variety of behavioral and neurological disorders have been related to soft-sign find-ings, and these are discussed later in the chapter. Very few individuals presently use MBD as a diagnostic category (see Kalverboer, 1993).

Classification of Soft Signs

To make meaning out of the quagmire associated with soft signs, some individuals have suggested the need for a classification of soft-sign items. One of the earliest attempts to decipher the meaning of soft signs was made by Rutter, Graham, and Yule (1970) in their Isle of Wight study. These authors proposed that there are not equally meaningful signs of brain dysfunction but rather that there are groupings of soft signs that indicate various factors:

1. Signs that indicate developmental delay and disappear with age, such as some associated movements.
2. Signs that are difficult to elicit and have poor reliability in the neurodevelopmental examination. These are generally considered difficult to test, irreproducible, or unreliable signs. They are the ones typically considered soft signs and suggest the presence of minor degrees of central nervous system (CNS) dysfunction. For example, choreiform movements

are not usually quantified and may be situation specific, leading to their less consistent identification.

3. Signs that result not from pathological neurological conditions but from causes other than neurological damage; for example, symptoms such as nystagmus or strabismus.

Denckla (1978), R. A. Gardner (1979), and Tupper (1986) also considered the theoretical basis of soft-sign classification and suggested at least two major categories of soft-sign items: soft signs that indicate abnormality and soft signs of a developmental nature. Soft signs of abnormality are those soft signs whose appearance at any age would be considered abnormal, although they are minor in degree with respect to hard signs. Denckla called these "pastel classics" of traditional pathognomonic signs, and they are considered mild abnormalities that one would find when conducting a typical neurological examination. Examples of some items that fit in this category are mild reflex asymmetries, hypokinesis, and mild incoordination. Some authors have referred to these signs as nonfocal neurological signs, because they generally do not have the localizing significance attributed to pathognomonic signs (Hertzig & Shapiro, 1987; Shapiro et al., 1978). Minor electroencephalographic abnormalities may also fit in this category (Hughes, 1987). Developmental soft signs consist of signs that are considered abnormal only if they persist beyond the age at which they are traditionally seen. This category makes the assumption that there are certain problems that the child outgrows and that are only problems when they continue. A second type of developmental soft sign is the delayed appearance of a developmental milestone, such as the late suppression of a primitive Babinski reflex or a slight delay in learning to walk. This type of soft sign is related more directly to the child's development, and it is expected that the child will outgrow the problem, so that the sign represents only a lag in development rather than a more pure deficit. Needless to say, the hypothesis that these signs represent only lags in development and disappear with age has yet to be sufficiently tested.

Another major way to consider the classification of soft signs is from an empirical perspective, that is, from studies that have examined statistically the grouping of soft sign items into meaningful categories using factor analysis. Unfortunately, there have been few studies done in this manner, but the research thus far suggests that researchers should also consider the content of the soft-sign items.

For example, Nichols (1987; Nichols & Chen, 1981), within the context of the NCPP, performed a total cohort analysis of the relationship between neurological soft signs and a variety of other neurological and neuropsychological variables in an effort to identify subtypes of soft signs. Interestingly, four factors emerged in a large-scale factor analysis and consisted of distinct factors reflecting learning difficulties, impulsive behavior, immature behavior, and — separately — neurological soft signs. Rie, Rie, Stewart, and Rettemnier (1978) factor analyzed soft signs in a sample of 80 children with learning disabilities and found three factors, related mostly to the content of the items. The first factor was a general ability factor with no neurological soft signs; the second factor consisted of verbal–motor items; and the third factor consisted of visual–motor items. The last two factors were composed primarily of soft-sign items, and the signs were otherwise related to age. Finally, a third factor analytic study of soft signs was reported by Spreen (1988) during a follow-up study of children with learning disabilities (LDs) into adulthood. Using 203 children with LDs, he found five distinct groupings of soft sign items during a factor analysis. Factor 1 consisted of motor items such as ataxia, tremor, tone, and dysdiadokokinesis; Factor 2 was sensory, consisting of position sense and graphesthesia; Factor 3 was a motor–speech factor, consisting of tongue dyspraxia and dysarthria; Factor 4 was visual and included strabismus and nystagmus; and Factor 5 was considered motor/peripheral/asymmetry and consisted of Babinski and tendon reflexes items. Although these studies are limited and have been primarily completed in samples of children with learning problems, factor analysis has been shown to be a useful tool in soft-sign classification.

Hence, theoretical suggestions as well as empirical studies have indicated that soft signs can be meaningfully classified into several categories. Table 6.3 provides an integrative summary of the major categories and content domains of soft signs as suggested by these studies. This preliminary classification can guide future research, with the assumption that valid and reliable signs can be identified in each category.

In addition, before reviewing the evidence relating soft signs to various CNS and developmental disorders, a summary of specific proposed criteria for an adequate soft sign can be provided. Hertzig and Shapiro (1987)

TABLE 6.3
Theoretical Soft-Sign Classification

Categories
Nonfocal signs
Slight abnormalities that are difficult to detect
Soft signs of developmental delay
Soft signs of neurological abnormality
Soft signs due to both neurological and nonneurological factors

Content
Asymmetries
Cognitive/integrative
Electroencephalographic
Personality/stylistic
Sensorimotor

described both inclusion and exclusion criteria for the development of a soft-sign item or battery, and the following should be the minimum requirements for use of a soft-sign examination in future research. Excluded from a neurological soft-sign battery should be: (a) items from IQ or other psychometric tests (at least those not from traditional soft sign domains); (b) items that may not be purely of neurological origin, such as nystagmus; (c) clearly inadequate indicators of neurological function, such as laterality; (d) items that are influenced significantly by other moderator variables (e.g., medications, attention, intelligence); and (e) unreliable or difficult-to-assess items. Also included are: (a) items from a range of functional areas, such as motor, sensory, and integrative items; (b) developmentally based items such as associated movements; (c) items that are able to be performed without marked deviation by the majority of normal children; and (d) especially, psychometrically sound, standardized, and normed items.

Raised Incidence of Soft Signs in Various Disorders

Soft neurological signs have been associated, in a multitude of studies, with an astonishing array of behavioral, psychiatric, cognitive, and neurological disorders (see Table 6.4). The existence of soft signs was known at the end of the 19th century (Kennard, 1960), but very little empirical work was done regarding these signs. Bender (1947) was the first to actually use the term soft neurological signs during a neurologic investigation of 100 children with schizophrenia. Investigators supportive of soft-sign research, searching for the indirect evidence suggestive of biological factors in behavioral disorders, contend that children with learning or behavioral disorders tend to have a greater number of soft signs than do normal children. Thus, stemming from Bender's origin, a great many studies have compared normal children with hyperactive, learning-disabled, language-disordered, or motor-disordered children, all in search of the indirect link between neurological and behavioral status.

For example, Hertzig et al. (1969) compared 90 children with LDs with children without LDs and found that 69% of the children with LDs demonstrated soft signs, whereas only 6% of the children without LDs demonstrated soft signs. Admission to their facility was based on a confirmed diagnosis of brain damage (see also Bortner, Hertzig, & Birch, 1972; Copple & Isom, 1968). However, Kenny and Clemmens (1971) concluded on the basis of evaluations of 100 children with learning and/or behavioral problems that there was no significant relation between neurological examination (including soft signs) and final diagnosis.

Other investigators at about the same time were arguing that involvement

TABLE 6.4
Clinical Disorders and Associated Variables Linked to Soft Signs

Clinical Disorder	Reference
ADHD/hyperactivity	Denckla & Rudel, 1978; Hern, 1988; Lerer & Lerer, 1976; Reeves & Werry, 1987; Werry, 1968
Articulation disorder	Cermak, Ward, & Ward, 1986
Borderline disorder	D. Gardner et al., 1987
Compulsive eaters	Rau & Green, 1976
Death row inmates	Lewis, et al., 1986
Delinquency	Karniski, Levine, Clarke, Palfrey, & Meltzer, 1982
Encopresis and eneuresis	Mikkelsen, Brown, Minichiello, Millican, & Rapoport, 1982
Hearing impairment	Kammerer, 1988
Learning disabilities	Adams et al., 1974; Barlow, 1974; Hadders-Algra & Touwen, 1992; Kenny & Clemmens, 1971; Peters et al., 1975; Rie et al., 1978; Spreen, 1981, 1988
Low birthweight	Dunn, 1986; Hertzig, 1981, 1987
Mania	Nasrallah, Tippin, & McCalley-Whitters, 1983
Measles sequelae	Wilner, Cannon, & Brody, 1969
Minimal brain dysfunction	Bortner et al., 1972; Clements, 1966; Denckla, 1978
Motor disorders and clumsiness	Abercrombie, Lindon, & Tyson, 1964; Cohen, Taft, Mahadeviah, & Birch, 1967; Denckla, 1984; Denckla & Rudel, 1978; Deuel & Robinson, 1987; Henderson, 1993; Henderson & Hall, 1982; Losse et al., 1991
Obsessive–compulsive disorder	Bihari, Pato, Hill, & Murphy, 1991; Hollander et al., 1990
Psychiatric disorders or behavior problems	Bender, 1947, 1956; Chess, 1972; Neeper & Greenwood, 1987; Quitkin et al., 1976; Shaffer, 1978; Shaffer et al., 1986
Schizophrenia	Awad, 1989; Bartko, Frecska, Zador, & Herczeg, 1989; Bender, 1947; Cox & Ludwig, 1979; Gureje, 1987, 1988; Heinrichs & Buchanan, 1988; Johnstone, Macmillan, Frith, Benn, & Crow, 1990; Marcuse & Cornblatt, 1986; Nasrallah, Tippin, McCalley-Whitters, & Kuperman, 1982; Rossi et al., 1990

Variable	
Age	Cohen et al., 1967; Connolly & Stratton, 1968; Rie et al., 1978
Drug response	Awad, 1989; Bartko et al., 1989; Lerer & Lerer, 1976
EEG abnormality	Agarwal, Das, Agarwal, Upadhyay, & Mishra, 1989; Kennard, 1969
Impulsivity (attention)	Levine, Busch, & Aufseeser, 1982; Paulsen & O'Donnell, 1979; Schonfeld et al., 1989; Vitiello, Stoff, Atkins, & Mahoney, 1990
Infant neurological scores	Ellison, 1983; Hadders-Algra et al., 1988a, 1988b; Hadders-Algra et al., 1986; Touwen, Lok-Meijer, Huisjes, & Olinga, 1982

(Continued)

141

TABLE 6.4 (Continued)

Variable	Reference
Intelligence	Bortner et al., 1972; Quitkin et al., 1976; Shaffer et al., 1985
Minor physical anomalies	Paulsen & O'Donnell, 1980; Quinn & Rapoport, 1974
Neuroimmaturity	Dunn, 1986; Kalverboer, 1979; Kinsbourne, 1973; Landman, Levine, Fenton, & Solomon, 1986; Mikkelsen et al., 1982; Younes, Rosner, & Webb, 1983
School achievement	Berger & Berger-Margulies, 1978; Blondis, Snow, & Accardo, 1990; Copple & Isom, 1968; Landman, 1986; Lucas, Rodin, & Simson, 1965; Schonfeld et al., 1989; Snow, Blondis, & Brady, 1988; Stine et al., 1975
Sex	Camp, Bialer, Press, & Winsberg, 1977; Camp, Bialer, Sverd, & Winsberg, 1978; Shaffer, O'Connor, Shafer, & Prupis, 1983

of the CNS is a common denominator in learning disabilities, and a variety of studies compared control groups with groups of children with LDs (Adams, Kocsis, & Estes, 1974; Page-El & Grossman, 1973; Peters et al., 1975; Rie et al., 1978), finding an increased incidence of soft signs in this group of children. Similar results have been obtained for children with other developmental abnormalities, specifically hyperactivity, language or reading disorders, or others, including schizophrenia (e.g., Quitkin, Rifkin, & Klein, 1976) and other psychiatric disorders (Shaffer, 1978). In an early classic investigation, Prechtl and Stemmer (1962) found a high incidence of reading difficulties in children with excessive clumsiness and choreiform movements. Wolff and Hurwitz (1973) also compared a group of normal boys with boys who demonstrated choreiform movements and found that the choreiform group (measured with soft signs) demonstrated more reading, spelling, and behavioral difficulties than the control children. Werry (1968) found a greater frequency of soft signs in a group of hyperactive children compared to a group of children with a neurosis but without hyperactivity. The most differentiating signs included those reflecting sensorimotor incoordination. See also Denckla and Rudel (1978) for similar findings in hyperactive children. Further studies include that of Stine, Saratsiotis, and Mosser (1975), who reported in a large-scale investigation that neurological signs are not predictive of any particular form of behavior.

More recent research has exploded, with soft signs being correlated with a wide range of disorders. Everything from disorders thought to relate directly to the CNS, such as MBD (see Touwen & Sporrell, 1979) and low birthweight (Hertzig, 1981), and psychiatric or behavioral disturbances (e.g., Bartko, Zador, Horvath, & Herczeg, 1988; Heinrichs & Buchanan, 1988; and many others), to more obscure and indirect correlations such as with hearing impairment (Kammerer, 1988), borderline personality disorder (D. Gardner, P. B. Lucas, & Cowdry, 1987), or even the status of death row inmates (Lewis, Pincus, Feldman, Jackson, & Bard, 1986), have been proposed. Recent reviews of the increased incidence and meaning of soft neurological signs in both neurological and behavioral disturbances have been provided (Neeper & Greenwood, 1987; Shaffer, 1978; Taylor, 1987; Touwen, 1987).

Table 6.4 also provides a list of moderating and outcome variables identified in more recent investigations of soft signs. Significant influences on soft signs include age, drug response, attention and impulsivity, and intellectual level. Soft signs have been linked directly, without study of specific disability groups, to such important findings as EEG abnormality, infant neurological scores, neuroimmaturity, and school achievement. Follow-up studies of these more important links is discussed in the next section relating soft signs to early developmental risk factors.

What then is the link between soft signs and clinical disorders? Clearly, most studies have been able to find an increased incidence of soft signs among a variety of exceptional children and adults. The overlap of soft signs in both abnormal and normal groups is significant at times and cause for concern (Helper, 1980). With regard to the hypothesis of a soft signs–MBD (using the term as a neurological term) correlation, soft signs are at best presumptive evidence of nonspecific cerebral dysfunction (Taylor, 1983; Taylor & Fletcher, 1983) and cannot be used to argue for clear-cut neurological dysfunction. Soft signs are affected significantly by important moderator variables and should be placed in appropriate context in a clinical situation. As Benton (1973) noted, soft signs may at best be infrabehavioral indicators, that is, markers for responses by the organism that are suspected to be more direct reflections of brain status than regular behavior. Soft signs as markers imply but do not prove a greater association between a disorder and a biological mechanism.

EARLY DEVELOPMENTAL RISK FACTORS FOR NEUROLOGICAL AND NEUROPSYCHOLOGICAL DISORDERS

Early Developmental Risk Factors

The other major hypothesis considered in this chapter is the presumed relationship of soft neurological signs to early developmental events and risk factors. There are many pre, peri, and postnatal influences on the proper development of the brain in early life (Freeman, 1985). The growing nervous system is vulnerable to a host of biological and environmental factors that increase the risk of neurological or neuropsychological deficit. This section outlines the relationship between several specific early neuro-developmental risk factors and the later development of neurological and neuropsychological disorder, as manifested by soft signs. Table 6.5 displays some of the common early developmental risk factors.

The developing fetus and infant are at risk for both traumatic and biological factors affecting their functioning and subsequent development. Major handicapping conditions are easily attributed to many of the factors in Table 6.5, but slight neurological deviations may interact with external factors to render causal connections between the pre and perinatal hazard and ultimate outcome difficult to discern. Longitudinal research is difficult to perform (Kopp, 1983; Molfese, 1989) but is clearly needed to address this situation, and follow-up studies related to soft signs are reviewed in the next section. The most frequent early developmental risk factors are asphyxia, low birthweight, and preterm birth—all nonfocal disorders—and their general neuropsychological outcomes are described here. Results of early focal brain injury are not discussed.

Asphyxia (anoxia, hypoxia) is considered a biochemical increase in blood carbon dioxide levels subsequent to a decrease in blood oxygen levels, and it is considered to be the single most influential event causing adverse developmental sequelae (Aylward & Pfeiffer, 1991). Asphyxia is not a single causative factor, and many bodily systems are also affected, which may relate to its neuropsychological outcome (see Gluck, 1977). Asphyxia is traditionally assumed to be indicated by low Apgar scores, although this relationship is not definitive. Much of the outcome data on asphyxia is derived from the NCPP, which was a large-scale prospective study with enrollment from 1959 to 1966 (Broman, 1981; Broman, Nichols, & Kennedy, 1975). Cognitive and motor development were assessed at 8 months, neurological function (including soft signs) was assessed at 1 year and at 7

TABLE 6.5
Early Developmental Risk Factors for
Neurological/Neuropsychological Disorder

Pre and Perinatal	Postnatal
Harmful drugs	Accidents
Maternal infections	Infections
Nutritional deprivation	Toxic substances
Asphyxia	Poverty
Disorders of labor and delivery	Parental psychopathology
Low birthweight	
Preterm birth	
Neonatal intracranial hemorrhage	

years, and later cognitive and intellectual function was assessed at 4 years and at 7 years.

Aside from a high rate of mortality in the NCPP infants with severe birth asphyxia, significant correlations were found between Apgar scores and neurobehavioral outcomes of infants at 1 year, and perinatal variables, including Apgar scores, accounted for a small proportion of the variance in intellectual functioning at 8 months (Broman et al., 1975). The most significant perinatal variable was birthweight. Later correlations showed weak relationships between asphyxia and intellectual development at 4 years (using the Stanford–Binet Intelligence Test). By 7 years of age, perinatal asphyxia was the basis of less than 1% of the variance in IQ on the Wechsler Intelligence Scale for Children (WISC); however, approximately 25% of the poor neurologic outcome in the severely retarded group of children could be attributed to asphyxia. Nichols and Chen (Nichols, 1987; Nichols & Chen, 1981) more specifically evaluated the relationship of asphyxia and neurological soft signs in approximately 30,000 7-year-old children from the NCPP. Indicators of asphyxia such as Apgar scores were very weak predictors of learning difficulties and soft signs, and family-related variables (e.g., SES) were most predictive. Overall, findings from studies of early developmental asphyxia, except in severe cases, show a minor role for neurological insult and soft signs. Environmental and behavioral variables outweigh the influence of asphyxia in later outcome (see Aylward & Pfeiffer, 1991). Mild encephalopathy in these cases appears to show little risk of major impairment, but severe encephalopathy leads to major deficit or death. A continuum of brain injury severity is suggested in asphyxia, although clearly a multivariate model is needed for predicting outcome.

Low and very low birthweight infants are usually classified by their criterion birthweights of less than 2,500 grams and 1,500 grams, respectively. Decreased birth weight is likely caused by a variety of pathophysiological mechanisms and frequent comorbidity of medical complications is seen. Many low birthweight infants are also small-for-gestational age or preterm. Hence, analysis of the specific impact of low birthweight on nervous system outcome is problematic, and methodological concerns abound. Nevertheless, a variety of studies have demonstrated a mixture of neurobehavioral outcomes ranging from poor to good, with most studies demonstrating an equivocal outcome (see Aylward & Pfeiffer, 1991). Low birthweight itself appears to represent the endpoint of many prenatal and perinatal influences, and some maternal and environmental variables may be necessary to consider when assessing ultimate outcome. The exact birthweight of the infant (low or very low) is also likely to be an important consideration.

Epidemiologically based investigations of low birthweight children have clearly documented an increased frequency of occurrence of nonfocal neurological signs (e.g., Nichols & Chen, 1981), but the overall neurobe-havioral consequences of low birthweight are not uniform. A variety of reports (see Hertzig, 1987) indicate wide variability in both neurological impairment and behavioral dysfunction exhibited by low birthweight children.

A study by Hertzig (1987) followed 66 of 74 infants originally identified with low birthweight (between 1,000 and 1,750 grams) to at least 8 years of age, but with no control group. Fifty-three children (80%) were found to be without localizing findings on neurological examination, but 20 children (38%) had two or more nonfocal neurological signs by 8 years. Hertzig concluded that her data confirmed the etiologic importance of perinatal risk conditions for neurological abnormality but suggested that the pattern of association between type of neurological finding and type of perinatal risk may be different for nonfocal versus focal signs. Nonfocal findings were suggested as emerging as a consequence of general developmental disability associated with the complications of pregnancy, whereas localizing findings (seen in 13 children) may be associated more directly with the specific effects of postnatal conditions on a growing and developing nervous system (e.g., respiratory distress, seizures).

Hertzig's (1987) data also demonstrate that the presence of nonfocal signs is compatible with the normal development of intellectual function, school achievement, and behavioral organization in at least half the children affected. However, despite normal intelligence and no significant differ-ences in IQ between the hard and nonfocal signs groups, almost half of the children with nonfocal signs required special educational interventions to reach the same overall level of academic performance achieved by the 33 children who were neurologically intact. Thus, although some children can achieve good outcome from low birthweight early in development, Hertzig's study provides support for the view that these children are indeed at greater risk for the emergence of behavioral and/or school learning problems.

Another group of studies considering the impact of pre and perinatal influences on future development have been performed with preterm infants (i.e., those infants born before 37 weeks of gestation). These infants are considered at risk for neurobehavioral dysfunction due to the common respiratory complications experienced by the preterm infant, and frequently associated biological factors include asphyxia and low or very low birth-weight. Epidemiological studies also indicate that prematurity and low birthweight are features of poor social and environmental conditions. As with many disadvantaged infants, a combination of biological and environ-mental factors in early development is the likely mechanism affecting the outcome of preterm children.

Few studies of soft signs or minor neurological impairment have been completed with preterm children, and much research has recognized the methodological limitations in separating prematurity from low birthweight and other perinatal conditions. It is clear that for very premature infants (less than 33 weeks gestation), as birthweight decreases, the mortality and frequency of major impairments rises. A significant proportion of premature infants appear free of major problems at follow-up, and neurological findings are much less pronounced in subtle cases (Casaer, de Vries, & Marlow, 1991). For instance, a recent large scale study found an association between growth and mild neurological dysfunction but no worsening of school performance or behavior at 6 years of age (Hadders-Algra, Huisjes, & Touwen, 1988c).

The association between pre/perinatal factors and minor neurological dysfunction, as evidenced by soft signs, has been weak in the conditions considered thus far. It appears that perinatal factors, although important for some children, are certainly influenced by a multitude of subsequent developmental events, and at most, soft signs represent nonspecific indicators of developmental concern. Better, more direct, longitudinal investigation of soft signs in minor neurological dysfunction is needed, and the few complete follow-up studies that have been performed are reviewed in the next section.

Neurodevelopmental Follow-Up Studies of Soft Signs

To date, there have been seven major longitudinal neurodevelopmental investigations of soft signs in association with various neuropsychological conditions (see Table 6.6). These studies have been selected for review here because they each: (a) include discussion of soft sign findings, (b) have a control group (with or without neurological findings), and (c) have followed children over time, and thus have assessed the relationship of soft signs both to perinatal events and to current performances. Follow-up periods have been variable, however, and the groups of children followed have been identified on the basis of several relevant clinical disorders or risk factors.

Dunn and colleagues (1986), in a study conducted in a large hospital in Vancouver, British Columbia, Canada, studied 335 children identified at birth with low birthweight following them to age 6.5 years and comparing them to 139 full birthweight children. Sixty-one (18%) of the low birthweight children demonstrated signs of minimal brain dysfunction diagnosed by neurological, behavioral, psychological, or EEG abnormality. At 6.5 years, early neurological abnormalities were important to the diagnosis, with particular antecedants of MBD being an increased frequency of abnormal initial Moro reflexes, hypothermia, and abnormal movements. The neurologically normal LBW children also demonstrated higher Full

TABLE 6.6
Neurodevelopmental Follow-Up Studies of Soft Signs

Authors	Group	Ages Followed	N (Follow-Up)
Vancouver, Canada			
Dunn (1986); Dunn, Ho & Schulzer (1986)	Children with minimal brain dysfunction	6.5 to 12–15	40
New York, United States			
Shafer, Stokman, Shaffer, Ng, O'Connor, & Schonfeld (1986); Shaffer, Stokman, O'Connor, Shafer, Barmack, Hess, Spalten, & Schonfeld (1986)	Children without focal neurological dysfunction	7 to 17	82
Göteborg, Sweden			
C. Gillberg, Carlstrom, Rasmussen, & Waldenstrom (1983); C. Gillberg, Matousek, Petersen, & Rasmussen (1984); C. Gillberg & Rasmussen (1982); I. C. Gillberg (1985); I. C. Gillberg & C. Gillberg (1989); I. C. Gillberg, C. Gillberg, & Groth (1989); Rasmussen, C. Gillberg, Waldenstrom, & Svenson (1983)	Children with minor perceptual, motor, and attentional disorders	7 to 13	52
London, U.K.			
Henderson & Hall (1982); Losse et al. (1991)	"Clumsy" children	6 to 16	16
Groningen, The Netherlands			
Hadders-Algra, Huisjes, & Touwen (1988a, 1988b, 1988c); Hadders-Algra, & Touwen (1992); Hadders-Algra, Touwen, & Huisjes (1986)	Infants with major and minor neurological dysfunction	birth to 9	300

(Continued)

148

TABLE 6.6 (*Continued*)

Authors	Group	Ages Followed	N (Follow-Up)
Victoria, Canada			
Spreen (1988)	Children with learning disabilities (two groups with neurological impairment)	10 to 19 (Phase 1) to mid-20s (Phase 2)	203
Helsinki, Finland			
Michelsson & Lindahl (1993); Lindahl (1987)	At risk for motor problems (neonatal risk)	birth to 5 and 9 years	837 (age 5) 755 (age 9)

Scale IQs than the MBD children. These authors were also able to follow 40 of the MBD children to 12–15 years (mean about 13 years). They again found that the MBD/LBW children had lower IQ scores (verbal, performance, and Full Scale) and that the MBD group also had an increased number of abnormal and borderline EEGs at 6.5 and 13 years, as well as increased maladaptive behavior. Interestingly, 8 of the 40 MBD children demonstrated no soft signs, and 6 low birthweight and 2 full birthweight children who were normal at 6.5 years were reclassified based on test findings as MBD at 13 years. Dunn and colleagues concluded that the soft neurological signs, especially signs of motor proficiency, demonstrated usefulness as they remained in the teenagers with MBD relative to the neurologically normal LBW children.

A subgroup of children from the National Collaborative Perinatal Project was the basis of a series of investigations concerning soft signs and minor neurological dysfunction by Shaffer and colleagues (O'Connor, Shaffer, Shafer, & Stokman, 1984; Shafer et al., 1986; Shaffer et al., 1985; Shaffer et al., 1986). From the Columbia Presbyterian Hospital component of the NCPP, 126 participants were selected. Black males from the young part of the cohort were selected because they were still in school at the time of the follow-up evaluation. Experimental participants ($N = 63$) were selected on the basis of positive soft sign findings at their 7-year-old examination, and the outcome of soft signs and other variables was assessed at 17 years. Also included were 63 matched controls without evidence of neurological findings.

At the 17-year-old follow-up, the participants were evaluated for the presence of three soft signs (astereognosis, mirror movements, dysdiadochokinesis), intellectual disturbance, psychiatric disorder, and social and family characteristics. Of the three soft signs followed, the two motor signs, dysdiadochokinesis and mirror movements, showed significant stability and were found in greater than half of the participants known to have the signs at 7 years. Astereognosis did not persist until adolescence, but the task used was thought to be more difficult at 17 years, because a high proportion of the participants in both groups failed. The implication of these findings is that soft signs persist and are generally stable at least from childhood through adolescence. In related data from the same longitudinal study, soft signs were shown to be correlated with intelligence (Shaffer et al., 1985), school achievement (Schonfeld et al., 1989), and later psychopathology and depression (Shaffer et al., 1986).

Children with minor perceptual, motor, and attentional disorders were the participants of a series of investigations by Gillberg, Rasmussen, and colleagues (C. Gillberg, Carlstrom, Rasmussen, & Waldenstrom, 1983; C. Gillberg, Matousek, Petersen, & Rasmussen, 1984; C. Gillberg & Rasmussen, 1982; I. C. Gillberg, 1985; I. C. Gillberg & C. Gillberg, 1989; I. C. Gillberg, C. Gillberg, & Groth, 1989; Rasmussen, C. Gillberg, Waldenstrom, & Svenson, 1983). These studies, conducted in Göteborg, Sweden, identified three groups of children (group Ns = 141) in a total population screening of about 3,500 children performed at 7 years. The first group of children, considered an MBD group, consisted of 42 children, 14 of whom demonstrated "severe" MBD and 28 of whom demonstrated "mild to moderate" MBD. The second group of 7 children demonstrated more specific problems in perceptual functioning and were described as a "minimal perceptual dysfunction" (MPD) group, whereas the third group consisted of 12 children with attention deficit disorder (ADD). A randomly selected comparison group of 51 children was also utilized.

These groups of children were identified by the investigators at age 7, and were followed and evaluated again at ages 10 and 13 years. At the start of the study, approximately 20% of the children demonstrated neurological findings (choreoathetosis, hemiparesis, etc.), but by age 10 about 25% of the severe MBD and 55% of the mild-to-moderate MBD children had grown out of their neurological deficit. The findings were similar in the MPD group, and the neurological status of the ADD group was similar to controls. High rates of behavioral and school achievement problems were seen in the MBD groups, leading the authors to speculate that although 3-year prognosis with regard to neurological dysfunction is reasonably good, it is gloomy with regard to behavioral and school achievement.

The authors measured a variety of soft signs and found that more than two thirds of the index children had no detectable motor soft signs at age 13, although they still had longer complex (choice) visual reaction times. The MBD groups still had high rates of behavioral and academic achievement problems, as measured by teacher and parent rating questionnaires, compared to the control group, but there were slightly fewer problems seen at age 13 than at age 10. The authors concluded that MBD children with early deficits have a fair biological/neurological prognosis by their early teen years, but that behavioral and academic achievement problems persist.

Henderson and Hall (1982) completed an initial cross-sectional study of 16 clumsy children and matched controls, which was then followed up by Losse et al. (1991); the later study included a battery of motor measures and neurological soft-sign testing from Shaffer's group (Stokman et al., 1986). These children, who were identified initially by their teachers as having poor motor coordination at age 6, were reassessed at 16 years of age. Whereas initially at 6 years the clumsy children performed poorly on neurodevelopmental testing, variability was seen with some children doing well, whereas others demonstrated academic difficulty. The children continued to demonstrate substantial motor difficulties at age 16, as well as a variety of educational, social, and emotional problems. However, various component soft-sign items from the neurodevelopmental testing showed differential findings, with only three of the items (dysdiadochokinesis, dysgraphesthesia, and motor slowness) demonstrating significant differences between the groups. The authors concluded that clumsy children tend to demonstrate persisting motor as well as educational difficulties in adolescence but that notable individual differences in both soft signs and coping with clumsiness can be seen.

Hadders-Algra, Touwen, and Kalverboer have been involved in one of the most ambitious prospective investigations yet of the outcome of various perinatal risk factors. Several important publications have resulted from this investigation, termed the Groningen Perinatal Project (Hadders-Algra, Huisjes, & Touwen, 1988a, 1988b, 1988c; Hadders-Algra & Touwen, 1992; Hadders-Algra, Touwen, & Huisjes, 1986; Kalverboer, 1979, 1988; Touwen, 1993). In 1975, these authors initiated a longitudinal population study of infants consecutively born in the Obstetric Department of Groningen University Hospital, to determine relationships between the perinatal obstetric conditions and early neurological status, and the later neonatal and developmental condition of the child. These children have been followed to 9 years of age in published reports.

Of the total group of 3,162 newborns, the initial neurological morbidity rate was 5% ($N = 160$); another 21.5% were considered suspect for abnormality. At the 9-year-old follow-up, 147 of the initial 160 abnormal newborns were reexamined, along with 300 normal controls and 300 neonatally neurologically suspect infants. Severe neurological deviations (e.g., cerebral palsy) and minor neurological dysfunction (called MND by the authors and denoting the presence of soft signs) were expectedly found proportionally more often in the abnormal and suspect groups of infants. Later neurological handicap was found to be related to low Apgar scores, neonatal neurological abnormality, disturbed neonatal course, and low social class. Two forms of MND were found; MND-1 ($N = 113$), a milder form with the presence of one or two abnormal neurological clusters and consisting primarily of males with very LBW; and MND-2 ($N = 72$), presenting with greater than two abnormal neurological clusters and demonstrating abnormal neonatal findings and lowered social class. In addition, in multivariate analyses behavioral and cognitive development at age 9 was related at least indirectly to the presence of either MND subtype, sex, and social class.

A summary of findings from the Groningen studies thus demonstrates the following (Touwen, 1993): (a) there is no direct relationship between perinatal events and later outcome; (b) the majority of neonatally deviant infants do not develop a neurologically handicapping condition; (c) the proportion of children with MND increases gradually, mainly in the neonatally deviant children; and (d) mild MND (MND–1) was found in the same proportion across normal, suspect, and abnormal groups, but more significant MND (MND–2) showed greater relationship with neonatal neurological condition. The authors concluded that by itself MND need not be considered pathological but is instead a sign of increased vulnerability, which may escape early life detection but be brought forth by later complications.

Children growing up with learning disabilities formed another major follow-up study of soft signs conducted by Spreen (1988). This study consisted of two phases, conducted at two points in time (the teen years and the mid-20s) in 203 children initially referred for assessment of learning disabilities (LDs). Spreen more directly evaluated the role of neurological impairment in participants with LDs by dividing the sample into three groups based on the degree of neurological impairment. Group 1 demonstrated definite neurological impairment; Group 2 demonstrated suspected neurological impairment documented with soft signs; and Group 3 demonstrated a learning disability without clinically demonstrated neurological impairment. A control group of 52 youngsters (Group 4), matched for age, sex, SES, and schools, was also included.

The most important finding of the Phase 1 follow-up was that on a majority of outcome variables (educational, behavioral, health, etc.), there was generally a linear relationship to group membership, such that Group 4 (controls) fared better than Group 3 (LDs, no soft signs), who fared better than Group 2 (soft evidence of neurological impairment), and Group 1 (the definitely brain-damaged group) demonstrated the poorest outcome. This data clearly demonstrates a strong correlation between degree of neurological impairment and ultimate outcome, but the neurological exam was initially performed at 8–12 years, so it cannot necessarily generalize to suspect neurological findings at earlier ages.

These same children were followed an average of 6.5 years further, into their mid-20s, and very similar findings resulted in Phase 2. Most outcome difficulties for all the LD groups persisted and apparently placed them at significant social disadvantage. The role of neurological impairment was similar to phase one findings with the MBD group falling between the LD and definite brain-damage groups. Most of the soft signs assessed did not disappear in adulthood but actually increased in frequency, contrary to the idea that they may be maturational in nature.

In the Helsinki Longitudinal Study, which began in 1971–1974, 1,196 at-risk infants with any of a variety of perinatal risk factors (LBW, low Apgar score, neurological symptoms, etc.) were prospectively enrolled during their hospital stay and consisted of 5.4% of the live births (Michelsson & Lindahl, 1993). Follow-up examinations of motor, neurodevelopmental, and cognitive functioning were performed in many of these children at 5 and 9 years of age (Lindahl, 1987; Lindahl, Michelsson, & Donner, 1988; Lindahl, Michelsson, Helenius, & Parre, 1988). Of the potential risk group, 147, or 10.7%, were not seen at either follow-up examination, but 837 children were examined at 5 years, and 755 children were examined at 9 years. Two control groups without perinatal risk factors, but born at the same hospital during the same years, were formed; 57 control children were examined at age 5, and 154 control children were examined at age 9 (including 43 of the 5-year-old control children who were reexamined).

Results of the neurodevelopmental testing (including many soft signs) at age 5 showed greater impairment for the risk group, with especially impaired scores for the children with early neurological symptoms and several diagnoses. Objective testing of motor impairment and intelligence also showed greater impairment in the risk group. Similar differences between groups was seen at age 9. Multivariate analyses at age 9 showed that poor performance at age 5 was significantly associated with failure in the 9-year-old examinations and with school problems. Predictively, the neurodevelopmental examination was accurate in identifying children without later problems but less satisfactory in identifying those who did develop problems. Other factors, in particular social class, also clearly affected outcome (Lindahl, Michelsson, Helenius, & Parre, 1988).

These few follow-up investigations support the hypothesis of a weak but important relationship between neurological risk factors during early development and the later vulnerability of the child to psychiatric, academic, motoric, and social difficulties. Apparently, children with early minor neurological deviations as assessed by soft signs are at risk for increased problems throughout their upbringing, although the mechanisms of nervous system–environment interaction are far from clear.

RESEARCH AND CONCEPTS IN NEUROPSYCHOLOGICAL DEVELOPMENT

Research and the conceptualization of the relationship between soft signs and various clinical disorders and risk factors has proven to be quite difficult and fraught with nonspecificity. The two hypotheses considered in this chapter, namely a soft signs–subtle neurological deficit correlation and the direct influence of perinatal risk factors on subsequent neurodevelopmental status, have not yet been neatly demonstrated to be true, and the interactive mechanisms in the relationship have yet to be identified. Studies of early neuropsychological development have assumed a relatively linear relationship, based on some of Sameroff and Chandler's (1975) writings about a "continuum of reproductive casualty" (p. 187).

However, the reviews of hypotheses related to soft signs and minor neurological dysfunction in this chapter would imply instead that the relationship is not a direct one and that early biological mechanisms or dysfunctions are not always expressed later in development in the same magnitude or to the same degree as measured earlier. Certainly, environmental influences are important in determining whether a risk turns into a deficit or just a lag. The plasticity or resiliency of the nervous system (Finger & Almli, 1985; Miller, 1992) has not yet entered many discussions of soft-signs research, but the studies reviewed in this chapter suggest that the nonspecific relationship to disorders and outcomes demonstrated by soft signs indicates the influence of many important factors that are external to the organism during development. As suggested by a variety of researchers in this area (Kalverboer, 1988; Taylor & Fletcher, 1983), a multivariate model is sorely needed to explain the diverse relationships and transactions in the expression of neurobehavioral deficit. A combination of microgenetic, factor analytic, cross-sectional, and longitudinal studies are needed.

CONCLUSIONS

Several general and more specific conclusions and suggestions can be provided based on the review presented in this chapter:

1. The psychometric foundation for soft signs still needs to be addressed, although greater reliability and agreement has been established.
2. Soft signs are seen with increased frequency in a variety of clinical populations; however, the meaning of these signs is often influenced by moderating variables.
3. A taxonomy of soft sign items needs to be established, using reliable items, preferably scored on a continuum.
4. The prognostic significance of soft signs needs to be determined; soft signs, particularly nonfocal signs, appear to signal neurobehavioral risk rather than actual impairment.

5. Although the research conducted to the present time has been useful and suggests important biological mechanisms, soft signs still need to be investigated further for their relationship to early developmental risk factors and broader neuropsychological outcome.
6. A multivariate model using soft signs as infrabehavioral markers holds the most promise for future investigations of the elusive soft signs–minor neurological dysfunction connection.

Discussion and consideration of soft signs touches on concerns regarding the detection and importance of mild degrees of brain pathology that appear to have a subtle but measureable impact on development and functioning. A better understanding of these soft signs — because they are a more exaggerated example of more general difficulties in neurobehavioral measurement and conceptualization — will ultimately help us to better understand brain–behavior relationships in developing children.

REFERENCES

Abercrombie, M., Lindon, R., & Tyson, M. (1964). Associated movements in normal and physically handicapped children. *Developmental Medicine and Child Neurology, 6,* 573–580.

Adams, R., Kocsis, J., & Estes, R. E. (1974). Soft neurological signs in learning disabled children and controls. *American Journal of Diseases of Children, 128,* 614–618.

Agarwal, K. N., Das, D., Agarwal, D. K., Upadhyay, S. K., & Mishra, S. (1989). Soft neurological signs and EEG pattern in rural malnourished children. *Acta Paediatrica Scandinavica, 78*(6), 873–878.

Awad, A. G. (1989). Drug therapy in schizophrenia — variability of outcome and prediction of response. *Canadian Journal of Psychiatry, 34*(7), 711–720.

Aylward, G. P., & Pfeiffer, S. I. (1991). Perinatal complications and cognitive/neuropsychological outcome. In J. W. Gray & R. S. Dean (Eds.), *Neuropsychology of perinatal complications* (pp. 128–160). New York: Springer.

Barlow, C. F. (1974). Soft signs in children with learning disorders. *American Journal of Diseases of Children, 128,* 605–606.

Bartko, G., Frecska, E., Zador, G., & Herczeg, I. (1989). Neurological features, cognitive impairment and neuroleptic response in schizophrenic patients. *Schizophrenia Research, 2*(3), 311–313.

Bartko, G., Zador, G., Horvath, S., & Herczeg, I. (1988). Neurological soft signs in chronic schizophrenic patients: Clinical correlates. *Biological Psychiatry, 24*(4), 458–460.

Bender, L. (1947). Childhood schizophrenia: Clinical study of one hundred schizophrenic children. *American Journal of Orthopsychiatry, 17,* 40–56.

Bender, L. (1956). *Psychopathology of children with organic brain disorders.* Springfield, IL: Thomas.

Benton, A. L. (1973). Minimal brain dysfunction from a neuropsychological point of view. *Annals of the New York Academy of Sciences, 205,* 29–37.

Berger, E., & Berger-Margulies, J. (1978). Frequency of minor nervous dysfunction in school children. *Journal of Neurology, 219,* 205–212.

Bihari, K., Pato, M. T., Hill, J. L., & Murphy, D. L. (1991). Neurologic soft signs in obsessive–compulsive disorder. *Archives of General Psychiatry, 48(*3), 278–279.

Blondis, T. A., Snow, J. H., & Accardo, P. J. (1990). Integration of soft signs in academically normal and academically at-risk children. *Pediatrics, 85,* 421–425.

Bortner, M., Hertzig, M. E., & Birch, H. G. (1972). Neurologic signs and intelligence in brain-damaged children. *Journal of Special Education, 6*(4), 325–333.

Broman, S. H. (1981). Risk factors for deficits in early cognitive development. In G. G. Berg & H. D. Maillie (Eds.), *Measurement of risks* (pp. 131–142). New York: Plenum.

Broman, S., Nichols, P., & Kennedy, W. (1975). *Preschool IQ: Prenatal and early development correlates.* Hillsdale, NJ: Lawrence Erlbaum Associates.

Camp, J. A., Bialer, I., Press, M., & Winsberg, B. G. (1977). The physical and neurological examination for soft signs (PANESS): Norms and comparisons between normal and deviant boys. *Psychopharmacology Bulletin, 13,* 39–41.

Camp, J. A., Bialer, I., Sverd, J., & Winsberg, B. (1978). Clinical usefulness of the NIMH physical and neurological examination for soft signs. *American Journal of Psychiatry, 135,* 362–364.

Casaer, P., de Vries, L., & Marlow, N. (1991). Prenatal and perinatal risk factors for psychosocial development. In M. Rutter & P. Casaer (Eds.), *Biological risk factors for psychosocial disorders* (pp. 139–174). Cambridge, England: Cambridge University Press.

Cermak, S. A., Ward, E. A., & Ward, L. M. (1986). The relationship between articulation disorders and motor coordination in children. *American Journal of Occupational Therapy, 40*(8), 546–550.

Chess, S. (1972). Neurological dysfunction and childhood behavioral pathology. *Journal of Autism and Childhood Schizophrenia, 2*(3), 299–311.

Clements, S. D. (1966). *Minimal brain dysfunction in children* (DHEW Publication No. NIH 76-349). Washington, DC: U.S. Department of Health, Education, and Welfare.

Cohen, H. J., Taft, L. T., Mahadeviah, M. S., & Birch, H. G. (1967). Developmental changes in overflow in normal and aberrantly functioning children. *Journal of Pediatrics, 71,* 39–47.

Connolly, K., & Stratton, P. (1968). Developmental changes in associated movements. *Developmental Medicine and Child Neurology, 10,* 49–56.

Copple, P. J., & Isom, J. B. (1968). Soft signs and scholastic success. *Neurology, 18,* 304.

Cox, S. M., & Ludwig, A. M. (1979). Neurological soft signs and psychopathology: I. Findings in schizophrenia. *Journal of Nervous and Mental Disease, 167*(3), 161–165.

Denckla, M. B. (1978). Minimal brain dysfunction. In J. S. Chall & A. F. Mirsky (Eds.), *Education and the brain* (pp. 223–268). Chicago: The National Society for the Study of Education.

Denckla, M. B. (1984). Developmental dyspraxia: The clumsy child. In M. D. Levine & P. Satz (Eds.), *Middle childhood: Development and dysfunction* (pp. 245–260). Baltimore: University Park Press.

Denckla, M. B. (1985). Revised Neurological Examination for Subtle Signs. *Psychopharmacology Bulletin, 21*(4), 773–800.

Denckla, M. B., & Rudel, R. G. (1978). Anomalies of motor development in hyperactive boys. *Annals of Neurology, 3,* 231–233.

Deuel, R. K., & Robinson, D. J. (1987). Developmental motor signs. In D. E. Tupper (Ed.), *Soft neurological signs* (pp. 95–129). Orlando: Grune & Stratton.

Dunn, H. G. (Ed.). (1986). *Sequelae of low birthweight: The Vancouver study.* Oxford, England: The MacKeith Press/Blackwell.

Dunn, H. G., Ho, H. H., & Schulzer, M. (1986). Minimal brain dysfunctions. In H. G. Dunn (Ed.), *Sequelae of low birthweight: The Vancouver study* (pp. 97–113). Oxford, England: The MacKeith Press/Blackwell.

Ellison, P. H. (1983). The relationship of motor and cognitive function in infancy, pre-school and early school years. *Journal of Clinical Child Psychology, 12*(1), 81–90.

Finger, S., & Almli, C. R. (1985). Brain damage and neuroplasticity: Mechanisms of recovery or development? *Brain Research Reviews, 10,* 177–186.

Foster, R. M., Margolin, L., Alexander, C., Benitez, O., & Carr, F. (1978). Equivocal neurological signs, child development and learned behavior. *Child Psychiatry and Human Development, 9,* 28–32.

Franzen, M., & Berg, R. (1989). *Screening children for brain impairment.* New York: Springer.

Freeman, J. M. (Ed.). (1985). *Prenatal and perinatal factors associated with brain disorders* (NIH Publication No. 85-1149). Bethesda, MD: National Institutes of Health.

Gardner, D., Lucas, P. B., & Cowdry, R. W. (1987). Soft sign abnormalities in borderline personality disorder and normal control subjects. *Journal of Nervous and Mental Disease, 175*(3), 177–180.

Gardner, R. A. (1979). *The objective diagnosis of minimal brain dysfunction.* Cresskill, NJ: Creative Therapeutics.

Gillberg, C., Carlstrom, G., Rasmussen, P., & Waldenstrom, E. (1983). Perceptual, motor, and attentional deficits in seven-year-old children: Neurological screening aspects. *Acta Paediatrica Scandinavica, 72,* 119–124.

Gillberg, C., Matousek, M., Petersen, I., & Rasmussen, P. (1984). Perceptual, motor, and attentional deficits in seven-year-old children: Electroencephalographic aspects. *Acta Paedopsychiatrica, 50,* 243–253.

Gillberg, C., & Rasmussen, P. (1982). Perceptual, motor, and attentional deficits in seven-year-old children: Background factors. *Developmental Medicine and Child Neurology, 24,* 752–770.

Gillberg, I. C. (1985). Children with minor neurodevelopmental disorders: III. Neurological and neurodevelopmental problems at age 10. *Developmental Medicine and Child Neurology, 27,* 3–16.

Gillberg, I. C., & Gillberg, C. (1989). Children with preschool minor neurodevelopmental disorders: IV. Behaviour and school achievement at age 13. *Developmental Medicine and Child Neurology, 31,* 3–13.

Gillberg, I. C., Gillberg, C., & Groth, J. (1989). Children with preschool minor neurodevelopmental disorders: V. Neurodevelopmental profiles at age 13. *Developmental Medicine and Child Neurology, 31,* 14–24.

Gluck, L. (Ed.). (1977). *Intrauterine asphyxia and the developing fetal brain.* Chicago: Year Book Medical Publishers.

Gureje, O. (1987). Tardive dyskinesia in schizophrenics: Prevalence, distribution and relationship to neurological "soft" signs in Nigerian patients. *Acta Psychiatrica Scandinavica, 76*(5), 523–528.

Gureje, O. (1988). Neurological soft signs in Nigerian schizophrenics: A controlled study. *Acta Psychiatrica Scandinavica, 78*(4), 505–509.

Guy, W. (1976). Physical and Neurological Examination for Soft Signs. In W. Guy (Ed.), *ECDEU assessment manual for psychopharmacology* (pp. 383–406). Rockville, MD: National Institutes of Mental Health.

Hadders-Algra, M., Huisjes, H. J., & Touwen, B. C. L. (1988a). Perinatal correlates of major and minor neurological dysfunction at school age: A multivariate analysis. *Developmental Medicine and Child Neurology, 30,* 472–481.

Hadders-Algra, M., Huisjes, H. J., & Touwen, B. C. L. (1988b). Perinatal risk factors and minor neurological dysfunction: Significance for behavior and school achievement at nine years. *Developmental Medicine and Child Neurology, 30,* 482–491.

Hadders-Algra, M., Huisjes, H. J., & Touwen, B. C. L. (1988c). Preterm or small for gestational age infants: Neurological and behavioural development at the age of 6 years. *European Journal of Pediatrics, 147,* 460–467.

Hadders-Algra, M., & Touwen, B. C. L. (1992). Minor neurological dysfunction is more closely related to learning difficulties than to behavioral problems. *Journal of Learning Disabilities, 25*(10), 649–657.

Hadders-Algra, M., Touwen, B. C. L., & Huisjes, H. J. (1986). Neurologically deviant newborns: Neurological behavioral development at the age of six years. *Developmental Medicine and Child Neurology, 28,* 569–578.

Heinrichs, D. W., & Buchanan, R. W. (1988). Significance and meaning of neurological signs in schizophrenia. *American Journal of Psychiatry, 145*(1), 11–18.

Helper, M. M. (1980). Follow-up of children with minimal brain dysfunctions: Outcomes and predictors. In H. E. Rie & E. D. Rie (Eds.), *Handbook of minimal brain dysfunctions: A critical view* (pp. 75–114). New York: Wiley-Interscience.

Henderson, S. E. (1993). Motor development and minor handicap. In A. F. Kalverboer, B. Hopkins, & R. H. Geuze (Eds.), *Motor development in early and later childhood: Longitudinal approaches* (pp. 286–306). Cambridge, England: Cambridge University Press.

Henderson, S. E., & Hall, D. B. (1982). Concomitants of clumsiness in young school children. *Developmental Medicine and Child Neurology, 24,* 448–460.

Hern, K. L. (1988). *Neurological soft signs and clinical differentiation of attention deficit disorder with and without hyperactivity.* Unpublished master's thesis, University of Georgia.

Hertzig, M. E. (1981). Neurological "soft" signs in low birthweight children. *Developmental Medicine and Child Neurology, 23,* 778–791.

Hertzig, M. E. (1982). Stability and change in non-focal neurological signs. *Journal of the American Academy of Child Psychiatry, 21,* 231–236.

Hertzig, M. E. (1987). Nonfocal neurological signs in low birthweight children. In D. E. Tupper (Ed.), *Soft neurological signs* (pp. 255–278). Orlando: Grune & Stratton.

Hertzig, M. E., Bortner, M., & Birch, H. G. (1969). Neurologic findings in children educationally designated as "brain-damaged." *American Journal of Orthopsychiatry, 39*(3), 437–446.

Hertzig, M. E., & Shapiro, T. (1987). The assessment of nonfocal neurological signs in school-aged children. In D. E. Tupper (Ed.), *Soft neurological signs* (pp. 71–93). Orlando: Grune & Stratton.

Hollander, E., Schiffman, E., Cohen, B., Rivera-Stein, M. A., Rosen, W., Gorman, J. M., Fyer, A. J., Papp, L., & Liebowitz, M. R. (1990). Signs of central nervous system dysfunction in obsessive–compulsive disorder. *Archives of General Psychiatry, 47*(1), 27–32.

Hughes, J. R. (1987). Electroencephalography soft signs. In D. E. Tupper (Ed.), *Soft neurological signs* (pp. 131–154). Orlando: Grune & Stratton.

Ingram, T. T. S. (1973). Soft signs. *Developmental Medicine and Child Neurology, 15,* 527–530.

Johnstone, E. C., Macmillan, J. F., Frith, C. D., Benn, D. K., & Crow, T. J. (1990). Further investigation of the predictors of outcome following first schizophrenic episode. *British Journal of Psychiatry, 157,* 182–189.

Kalverboer, A. F. (1979). Neurobehavioral findings in preschool and school-aged children in relation to pre- and perinatal complications. In D. Shaffer & J. Dunn (Eds.), *The first year of life: Psychological and medical implications of early experience* (pp. 55–67). Chichester, England: Wiley.

Kalverboer, A. F. (1988). Follow-up of biological high-risk groups. In M. Rutter (Ed.), *Studies of psychosocial risk: The power of longitudinal data* (pp. 114–137). Cambridge, England: Cambridge University Press.

Kalverboer, A. F. (1993). Neurobehavioural relationships in children: New facts, new fictions. *Early Human Development, 34,* 169–177.

Kammerer, E. (1988). Zur Pravalenz und Aussagekraft sog. neurologischer soft signs bei einer grosseren Stichprobe stark horgeschadigter 10–13jahriger Kinder [Prevalence and diagnostic value of so-called neurologic soft signs in a larger sample of severely hearing impaired 10 to 13-year-old children]. *Monatsschrift Kinderheilkunde, 136*(4), 186–189.

Karniski, W. M., Levine, M. D., Clarke, S., Palfrey, J. S., & Meltzer, L. J. (1982). A study of neurodevelopmental findings in early adolescent delinquents. *Journal of Adolescent Health Care, 3,* 151–159.

Kennard, M. A. (1960). Value of equivocal signs in neurologic diagnosis. *Neurology, 10,* 753–764.

Kennard, M. A. (1969). EEG abnormality in first grade children with "soft" neurological signs. *Electroencephalography and Clinical Neurophysiology, 27,* 544.

Kenny, T. J., & Clemmens, R. L. (1971). Medical and psychological correlates in children with learning disabilities. *Journal of Pediatrics, 78*(2), 273–277.

Kinsbourne, M. (1973). Minimal brain dysfunction as a neurodevelopmental lag. *Annals of the New York Academy of Sciences, 205,* 268–273.

Kopp, C. B. (1983). Risk factors in development. In M. M. Haith & J. J. Campos (Eds.), *Handbook of child psychology: Vol. II. Infancy and developmental psychobiology* (4th ed., pp. 1081–1188). New York: Wiley.

Kuhns, J. W. (1979). *Neurological dysfunctions of children.* Monterey, CA: Publishers Test Service.

Landman, G. B. (1986). Preventing school failure: The physician as child advocate. *Pediatric Clinics of North America, 33*(4), 935–953.

Landman, G. B., Levine, M. D., Fenton, T., & Solomon, B. (1986). Minor neurological indicators and developmental function in preschool children. *Journal of Developmental and Behavioral Pediatrics, 7*(2), 97–101.

Lerer, R. J., & Lerer, M. D. (1976). The effects of methylphenidate on the soft neurologic signs of hyperactive children. *Pediatrics, 57,* 521–525.

Levine, M. D., Busch, B., & Aufseeser, C. (1982). The dimension of inattention among children with school problems. *Pediatrics, 70*(3), 387–395.

Levine, M. D., Meltzer, L. J., Busch, B., Palfrey, J., & Sullivan, M. (1983). The Pediatric Early Elementary Examination: Studies of a neurodevelopmental examination for 7- to 9-year-old children. *Pediatrics, 71*(6), 894–903.

Lewis, D. O., Pincus, J. H., Feldman, M., Jackson, L., & Bard, B. (1986). Psychiatric, neurological, and psychoeducational characteristics of 15 death row inmates in the United States. *American Journal of Psychiatry, 143*(7), 838–845.

Lindahl, E. (1987). Motor performance of neonatal risk and non-risk children at early school-age. *Acta Paediatrica Scandinavica, 76,* 809–817.

Lindahl, E., Michelsson, K., & Donner, M. (1988). Prediction of early school-age problems by a preschool neurodevelopmental examination of children at risk neonatally. *Developmental Medicine and Child Neurology, 30,* 723–734.

Lindahl, E., Michelsson, K., Helenius, M., & Parre, M. (1988). Neonatal risk factors and later neurodevelopmental disturbances. *Developmental Medicine and Child Neurology, 30,* 571–589.

Losse, A., Henderson, S. E., Elliman, D., Hall, D., Knight, E., & Jongmans, M. (1991). Clumsiness in children – Do they grow out of it? A 10-year follow-up study. *Developmental Medicine and Child Neurology, 33,* 55–68.

Lucas, A. R., Rodin, E. A., & Simson, C. B. (1965). Neurological assessment of children with early school problems. *Developmental Medicine and Child Neurology, 7,* 145–156.

Marcuse, Y., & Cornblatt, B. (1986). Children at high risk for schizophrenia: Predictions from infancy to childhood functioning. In L. Erlenmeyer-Kimling & N. E. Miller (Eds.), *Life-span research on the prediction of psychopathology* (pp. 81–100). Hillsdale, NJ: Lawrence Erlbaum Associates.

Michelsson, K., & Lindahl, E. (1993). Relationship between perinatal risk factors and motor development at the ages of 5 and 9 years. In A. F. Kalverboer, B. Hopkins, & R. Geuze

(Eds.), *Motor development in early and later childhood: Longitudinal approaches* (pp. 266–285). Cambridge, England: Cambridge University Press.

Mikkelsen, E. J., Brown, G. L., Minichiello, M. D., Millican, F. K., & Rapoport, J. L. (1982). Neurologic status in hyperactive, enuretic, encopretic, and normal boys. *Journal of the American Academy of Child Psychiatry, 21*(1), 75–81.

Miller, E. (1992). Vulnerability and resilience to early cerebral injury. In B. Tizard & V. Varma (Eds.), *Vulnerability and resilience in human development* (pp. 151–162). London: Kingsley.

Molfese, V. (1989). *Perinatal risk and infant development: Assessment and prediction.* New York: Guilford.

Mutti, M., Sterling, H. M., & Spalding, N. V. (1978). *QNST: Quick Neurological Screening Test* (Rev. ed.). Novato, CA: Academic Therapy.

Nasrallah, H. A., Tippin, J., & McCalley-Whitters, M. (1983). Neurological soft signs in manic patients. *Journal of Affective Disorders, 5,* 45–50.

Nasrallah, H. A., Tippin, J., McCalley-Whitters, M., & Kuperman, S. (1982). Neurological differences between paranoid and nonparanoid schizophrenia: Part III. Neurological soft signs. *Journal of Clinical Psychiatry, 43*(8), 310–312.

Neeper, R., & Greenwood, R. S. (1987). On the psychiatric importance of neurological soft signs. In B. B. Lahey & A. E. Kazdin (Eds.), *Advances in clinical child psychology* (Vol. 10, pp. 217–258). New York: Plenum.

Nichols, P. L. (1987). Minimal brain dysfunction and soft signs: The Collaborative Perinatal Project. In D. E. Tupper (Ed.), *Soft neurological signs* (pp. 179–199). Orlando: Grune & Stratton.

Nichols, P. L., & Chen, T. C. (1981). *Minimal brain dysfunction: A prospective study.* Hillsdale, NJ: Lawrence Erlbaum Associates.

O'Connor, P. A., Shaffer, D., Shafer, S., & Stokman, C. (1984). A neuropsychiatric follow-up of children in the Collaborative Perinatal Project population. In S. A. Mednick, M. Harway, & K. M. Finello (Eds.), *Handbook of longitudinal research: Vol. 1. Birth and childhood cohorts* (pp. 216–227). New York: Praeger.

Page-El, E., & Grossman, H. J. (1973). Neurologic appraisal in learning disorders. *Pediatric Clinics of North America, 20,* 599–605.

Paulsen, K., & O'Donnell, J. P. (1979). Construct validation of children's behavior problem dimensions: Relationship to activity level, impulsivity, and soft neurological signs. *Journal of Psychology, 101,* 273–278.

Paulsen, K. A., & O'Donnell, J. P. (1980). Relationship between minor physical anomalies and "soft signs" of brain damage. *Perceptual and Motor Skills, 51,* 402.

Peters, J. E., Davis, J. S., Goolsby, C. M., Clements, S. D., & Hicks, T. J. (1973). *Physician's handbook: Screening for MBD.* Summit, NJ: CIBA Pharmaceuticals.

Peters, J. E., Romine, J. S., & Dykman, R. A. (1975). A special neurological examination of children with learning disabilities. *Developmental Medicine and Child Neurology, 17,* 63–78.

Prechtl, H. F. R., & Stemmer, C. J. (1962). The choreiform syndrome in children. *Developmental Medicine and Child Neurology, 4,* 119–127.

Quinn, P. Q., & Rapoport, J. L. (1974). Minor physical anomalies and neurologic status in hyperactive boys. *Pediatrics, 53*(5), 742–747.

Quitkin, F., Rifkin, A., & Klein, D. F. (1976). Neurologic soft signs in schizophrenia and character disorders. *Archives of General Psychiatry, 33,* 845–853.

Rasmussen, P., Gillberg, C., Waldenstrom, E., & Svenson, B. (1983). Perceptual, motor, and attentional deficits in seven-year-old children: Neurological and neurodevelopmental aspects. *Developmental Medicine and Child Neurology, 25,* 315–333.

Rau, J. H., & Green, R. S. (1976). Soft neurological correlates of compulsive eaters. *Journal of Nervous and Mental Disease, 166*(6), 435–437.

Reeves, J. C., & Werry, J. S. (1987). Soft signs in hyperactivity. In D. E. Tupper (Ed.), *Soft neurological signs* (pp. 225–245). Orlando: Grune & Stratton.

Rie, E. D., Rie, H. E., Stewart, S., & Rettemnier, S. C. (1978). An analysis of neurological soft signs in children with learning problems. *Brain and Language, 6,* 32–46.

Rossi, A., DeCataldo, S., DiMichele, V., Manna, V., Ceccoli, S., Stratta, P., & Casacchia, M. (1990). Neurological soft signs in schizophrenia. *British Journal of Psychiatry, 157,* 735–739.

Rutter, M., Graham, P., & Yule, W. (1970). *A neuropsychiatric study in childhood* (Clinics in Developmental Medicine, Nos. 35/36). London: Heineman.

Sameroff, A. J., & Chandler, M. J. (1975). Reproductive risk and the continuum of caretaking casualty. In F. D. Horowitz (Ed.), *Review of child development research* (Vol. 4, pp. 187–244). Chicago: University of Chicago Press.

Schonfeld, I. S., Shaffer, D., & Barmack, J. E. (1989). Neurological soft signs and school achievement: The mediating effects of sustained attention. *Journal of Abnormal Child Psychology, 17*(6), 575–596.

Shafer, S. Q., Shaffer, D., O'Connor, P. A., & Stokman, C. J. (1983). Hard thoughts on neurological "soft signs." In M. Rutter (Ed.), *Developmental neuropsychiatry* (pp. 133–143). New York: Guilford.

Shafer, S. Q., Stokman, C. J., Shaffer, D., Ng, S. K., O'Connor, P. A., & Schonfeld, I. S. (1986). Ten-year consistency in neurological test performance of children without focal neurological deficit. *Developmental Medicine and Child Neurology, 28,* 417–427.

Shaffer, D. (1978). Soft neurologic signs and later psychiatric disorder—a review. *Journal of Child Psychology and Psychiatry, 19,* 63–65.

Shaffer, D., O'Connor, P. A., Shafer, S. Q., & Prupis, S. (1983). Neurological "soft signs": Their origins and significance for behavior. In M. Rutter (Ed.), *Developmental neuropsychiatry* (pp. 144–163). New York: Guilford.

Shaffer, D., Schonfeld, T., O'Connor, P. A., Stokman, C., Trautman, P., Shafer, S., & Ng, S. (1985). Neurological soft signs: Their relationship to psychiatric disorder and intelligence in childhood and adolescence. *Archives of General Psychiatry, 42,* 342–351.

Shaffer, D., Stokman, C. S., O'Connor, P. A., Shafer, S., Barmack, J. E., Hess, S., Spalten, D., & Schonfeld, I. S. (1986). Early soft neurological signs and later psychopathology. In L. Erlenmeyer-Kimling & N. E. Miller (Eds.), *Life-span research on the prediction of psychopathology* (pp. 31–48). Hillsdale, NJ: Lawrence Erlbaum Associates.

Shapiro, T., Burkes, L., Petti, T. A., & Ranz, J. (1978). Consistency of "nonfocal" neurological signs. *Journal of the American Academy of Child Psychiatry, 17,* 70–79.

Snow, J. H., Blondis, T., & Brady, L. (1988). Motor and sensory abilities with normal and academically at-risk children. *Archives of Clinical Neuropsychology, 3,* 227–238.

Spreen, O. (1981). The relationship between learning disability, neurological impairment and delinquency: Results of a follow-up. *Journal of Nervous and Mental Diseases, 169,* 791–799.

Spreen, O. (1988). *Learning disabled children growing up: A follow-up into adulthood.* Oxford, England: Oxford University Press.

Stine, O. C., Saratsiotis, J. B., & Mosser, R. S. (1975). Relationships between neurological findings and classroom behavior. *American Journal of Diseases of Children, 129,* 1036–1040.

Stokman, C. J., Shafer, S. Q., Shaffer, D., Ng, S., O'Connor, P. A., & Wolff, R. R. (1986). Assessment of neurological "soft signs" in adolescents: Reliability studies. *Developmental Medicine and Child Neurology, 28,* 428–439.

Taylor, H. G. (1983). MBD: Meanings and misconceptions. *Journal of Clinical Neuropsychology, 5(3),* 271–287.

Taylor, H. G. (1987). The meaning and value of soft signs in the behavioral sciences. In D. E. Tupper (Ed.), *Soft neurological signs* (pp. 297–335). Orlando: Grune & Stratton.

Taylor, H. G., & Fletcher, J. M. (1983). Biological foundations of "specific developmental disorders": Methods, findings, and future directions. *Journal of Clinical Child Psychology, 12*(1), 46–65.

Touwen, B. C. L. (1979). *Examination of the child with minor neurological dysfunction* (2nd ed.). London/Philadelphia: Heineman/Lippincott.

Touwen, B. C. L. (1987). The meaning and value of soft signs in neurology. In D. E. Tupper (Ed.), *Soft neurological signs* (pp. 281–295). Orlando: Grune & Stratton.

Touwen, B. C. L. (1993). Longitudinal studies on motor development: Developmental neurological considerations. In A. F. Kalverboer, B. Hopkins, & R. Geuze (Eds.), *Motor development in early and later childhood: Longitudinal approaches* (pp. 15–34). Cambridge, England: Cambridge University Press.

Touwen, B. C. L., Lok-Meijer, T. Y., Huisjes, H. J., & Olinga, A. A. (1982). The recovery rate of neurologically deviant newborns. *Early Human Development, 7,* 131–148.

Touwen, B. C. L., & Sporrell, T. (1979). Soft signs and MBD. *Developmental Medicine and Child Neurology, 21,* 528–530.

Tupper, D. E. (1986). Neuropsychological screening and soft signs. In J. Obrzut & G. Hynd (Eds.), *Child neuropsychology* (Vol. 2, pp. 139–186). Orlando, FL: Academic Press.

Tupper, D. E. (Ed.). (1987). *Soft neurological signs.* Orlando: Grune & Stratton.

Vitiello, B., Stoff, D., Atkins, M., & Mahoney, A. (1990). Soft neurological signs and impulsivity in children. *Journal of Developmental and Behavioral Pediatrics, 11,* 112–115.

Werry, J. S. (1968). Studies on the hyperactive child: IV. An empirical analysis of the minimal brain dysfunction syndrome. *Archives of General Psychiatry, 19,* 9–16.

Wilner, E., Cannon, J., & Brody, J. A. (1969). Measles, minor neurological signs, and intelligence. *Developmental Medicine and Child Neurology, 11,* 449–454.

Wolff, P. H., & Hurwitz, I. (1973). Functional implications of the minimal brain damage syndrome. In S. Walzer & P. H. Wolff (Eds.), *Minimal cerebral dysfunction in children* (pp. 105–115). New York: Grune & Stratton.

Younes, R. P., Rosner, B., & Webb, G. (1983). Neuroimmaturity of learning disabled children: A controlled study. *Developmental Medicine and Child Neurology, 25,* 574–579.

7

Early Physiological Patterns and Later Behavior

Stephen W. Porges
Jane A. Doussard-Roosevelt
University of Maryland

During early infancy, physiological vulnerabilities associated with medical risk (low birthweight, fetal distress, neonatal hypoxia, etc.) are assumed to be potent marker variables capable of predicting difficulties in developmental outcome (e.g., mental retardation and difficulties in learning, poor motor coordination, attention problems, and poor social interactions). However, the specific physiological mechanisms that promote or ameliorate subsequent developmental difficulties have not been identified. Why two children experiencing the same specific risk factors at birth or during early infancy have different outcomes is not well understood. Vague statements regarding the complex interaction between the infant and postpartum environmental factors are often provided in place of an explanation. In the child development literature, the role of the nervous system in the regulation of stress responses has received little attention. In this chapter, we propose that the central regulation of the autonomic nervous system plays a critical role in the child's ability to respond adaptively to stress events and to organize behavioral outcomes. The chapter is based on the hierarchical model of neurobehavioral organization proposed by Porges (1983) and incorporates portions of the recent Polyvagal Theory (Porges, 1995).

Responses to Stress

Research on stress in adults has often focused on the description of events that are considered stressful (death of a spouse, loss of a job, etc.) and not on the functional impact of these events on physiology. With adults and older children, clinical interview techniques effectively elicit the patients' verbal description of the stressful events. With younger patients, especially with the preverbal infant, the evaluation of stress is more difficult and relies on the ability to interpret clinical signs of behavioral and physiological reactivity. With young infants, stress is often observed when behavior becomes disorganized (e.g., irregular sleep–wake patterns, difficulties in regulating behavior in social settings, extended bouts of crying, and general irritability) and homeostatic physiological processes are disrupted (e.g., difficulties in digestion and elimination and other problems with autonomic processes). Unlike the behavioral and psychological emphasis of stress responses in adults, research with infant populations has focused on assessments of behavior (e.g., crying, facial affect) and physiology (e.g., heart rate, cortisol) in response to procedures that are presumed painful. Many researchers assume that global measures of physiological systems reflecting cardiovascular activity and the hypothalamic-pituitary-adrenal axis will be sensitive to stressful events. How these systems register stress or stress vulnerability is seldom discussed.

In contrast, the Polyvagal Theory (Porges, 1995) provides the neurophysiological justification for new definitions and explanations of stress and stress vulnerability. The theory emphasizes the functional difference between vagal fibers originating in two areas of the brain stem, the nucleus ambiguus and the dorsal motor nucleus of the vagus. The two types of pathways have different embryological origins and mediate different response strategies to stressors. The neomammalian nucleus ambiguus vagal pathways mediate a response characterized by a rapid withdrawal of vagal tone. This functionally removes the potent "vagal brake" from the heart and facilitates an instantaneous increase in metabolic output (i.e., increased heart rate) to mobilize energy resources. While the vagal brake is released, the organism is at risk for a stress response mediated by the dorsal motor vagal pathways and characterized by a massive increase in vagal tone. As discussed in the Polyvagal Theory, the nucleus ambiguus vagal response is adaptive for mammals, whereas the dorsal motor vagal response is not. Measurement of the nucleus ambiguus vagal response via its effect on control of heart rate can serve as an index of adaptive reactivity. Vagal fibers to the heart from the nucleus ambiguus produce a respiratory rhythm, known as respiratory sinus arrhythmia (RSA). By applying time-series statistics to the beat-to-beat heart rate pattern (Porges, 1985), it is possible to extract a measure of RSA that accurately represents vagal influences from the nucleus ambiguus.

Nucleus ambiguus vagal tone (V_{NA}) is a measure of the amplitude of RSA and can serve as an index of neurophysiological regulation prior to a stressor. In turn, the observation of changes in V_{NA} to a stressor can serve as an indicator of how adaptively the infants' systems respond. And, given a model in which complex behaviors are built on a foundation of physiological regulation (e.g., Porges, 1983; Porges, Doussard-Roosevelt, & Maiti, 1994), one can expect a relation between measures of V_{NA} (baseline and change to stressors) and later development. The model predicts that chronically low cardiac vagal tone and/or poor vagal regulation to stressors will be predictive of poor developmental outcomes. Following a brief description of the measurement of nucleus ambiguus vagal tone, we review the stability of these measures and their usefulness in predicting outcome.

Measurement of Nucleus Ambiguus Vagal Tone

Measurement of RSA requires detection of the heart beat from the electrocardiogram (i.e., R-wave) and timing between heart beats (i.e., heart periods). To quantify the cardiac vagal tone index (V_{NA}) from RSA, it is necessary to detect and time with ms accuracy. V_{NA} is extracted via time-series procedures. These procedures require heart period rather than heart rate data. On a beat-to-beat level, heart periods are the sequential time intervals between heart beats. These interbeat-interval data are processed by a patented method (Porges, 1985). The technique includes the application of time domain filters designed to extract only RSA. The resulting heart period pattern is sinusoidal with an amplitude and time period. The amplitude represents the changing vagal influences to the sinoatrial node, and the period represents the medullary inspiratory drive frequency also originating from the nucleus ambiguus (Haselton, Solomon, Motekaitis, & Kaufman, 1992). An excellent measure of cardiac vagal tone (V_{NA}) is derived by calculating the amplitude of RSA.

Summary

Although recent modeling (e.g., Porges, 1995) has led to a change in terminology and statistical notation (i.e., from cardiac vagal tone and $\hat{V}$ to nucleus ambiguus vagal tone and V_{NA}) the calculation of vagal tone has remained unchanged. Thus, we are able to review a continuous literature regarding vagal tone and its role in the child's ability to respond adaptively to stress events and to organize both physiological and behavioral outcomes. We begin with a look at stress responses in neonates, followed by questions of stability of neonatal V_{NA} measures, and then examine the relation of neonatal V_{NA} measures to developmental outcome. Following the review of the neonatal literature, we review the infant and toddler literature in the same manner.

NEONATES

Vagal Tone as an Index of Stress

Porges (1992) presented a test of the hypothesis that V_{NA} is related to clinical health status by evaluating cardiac vagal tone in two large samples of neonates: a full-term, low-risk group residing in a normal nursery (*n* = 125) and a high-risk group primarily composed of premature neonates residing in the neonatal intensive care unit (*n* = 112). All full-term infants were born via spontaneous vaginal delivery, had an absence of indications of neurological or medical pathology, and had a 5-min Apgar score of 8 or higher. The high-risk sample represented a range of diagnostic and risk factors: 56% had intraventricular hemorrhage Grades I–IV, 12% had other central nervous system pathology, and 47% had respiratory distress syndrome or other pulmonary dysfunction. Term neonates were monitored between 21 and 48 hours postpartum while in a sleep state. The high-risk neonates were preterm, ranging in gestational age from 26 to 34 weeks and were tested at a corrected gestational age (i.e., gestational age + postpartum age) of between 35 and 37 weeks. The high-risk infants were not receiving ventilatory assistance during the study. The high-risk infants were monitored during a period free of nursing procedures during sleep. Approximately 10 min of continuous electrocardiogram data were quantified for the vagal tone analyses.

The distributions of the vagal tone index for these two groups, illustrated in Fig. 7.1 (designated as preterm and full term), were signficantly different, $F(1, 235) = 226.3$, $p < .0001$. The means of the vagal tone distributions

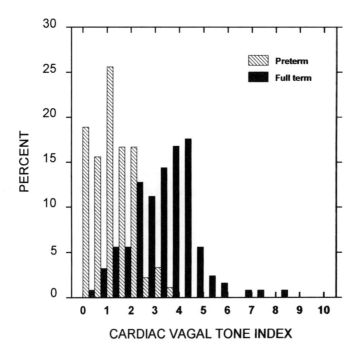

FIG. 7.1.   Distribution of cardiac vagal tone in preterm and full-term samples.

were 3.86 for the full-term, healthy neonates and 1.70 for the preterm neonates. The standard deviation of the vagal tone values was about 1.0 for each group. Similar values have been derived via analyses in Porges' laboratory of a sample of 74 full-term neonates who had a mean vagal tone of 3.94 and a standard deviation of .97 (Fox & Stifter, 1989) and for an additional high-risk sample of 99 preterm neonates with a mean vagal tone at 36 weeks corrected gestational age of 1.18 and a standard deviation of .84 (Doussard-Roosevelt, Porges, Scanlon, Alemi, & Scanlon, in press).

To investigate the possible contribution of group differences in respiration frequency to the observed vagal tone differences, respiratory frequency was calculated for a subset of the infants (48 full-term and 69 preterm). The full-term neonates breathed significantly slower (0.7 Hz or 42 breaths per min) than the preterm neonates (0.9 Hz or 53.5 breaths per min). All infants were breathing within the frequency band of .3 to 1.3 Hz used for the calculation of V_{NA}. These findings lead to the question of whether the observed group differences in vagal tone are dependent on respiration frequency. An analysis of covariance was conducted to determine whether there were significant group differences in vagal tone when the influence of respiration frequency was statistically removed. The analysis confirmed that even when the influence of respiration is removed, there are highly significant differences between the two groups in vagal tone, $F(1, 107) = 82.2$, $p < .0001$. Group classification accounted for 53.1% of the variance of vagal tone in the initial analysis of variance. When the influence of respiration was removed, group classification still accounted for 43.7% of the variance of vagal tone.

DiPietro, Cusson, Caughy, and Fox (1994) examined neonatal response to routine handling and to gavage feeding, in a sample of 36 preterm neonates. In response to handling, heart period and vagal tone decreased. Vagal tone further decreased in response to gavage feeding. Although nonnutritive sucking on a pacifier calmed behavioral state during these procedures, there was no similar effect on the physiological response. Thus, the vagal tone index allowed for a measure of physiological response to stress apart from the observed behavioral response.

Porter, Porges, and Marshall (1988) found a relation between the vagal response to the stress of circumcision and the behavioral response to the same procedures in full-term newborns. In response to circumcision, there were parallel changes in newborn pain cries and vagal tone. Again, onset of the stressor resulted in a decrease in vagal tone.

Thus, two points are extracted from studies of neonatal vagal responses. First, tonic levels of V_{NA} are lower in preterm neonates than in full-term neonates, supporting the model of baseline V_{NA} associated with stress vulnerability. Second, changes in V_{NA} in response to disruptive and/or painful medical procedures are seen in both preterm and full-term neonates.

Stability of Vagal Tone Assessments

To understand whether V_{NA} can be used as a clinical indicator or risk factor, it is necessary to evaluate both developmental influences and test–retest stability. Repeated weekly assessments of a second preterm sample ($n = 99$) provided an initial indicator of week-to-week stability. Although there were obvious developmental changes, after the first recording the vagal tone measure exhibited a reasonable degree of stability. Test–retest correlations for vagal tone over the first four recordings for the entire sample yielded significant findings for all comparisons. However, all contrasts with the first recording were low (.23, .22, .28) whereas the relationships among recordings 2, 3, and 4 were all approximately .50.

Our initial approach to the within-participant development question was addressed by categorizing these preterm neonates into groups based on gestational age at birth. The neonates were divided into four groups: 24–26 weeks (27 neonates), 27–29 weeks (37 neonates), 30–32 weeks (16 neonates), and 33–35 weeks (11 neonates). A repeated measures analysis of variance evaluated gestational age influence on the first two values and the discharge value. As seen in Fig. 7.2, there was a group by testing session interaction, $F(6, 174) = 3.84, p < .01$.

Similar to the correlations, the gestational age influence was muted

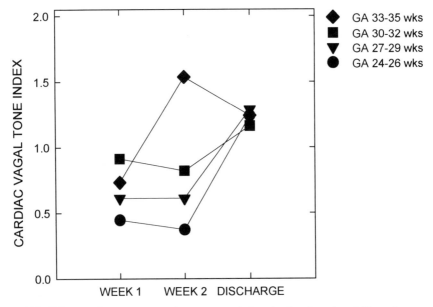

FIG. 7.2. Vagal tone measures for preterms during the first 2 weeks of life and at discharge from the neonatal intensive care unit, with infants grouped on gestational age (GA) in weeks at birth.

during the first recording, was maximally expressed during the second recording, and was nonexistent during the discharge recording. Simple effects analyses identified significant gestational age group differences only during the second recording. These data demonstrate that although there are significant gestational age influences on vagal tone during the early part of postpartum life, by the time the neonate has physiologically stabilized and is discharged, gestational age is not influencing vagal tone, and the younger gestational age neonates have "caught up" with the older preterm neonates.

In addition to theses analyses, we also examined maturational changes in vagal tone within participants from their weekly recordings. Fig. 7.3 illustrates the data for all neonates with gestational ages of 32 weeks or less. Note that the maturational increases in vagal tone between adjacent weeks are largest in the 33–35 week period.

Portales and Porges (1995) further explored the issue of stability of vagal tone within the neonatal intensive care unit, with sequential measurements during four recording sessions, 1 to 3 days apart, in two samples of low-birthweight infants. The mean correlation across the four sessions for the higher risk group ($n = 14$, mean birthweight $= 1365$ g, mean Hobel risk

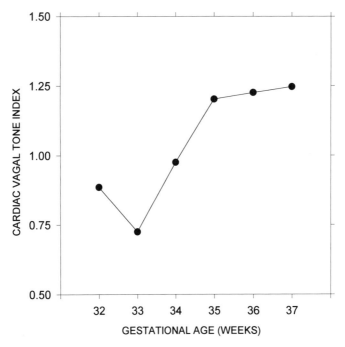

FIG. 7.3.   Mean of weekly vagal tone estimates plotted as a function of gestational age at time of testing.

score = 55) was .85 with correlations ranging from .77 to .95. The mean correlation across the four sessions for the lower-risk group (n = 12, mean birthweight = 1725 g, mean Hobel risk score = 30) was .78 with correlations ranging from .68 to .88. For the two groups combined, the mean correlation was .82 with correlations ranging from .76 to .86.

Although there are developmental–maturational effects observed in the neonatal intensive care unit (Fig. 7.2) for vagal tone, the magnitude of these effects is small relative to the group differences between high-risk neonates and extremely low-risk or full-term neonates (Fig. 7.1). Thus, the stability of the vagal tone index is statistically enhanced when calculating test–retest correlations of neonates containing a wide range of clinical conditions. The high stability is statistically caused by three factors: (a) the large range of vagal tone, (b) the strong relationship between vagal tone and general risk status (e.g., extremely low risk vs. high risk), and (c) the magnitude of the maturational effects. Maturational effects from birth to discharge for the very premature and clinically compromised neonates are small relative to the difference between high-risk and low-risk preterm groups. In general, if we were to include normals or extremely low-risk neonates in our sample, the test–retest correlations (deleting the recording immediately following birth for the neonates) would be approximately .90. If we evaluate only the high-risk neonates, given the physiological instability and truncated range, the test–retest correlations appear to be approximately .50. In conclusion, vagal tone exhibits stability within the neonatal intensive care unit. Stability is excellent (i.e., correlations approaching .90), if the sample is heterogeneous. Stability is moderate (i.e., correlations in the .50–.60 range) when test–retest stability is evaluated within a high-risk group with a limited range of individual differences in vagal tone. These findings refer to neonatal measures of vagal tone taken at least 24 hours after delivery. During the first day of life, the measures are affected by delivery and recovery.

Neonatal Vagal Tone and Developmental Outcome

Given that neonatal V_{NA} is a stable index and demonstrates a responsiveness to stressors, Porges' hierarchical model of behavior (e.g., Porges, 1983) suggests that there should be a relationship between neonatal V_{NA} (Level I and II processes reflecting underlying physiology) and developmental outcome (Level III and IV processes manifested in individual behaviors and coordination of behaviors). We assessed the hypothesized relationship in two independent samples, a full-term sample and a preterm sample. For the full-term group, we evaluated the relationship between term values of vagal tone and outcome measures. For the preterm group, weekly measures of vagal tone were used to calculate an Average Vagal Tone score as well as a

Maturation of Vagal Tone score, which were used in the prediction of outcome variables.

Full-term Neonates. At 15 months, 44 of the neonates from the full-term sample were tested in a follow-up study in which the Bayley scales (Mental Development Index, Psychomotor Development Index, Infant Behavior Record), the Bates (1984) Infant Characteristics Questionnaire, vagal tone, and developmental landmarks were assessed. Selection of the infants was based on their neonatal vagal tone. To ensure a range of individual differences, all infants with an extreme vagal tone as a newborn (i.e., vagal tone of .75 standard deviation or more above or below the mean) were recruited. The remaining participants were randomly selected from the group with newborn vagal tone scores within .75 standard deviation of the mean. Higher neonatal vagal tone was related to higher 15-month Mental Development Index ($r = .30$), earlier age that mother reported that the infant could sit up alone ($r = -.39$), and greater persistency as measured by the Infant Characteristics Questionnaire ($r = .32$). Moreover, for the Matheny (1980) clusters of the Infant Behavior Record, higher neonatal vagal tone was related to greater activity ($r = .33$) and better motor coordination ($r = -.34$). Behavior in the newborn nursery also provides information regarding 15-month behavior coded on the Infant Behavior Record. Neonates who were judged by the experimenters during the neonatal testing as having more aversive cries, exhibited poorer involvement with and orientation toward objects during the Bayley administration at 15 months ($r = -.37$). In contrast, higher scores on the Kansas addenda to the Neonatal Behavioral Assessment Scale were associated with greater task orientation ($r = .35$), more outgoing style ($r = .32$), and greater sensory awareness ($r = .38$) at 15 months.

Thus, the neonatal vagal tone index predicts neurophysiologically based response systems such as motor activity, coordination, and cognition. In contrast, the behavioral response "style" at birth seems to be related to reactivity and interaction with objects and persons. It is important to note that these reported relationships are based on an extremely healthy sample, and all infants had outcomes in the normal range. At 15 months, no infant had a Mental Development Index below 90; but even within this sample of infants who had outstanding developmental outcomes, the neonatal vagal tone was significantly associated with the Mental Development Index scores. Relationships might be stronger if high-risk participants were included in these analyses, because their outcomes are more variable (i.e., with greater representation of lower outcomes) and they have lower neonatal vagal tone, as reported previously. However, our objective was to evaluate, within a normal group of newborns, whether the neonatal vagal tone measure predicted variance in developmental outcome.

Preterm Neonates.   We took a different approach to the problem of relating neonatal vagal tone to outcome with the second preterm sample. Selection of the sample was based on extremely low birthweights, and measures of vagal tone were collected weekly from birth to discharge. The outcome measures represented five broad areas of development (behavior regulation, mental processing, achievement, motor skills, and social competency). Based on the findings of a developmental shift in vagal tone, measures of vagal tone represented Average Vagal Tone across the period of 33–35 weeks as well as a Maturation of Vagal Tone across this period.

Correlational analyses revealed significant ($p < .05$) relations among the vagal tone measures and the outcome measures. Average Vagal Tone was negatively correlated with Behavior Problems ($r = -.36$) as measured by the Parenting Stress Index (Abidin, 1983) and was positively correlated with Social Skills ($r = .44$) as measured by the California Preschool Social Competency Scale (Levine, Elzey, & Lewis, 1969) and gross motor skills ($r = .32$) as measured by the Revised Denver Prescreening Developmental Questionnaire (Frankenburg, 1986). The Vagal Maturation score was negatively correlated with Behavior Problems ($r = -.36$) as measured by the Revised Dimensions of Temperament Survey (Windle & Lerner, 1985) and positively correlated with Mental Processing ($r = .36$) as measured by the Mental Processing Composite of the Kaufman Assessment Battery for Children (Kaufman & Kaufman, 1983) and both Gross motor ($r = .33$) and Fine motor ($r = .33$) skills.

Socioeconomic status, birthweight, and medical risk were also correlated with various outcome measures. Multiple regression analyses were run to determine the best predictor of each outcome variable and whether or not either Vagal Tone measure added a unique source of variance. Vagal Maturation was the single best predictor for the Dimensions of Temperament score and added unique variance to the predictive model for the Mental Processing Composite. Average Vagal Tone was the single best predictor for the Social Competency Score and added unique variance to the predictive model for the Parenting Stress Index child subscale score.

Analyses by Birthweight Group: Extremely Low Birthweight Versus Very Low Birthweight

An assumption in using correlation and regression analyses to test the ability of early measures to predict outcome is that the relations tested are linear. However, the linear model may not fit the data within each birthweight group. Within-group correlations were conducted for each of two birthweight groups: extremely low birthweight infants (birthweights < 1000g) and very low birthweight infants (birthweights between 1000g and

1500g). The extremely low birthweight group consisted of 21 participants (mean birthweight = 781g) with mean gestational age of 26 weeks and mean Hobel Risk Index of 81. The very low birthweight group consisted of 18 participants (mean birthweight = 1105g) with mean gestational age of 30 weeks and mean Hobel Risk Index of 67. There were no differences in maternal age or socioeconomic level for the subgroups.

Results indicated that the vagal tone measures that were significantly related to outcome variables for the entire sample were not necessarily related to outcome within each of the two subsamples. Thus, the correlations for the entire sample were somewhat diluted by combining the extremely low birthweight and very low birthweight subsamples. For example, the Dimensions of Temperament Score was related to the Vagal Maturation Score in the extremely low birthweight subsample ($r = -.60$) but not in the very low birthweight subsample ($r = -.10$). Likewise, the Mental Processing Composite and Achievement Scale of the Kaufman were related to the Vagal Maturation Score in the very low birthweight subsample ($r = .62, .55$, respectively) but not in the extremely low birthweight subsample ($r = -.05, -.27$, respectively). Thus, Vagal Maturation appears to identify a different set of outcome problems for very low birthweight as opposed to extremely low birthweight neonates.

Hofheimer, Wood, Porges, Pearson, and Lawson (1995) examined the relation between neonatal vagal tone (V_{NA}) and behavioral organization in a sample of high-risk preterm infants ($n = 52$). Infants were categorized into three groups: (a) healthy infants (Apgar scores > 6; no respiratory problems or diseases), (b) infants with major respiratory disease but no overt disease of the central nervous system, and (c) infants with both major respiratory disease and disease of the central nervous system. Higher V_{NA} at 35 weeks was related to more focused attention during a mother–child interaction at 42 weeks for all infants.

These results support the hypothesis that higher V_{NA} is associated with better neurobehavioral organization and that this organization provides a foundation for later social, cognitive, and motor behaviors. Further, they introduce the concept of assessing the maturational development of the vagal tone measure during the neonatal period. Both baseline V_{NA} and shift in V_{NA} during the preterm period were related to measures of developmental outcome.

INFANTS AND TODDLERS

Infant/Toddler Vagal Responses to Stress

Fracasso, Porges, Lamb, and Rosenberg (1994) collected heart rate data in infants at 7, 10, and 13 months. At each age, infant heart rate was recorded during a quiet baseline and in response to emotion-eliciting stimuli. Describing the emotion-eliciting stimuli as a stressor, the authors noted decreases in both heart rate and vagal tone from pre-stress to post-stress conditions.

Richards (1987; Richards & Casey, 1991) noted the positive correlation between baseline vagal tone and vagal response to stimulation/stressors. That is, infants with greater RSA exhibit larger decreases in RSA in response to a stressor.

A recent study by Bazhenova (1995) emphasizes the dynamics of RSA change during shifting affective states. She noted a parallel between positive and negative affect shifts in 5-month-olds in response to baseline, social interaction, stillface, and visual stimulation conditions and concurrent shifts in RSA.

Thus, studies with infants and toddlers indicate that vagal tone measures index the child's response to external stimulation.

Stability

Fracasso et al. (1994) reported stability over the first year of life with assessments at 5, 7, 10, and 13 months. Correlations across the 5–7, 7–10, and 10–13 month periods were .50, .55, and .50, respectively. The correlation from 5 months to 13 months was not significant ($r = .10$). Thus, moderate stability is seen in across-month comparisons in the first year of life.

Porges, Doussard-Roosevelt, Portales, and Suess (1994) examined the stability of infant vagal tone beyond the first year of life as well as its role as a marker variable for preschool behavior problems. Stability was assessed along two dimensions. First, age effects were evaluated with analyses of variance to determine whether there were developmental shifts in heart period and vagal tone from 9 months to 3 years. Second, correlations between 9-month and 3-year measures were used to evaluate stability for each of the variables. The means and across-age correlations for the vagal tone and heart period measures are shown in Table 7.1.

Repeated measures analyses of variance indicated that there were developmental shifts in both heart period (baseline: $F[1, 19] = 125.41, p < .001$; testing: $F[1, 15] = 110.93, p < .001$) and vagal tone (baseline: $F[1, 19] = 43.56, p < .001$; testing $F[1, 15] = 50.09, p < .001$). With age, heart period and vagal tone both increased.

Correlational analyses of the 15 participants with complete temperament and physiological data at both 9 months and 3 years are presented in Table 7.1 and indicate that maternal perceptions of difficultness were stable across time. Heart period was stable over time whether assessed during baseline or testing conditions. Similarly, vagal tone was stable over time

TABLE 7.1
Correlations of Stability From 9 Months to 3 Years

Measure	r	r^2	p
Maternal perceptions			
Difficultness	.71	.50	< .01
Vagal tone (V_{NA})			
Baseline	.55	.30	< .05
Testing	.69	.48	< .01
Heart period			
Baseline	.68	.46	< .01
Testing	.66	.44	< .01

Note. Difficultness = raw score on the Infant Characteristics Questionnaire at 9 months (Bates, Freeland, & Lounsbury, 1979) and the Preschool Characteristics Questionnaire at 36 months (Finegan, 1989).

when assessed during baseline and developmental testing. Thus, although both heart period and vagal tone exhibited developmental shifts in level, the participants maintained their relative rank. In examining the stability of heart rate variability in infants from 14 to 20 to 26 weeks, Richards (1989) also noted a developmental increase in RSA with age and found that the measures were positively correlated across all three ages.

Fox and Field (1989) looked at vagal tone in a study of 3-year-olds' responses to the preschool setting. Using measures collected 6 months apart, they found stability within this period ($r = .89$).

Izard et al. (1991) reported intraindex stability for four physiological measures (vagal tone, heart period variance, heart period range, mean heart period) recorded at 3, 4.5, 6, 9, and 13 months. In comparing early measures (3, 4.5 months) to later measures (6, 9, 13 months), they found stability of vagal tone over time ($rs = .32$ to $.49$).

Infant Vagal Tone and Developmental Outcome

Fox (1989) and colleagues studied the relation between vagal tone and emotional reactivity. Stifter, Fox, and Porges (1989) found greater facial expressivity in 5-month-olds with higher vagal tone. Similarly, Stifter and Fox (1990; Fox & Stifter, 1989) observed that 5-month-olds with higher vagal tone exhibited greater negative reactivity to arm restraint and more positive reactivity to a "peek-a-boo" procedure than infants with lower vagal tone. However, by 14 months, these highly reactive infants had developed into sociable toddlers. Whereas high vagal tone at 5 months was associated with greater reactivity, at 14 months, higher vagal tone was associated with more approach behaviors (to a stranger and to a novel object). Calkins and Fox (1992) also assessed vagal tone and behavioral reactivity in 5-month-old infants. Infants who cried in response to two stressors exhibited higher vagal tone than infants who did not cry to the stressors, although the finding was not statistically significant ($.05 < p < .06$).

Fox and Field (1989) also showed a relationship between vagal tone and social behaviors. The vagal tone of 3-year-olds predicted their interactive behaviors over the first weeks of preschool. Higher vagal tone predicted a greater increase in interactive versus solitary play behaviors in preschool.

Izard et al. (1991) reported that infant vagal tone measures, but not heart rate measures, were related to later attachment behaviors. Vagal tone measures at 3, 6, and 9 months were related to level of attachment security at 13 months. Infants with higher V_{NA} exhibited more insecure attachment behaviors (contact resistance, proximity avoidance, crying), whereas infants with lower V_{NA} exhibited more secure attachment behaviors (proximity seeking, contact maintaining).

DeGangi, Porges, Sickel, and Greenspan (1993) found a different pattern of predictability for vagal tone measures based on the sample in question. In comparing 8- to 11-month-old regulatory-disordered ($n = 9$) and nonregulatory-disordered ($n = 13$) infants, they found a change in the relation of vagal tone with measures of behavioral organization at 4 years. For the nonregulatory-disordered group, higher infant V_{NA} was associated with 4-year ratings of better behavioral organization (e.g., attention, activity level, and self-calming abilities). However, for the regulatory disordered infants, higher V_{NA} was associated with behavioral difficulties at 4 years. It is suggested that, due to their inability to self-regulate, the increase in reactivity to the environment (reflected in high V_{NA}) results in behavioral difficulties. In support of this, at 9 months, the regulatory-disordered infants, relative to normal infants, showed less suppression of V_{NA} during administration of the Bayley scales.

Porges, Doussard-Roosevelt, Portales, and Greenspan (in press) found that 9-month vagal tone measures predicted later scores on syndrome scales of the Child Behavior Checklist (Achenbach, 1988). Higher infant vagal tone and a greater vagal response to a stressor (test administration) were associated with fewer behavior problems at 3 years.

Each of these studies demonstrates that infant measures of baseline V_{NA} and/or vagal response to stimulation/stressors are predictive of later behaviors. The outcome measures represent various areas, including social, cognitive, and self-regulatory behaviors.

CONCLUSIONS

High-risk neonates are compromised. Low birthweight, prematurity, and medical complications place the infants at risk for poor developmental outcome. However, not all high-risk preterm infants manifest poor outcomes. Similarly, infants diagnosed with regulatory disorders have been shown to have developmental deficits in childhood. But, again, not all infants with regulatory disorders demonstrate the same pattern of outcome. The model presented in this chapter suggests that measures of nucleus ambiguus vagal tone provide insight into physiological systems underlying complex behaviors. We have focused on interpreting the role of the nervous system in regulating physiological systems. For at-risk newborns, survival is based on their level of self-regulation. Moreover, in all infants, self-regulation of physiological systems provides the infrastructure for more complex levels of self-regulation of behavioral, social, emotional, and cognitive systems.

The assessment methods described in this chapter focus on a specific physiological system originating in the nucleus ambiguus. The nucleus ambiguus is a brain stem nucleus that coordinates sucking, swallowing, vocalizing, and breathing via vagal pathways. By monitoring RSA, it is possible to assess neural regulation competence. According to the hierarchical model, as proposed by Porges (1983), baseline measures of V_{NA} assess the first level of competence, which is successful regulation of internal bodily process via neural negative-feedback systems. The vagal response to stimulation/stressors assesses the second level of competence, which is the balance between homeostatic demands and the demands of the stimuli/stressor. The assessment of each of these levels leads to conclusions regarding the likelihood of successful negotiation of the third and fourth levels of competence, reflecting observable behaviors and the coordination of behaviors, respectively. The review of the vagal tone/RSA literature, divided into neonatal and infant/toddler areas, provides evidence in support of the hierarchical model and the usefulness of V_{NA} measures in the prediction of developmental outcome.

ACKNOWLEDGMENTS

Preparation of this chapter and much of the research surveyed herein were supported in part by NICHD Grant HD22628 and Maternal and Child Health Bureau Grant MCJ240622 awarded to S. W. Porges.

REFERENCES

Abidin, R. (1983). *Parenting Stress Index*. Charlottesville, VA: Pediatric Psychology Press.
Achenbach, T. M. (1988). *Child Behavior Checklist for Ages 2–3*. Burlington, VT: University Associates in Psychiatry.

Bates, J. E. (1984). *Infant Characteristics Questionnaire*. Bloomington: Indiana University Press.

Bates, J. E., Freeland, C. B., & Lounsbury, M. L. (1979). Measurement of infant difficultness. *Child Development, 50*, 794–803.

Bazhenova, O. V. (1995, March). *Vagal tone reactivity: A psychophysiological parallel of the dynamics of affect*. Paper presented at the biennial meeting of the Society for Research in Child Development, Indianapolis, IN.

Calkins, S. D., & Fox, N. A. (1992). The relations among infant temperament, security of attachment, and behavioral inhibition at twenty-four months. *Child Development, 63*, 1456–1472.

DeGangi, G. A., Porges, S. W., Sickel, R. Z., & Greenspan, S. I. (1993). Four-year follow-up of a sample of regulatory disordered infants. *Infant Mental Health Journal, 14*, 330–343.

DiPietro, J. A., Cusson, R. M., Caughy, M. O., & Fox, N. A. (1994). Behavioral and physiologic effects of nonnutritive sucking during gavage feeding in preterm infants. *Pediatric Research, 36*, 207–214.

Doussard-Roosevelt, J.A., Porges, S. W., Scanlon, J. W., Alemi, B., & Scanlon, K. (in press). Vagal regulation of heart rate in prediction of outcome for very low birthweight preterm neonates. *Child Development*.

Finegan, J. (1989). *Preschool Characteristics Questionnaire*. Unpublished manuscript. The Hospital for sick children, Toronto.

Fox, N. A. (1989). Psychophysiological correlates of emotional reactivity during the first year of life. *Developmental Psychology, 25*, 364–372.

Fox, N. A., & Field, T. M. (1989). Individual differences in preschool entry behavior. *Journal of Applied Developmental Psychology, 10*, 527–540.

Fox, N. A., & Stifter, C. A. (1989). Biological and behavioral differences in infant reactivity and regulation. In G. A. Kohnstamm, J. E. Bates, & M. K. Rothbart (Eds.), *Temperament in childhood* (pp. 169–183). New York: Wiley.

Fracasso, M. P., Porges, S. W., Lamb, M. E., & Rosenberg, A. A. (1994). Cardiac activity in infancy: Reliability and stability of individual differences. *Infant Behavior and Development, 17*, 277–284.

Frankenburg, W. K. (1986). *Revised Denver Prescreening Developmental Questionnaire*. Denver, CO: Denver Developmental Materials.

Haselton, J. R., Solomon, I. C., Motekaitis, A. M., & Kaufman, M. P. (1992). Bronchomotor vagal preganglionic cell bodies in the dog: An anatomic and functional study. *Journal of Applied Physiology, 73*, 1122–1129.

Hofheimer, J. A., Wood, B. R., Porges, S. W., Pearson, E., & Lawson, E. E. (1995). Respiratory sinus arrhythmia and social interaction patterns in preterm newborns. *Infant Behavior and Development, 18*, 233–245.

Izard, C. E., Porges, S. W., Simons, R. F., Haynes, O. M., Hyde, C., Parisi, M., & Cohen, B. (1991). Infant cardiac activity: Developmental changes and relations with attachment. *Developmental Psychology, 27*, 432–439.

Kaufman, A. S., & Kaufman, N. L. (1983). *Kaufman Assessment Battery for Children*. Circle Pines, MN: American Guidance Service.

Levine, S., Elzey, F. F., & Lewis, M. (1969). *California Preschool Social Competency Scale*. Palo Alto, CA: Consulting Psychologists Press.

Matheny, A. P. (1980). Bayley's Infant Behavior Record: Behavioral components and twin analyses. *Child Development, 51*, 1157–1167.

Porges, S. W. (1983). Heart rate patterns in neonates: A potential diagnostic window to the brain. In T. M. Field & A. Sostek (Eds.), *Infants born at risk: Physiological, perceptual, and cognitive processes* (pp. 3–22). New York: Grune & Stratton.

Porges, S. W. (1985). *Method and apparatus for evaluating rhythmic oscillations in aperiodic physiological response systems* (US patent no. 4520944). Washington, DC: US Government

Patent Office.

Porges, S. W. (1992). Vagal tone: A physiologic marker of stress vulnerability. *Pediatrics, 90*, 498–504.

Porges, S. W. (1995). Mammalian modifications of our evolutionary heritage: A polyvagal theory. *Psychophysiology, 32*, 301–318.

Porges, S. W., Doussard-Roosevelt, J. A., & Maiti, A. K. (1994). Vagal tone and the physiological regulation of emotion. In N. A. Fox (Ed.), *Emotion regulation: Behavioral and biological considerations, 59* (2–3, Serial No. 240). Monograph of the Society for Research in Child Development, pp. 167–186.

Porges, S. W., Doussard-Roosevelt, J. A., Portales, A. L., & Greenspan, S. I. (in press). Infant regulation of the vagal brake predicts child behavior problems: A psychobiological model of social behavior. *Developmental Psychobiology*.

Porges, S. W., Doussard-Roosevelt, J. A., Portales, A. L., & Suess, P. E. (1994). Cardiac vagal tone: Stability and relation to difficultness in infants and 3-year-olds. *Developmental Psychobiology, 27*, 289–300.

Portales, A. L., & Porges, S. W. (1995, March). *Cardiac vagal tone in assessing low birthweight neonates: Stability and usefulness.* Paper presented at the biennial meeting of the Society for Research in Child Development, Indianapolis, IN.

Porter, F. L., Porges, S. W., & Marshall, R. E. (1988). Newborn pain cries and vagal tone: Parallel changes in response to circumcision. *Child Development, 59*, 495–505.

Richards, J. E. (1987). Infant visual sustained attention and respiratory sinus arrhythmia. *Child Development, 58*, 488–496.

Richards, J. E. (1989). Development and stability in visual sustained attention in 14, 20, and 26 week old infants. *Psychophysiology, 26*, 422–430.

Richards, J. E., & Casey, B. J. (1991). Heart rate variability during attention phases in young infants. *Psychophysiology, 28*, 43–53.

Stifter, C. A., & Fox, N. A. (1990). Infant reactivity: Physiological correlates of newborn and five-month temperament. *Developmental Psychology, 26*, 582–588.

Stifter, C. A., Fox, N. A., & Porges, S. W. (1989). Facial expressivity and vagal tone in five- and ten-month-old infants. *Infant Behavior and Development, 12*, 127–137.

Windle, M., & Lerner, R. M. (1985). Reassessing the dimensions of temperamental individuality across the lifespan: The Revised Dimensions of Temperament Survey (DOTS-R). *Journal of Adolescent Research, 1*, 213–230.

8 The Development of Lateralization

Marcel Kinsbourne
New School for Social Research, New York

Massive evidence from studies of focal brain damage documents the many functional specializations in the human forebrain. Most if not all of these "modular" specializations are unilateral, that is, confined to one of the cerebral hemispheres. But little is known about the importance of the laterality involved. Is the asymmetry necessary for the modules to work effectively, or is it a trivial consequence of the fact that there are two cerebral hemispheres and that the modules do not need to be spread across both (even if they could be without detriment)?

Why might it be necessary for a module to be confined to one hemisphere? Perhaps the neuronal circuitry needs to be concentrated within a limited territory in order for its activity to be coordinated, or perhaps it is more feasible to insulate a focal facility from interfering informational neural cross-talk (Kinsbourne & Hicks, 1978). Perhaps bilaterally represented facilities are apt to compete for control of output mechanisms, causing dysfluencies (i.e., impaired timing) in rapidly executed sequential skills (Levy, 1969; Marler, 1970). If so, those control mechanisms that influence midline output (e.g., speech, song) should be the ones that are lateralized. Therefore, or for reasons that have not been articulated, it has been traditionally assumed that laterality, apparently so prominent in humans, in some way renders possible humans' superior behavioral control. Laterality might even itself be an emergent consequence of neural maturation. The older child is perhaps better able to process certain kinds of information precisely because the components of the relevant module have become concentrated within a hemisphere. But it is difficult to find out whether this is really so. Laterality cannot be manipulated within-

181

participant in order to test this hypothesis under controlled experimental conditions. However, it is possible to make some potentially informative between-group comparisons. These take three forms:

1. comparing groups that are more and less lateralized (right-handers and nonright-handers matched for age and gender). Do they differ in the efficacy of their cognitive processes?
2. comparing cognitively unequal groups (phylogenetic: species differing in degree of behavioral control, and ontogenetic: conspecific cohorts differing in age). Do they differ systematically in laterality?
3. examining the neuropsychological consequences of early hemisphere damage in humans. Are the deficits that result more differentiated between hemispheres the greater the age at which the damage occurred (assuming that modules become more lateralized with increasing maturity)?

This discussion considers lateralization from the developmental viewpoint. It considers the evidence from development subsumed under Items 2 and 3.

PHYLOGENETIC ASPECTS OF LATERALIZATION

Most animal studies have dealt with the target species in the adult phase of its development. Having discovered a lateralized function, a few have proceeded to find out how it developed.

It is surprising how many of these efforts to identify instances of animal laterality have met with success, when it is still unclear which particular animal capabilities are most likely to have a lateralized brain base. By analogy with human language lateralization, there are some obvious candidates, such as animal communication, bird song, and sensitivity to the characteristic cries of the young of one's own species (conspecific pup cries). But beyond these, the existing evidence is based on a miscellany of abilities nominated for test by experimenters whose working hypotheses or intuitions have been quite diverse and even contradictory. It seems probable, therefore, that lateralized abilities are plentiful among mammals and far greater in number than those that have been sampled to date.

The most thoroughly studied species (rodents, birds, primates) all have been shown to have functions that are lateralized, but it is not clear what (if anything) the lateralized functions have in common. Analogies with the principles of human hemisphere specialization have by and large failed to predict putative animal laterality. This is partly because the human specializations are so often formulated in an unduly anthropocentric fashion that is not amenable to animal analogy (verbal–nonverbal, propositional–appositional) and partly because these analogies appear in any case not to have the necessary generality. As we see later, the lateralizations that have been discovered in animals cannot readily be organized in terms of a discernable overriding phylogenetic principle. Most importantly, the behaviorally more sophisticated species do not necessarily manifest more plentiful or prominent instances of lateralization. Cognitive abilities and laterality in the brain do not emerge in parallel across species. Human laterality is not at the peak of an evolutionary progression of increasing asymmetry that parallels increasing control over behavior.

Nonprimate Studies

Many fishes have species-specific somatic asymmetries that involve the pectoral and pelvic fins (Hubbs & Hubbs, 1964). But no corresponding neurological asymmetries have been described. One central asymmetry found in fish, amphibians, and reptiles, though long known, remains unexplained. This is an asymmetry of the paired habenular nuclei, favoring the left in most cases (Braitenberg & Kemali, 1970). Although they are presumed to participate in autonomic control, the exact function of these structures is unknown.

Male passerine song birds (canaries, chaffinches, white-crowned sparrows) vocalize by vibrating membranes within paired syringeal structures in the left and right bronchi. The muscles that control each syrinx, and thus the phrase structure of the song, are innervated by the ipsilateral hypoglossal nerve. This is in turn controlled by the ipsilateral Higher Vocal Control Center (HVc). If the left hypoglossal nerve is sectioned, song is abruptly and permanently abolished. This does not occur after right-sided section (Nottebohm, 1971). These dramatic findings make it tempting to generalize across human speech and bird song and infer that there is an adaptive advantage in the unilateral generation of responses that are emitted in rapid sequence, whether they constitute bird song or speech acts. If so, the brain structures that control the imitative speech of the parrot should also be lateralized. But control of parrot utterances is bilateral (Nottebohm, 1976), disconfirming the generalization. Moreover, recent research has uncovered species of birds in whom song is controlled by the right brain and, most significantly, species in whom both half brains control independent, but coordinated song lines (reviewed by Hauser, 1996). The notion that rapid sequential responding mandates lateralized control has to be discarded.

Another classical assumption that can be tested for generality with respect to bird song is that a brain area that houses a lateralized function must be larger than its nonspecialized contralateral counterpart. Along these lines, much has been made of the temporal planum asymmetry, usually favoring the left, as integral to left-hemisphere specialization for human language (Geschwind & Levitsky, 1968). If the left of the paired plana is really larger because it subserves language, then by analogy, should not the communicatively functioning left HVc be larger than the barely functioning right? It is not. Morphological asymmetry is not a necessary condition for functional asymmetry in the bird brain (and has not been proven to be so in the human brain either).

Although it has no song, the domestic chick features numerous asymmetries (Arnold & Bottjer, 1985). Visual discrimination learning is lateralized to the left striatal hemisphere, whereas imprinting, at least in its initial stages, is related to the right intermediate medial hyperstriatum ventrale (imhv). However, with increasing familiarity of the imprinted object, control appears to shift to the left imhv (Cipolla-Neto, Horn, & McCabe, 1982). A comparable shift in humans from right to left brain control with increasing familiarity of repeatedly viewed stimuli has been suggested by Goldberg and Costa (1981) and illustrated by Kinsbourne and Bruce (1987).

Rodents exhibit asymmetries in brain morphology, behavior, and neurochemistry. Male rats have generally thicker cortex in the right hemisphere and hippocampus and female rats in the left hemisphere and hippocampus. These asymmetries are less or even reversed if the animal has been castrated at birth (Diamond, 1985). However, any functional implications that these asymmetries might have are unknown.

The right hemisphere controls the open field activity of rats but only if the rat has been handled early in life, and the direction of the effect depends on whether the animal was reared in an impoverished or an enriched environment (Denenberg & Yutzey, 1985). Fear appears to be subserved by the right hemisphere also. The left hemisphere inhibits fear and also mouse killing. The latter is more frequent after the callosum is cut (Denenberg, Gall, Berrebi, & Yutzey, 1986). This suggests transcallosal inhibition in the intact state, which will be seen to be a heuristic concept in humans when recovery from aphasia is considered.

Spontaneous activity in the running wheel increases after right but not left hemisphere injury, and this has been related to greater depletion of catecholamine concentrations bilaterally after the right sided lesion (Pearlson, Kubos, & Robinson, 1984). The effect is thought to be mediated by efferent projections from cortex to the striatum (Robinson, 1985).

These rodent asymmetries correspond poorly to those in humans. This is not only on account of species differences in behavior (e.g., mouse killing) but because behavioral parameters that are lateralized in rodents are not lateralized in humans (e.g., activity level).

In contrast to these species-specific asymmetries, asymmetries in mouse paw preference (Collins, 1985) and in direction of rat circling (Glick &

Shapiro, 1985) occur at the level of the individual; that is, they favor one side or the other in different animals. Asymmetric dopamine uptake between the striata makes for more circling, but in different animals the circling is either ipsilateral or contralateral to the more active side. There are no significant asymmetries at the population level.

Whereas in birds, lateralization is closely linked to communicative functions, the only known laterality finding in rodents that relates to communication is left hemisphere dominance for approach to the source of pup calls in lactating but not in virgin mice (Ehret, 1987). The asymmetry is confined to a phase in the life span during which the signals have adaptive significance.

Behavioral asymmetries in cats have been shown at the individual but not the population level. There are also asymmetries in cortical sulcal patterning, but these have not been related to paw preference (Webster, 1981). Dogs appear to rely on their right hemispheres to learn an auditory discrimination based on voice onset time (Adams, Molfese, & Betz, 1987). In this respect, they resemble monkeys and humans.

Primate Studies

Nonhuman primates show both morphological and behavioral asymmetries. Specifically, they share sundry brain asymmetries with humans, including those of the Sylvian fissures and temporal lobes, as well as the normal skewing ("petalia") that has the right hemisphere protrude anteriorly and the left posteriorly (LeMay, 1985). Not only humans, but also chimpanzees and orangutans (Beheim-Schwarzbach, 1975) and even monkeys (Heilbroner & Holloway, 1988), usually have a larger temporal planum on the left. Not being specific to our species, such asymmetries may therefore not be informative about the brain basis of abilities that are uniquely human, in particular language.

Studies of visual pattern discrimination in primates generally have shown the two hemispheres to be equally proficient, even for tasks chosen for their resemblance to ones known to elicit lateralization in humans, for instance, learning based on facial or perspective cues (Hamilton, 1977). This bisymmetry of function is still found when stimuli are presented sequentially (Hamilton & Vermeire, 1982). When lateralization is found, it has sometimes been the opposite of that in humans. For discrimination of line orientation (Hamilton, 1983) and of dot displacement (Jason, Cowey, & Weiskrantz, 1984), tasks that elicit right-hemisphere dominance in humans, left-hemisphere superiority was found in monkeys. Similarly, Vanclair, Fagot, and Hopkins (1993) found a left-hemisphere advantage for mental rotation in baboons. However, Hamilton and Vermeire's (1988) split-brain monkeys did show right-hemisphere superiority for discriminating monkey faces. Consistent with findings in humans, this asymmetry disappeared when the faces were inverted. Hopkins, Washburn, and Rumbaugh (1990) even found left-hemisphere dominance for nonface visual stimuli in chimpanzee and macaques. Clearly, if the nonhuman primate hemispheres have complementary specializations, they do not entirely correspond to those in humans, even after making allowance for the differences between the species in cognitive profile.

Auditory studies have been more analogous to human in outcome. Dewson (1977) found that left- but not right-temporal lesions disrupt auditory–visual matching. Peterson, Beecher, Zoloth, Moody, and Stebbins (1978) showed a right ear advantage for recognizing conspecific macaque calls. Additionally, the ability of Japanese macaques to discriminate vocalizations is impaired by removing the left, but not the right, superior temporal gyrus (Heffner & Heffner, 1984). Also, Pohl (1983) found a right-hemisphere advantage for discriminating diverse stimuli of no communicative significance to baboons, a finding that has its parallel in the human literature. Adult rhesus monkeys favor the right ear when listening to conspecific vocalizations, but the left ear when listening to the vocalizations of other species—complementary asymmetries that are not present in the infant rhesus monkey (Hauser & Andersson, 1994). Perhaps the left-sided specialization favors the more familiar patterns, as it appears to do in humans (discussed later).

Memory for tactile discriminations is represented bilaterally in the monkey brain (Ebner & Myers, 1962). But monkeys who elected to use their left hand for a tactual discrimination task outperformed those who used their right hand (Ettlinger, 1987). When monkeys produce emotional grimaces (e.g., indicating fear), the left side of the face precedes the right in assuming the expression (Hauser, 1993). This evidence of right-hemisphere dominance for emotional expression parallels similar findings in humans. Correspondingly, Ifune, Vermeire, and Hamilton (1984) elicited more emotional expression in split-brain rhesus monkeys when they stimulated the right hemisphere with emotive videotaped scenes.

Overview

In overview of the animal literature, the following can be concluded:

1. Central asymmetries in mammals are reasonably plentiful where looked for.
2. No trend is apparent for them to be more frequent or more pronounced in behaviorally relatively sophisticated species or in species that are phylogenetically relatively close to humans.

3. The functions that have been found to be lateralized appear not to be subsumed within a specific mental domain, such as communication, and not all correspond well to functions that are lateralized in humans.
4. Some striking analogies with human lateralization have been uncovered, especially in nonhuman primates, but then again some lateralizations are the precise opposite of those in humans.
5. The fact, though not the side, of lateralization, may be permitted by a lack of need to align the output in question with specific targets in ambient space.

It appears that lateralization is not necessarily related to the emergence of communicative or other higher mental functions. It does appear that specialized cortical machinery is more likely to be lateralized, regardless of its categorical nature. This finding can be accommodated within the following generalization (Kinsbourne, 1978). Functions are bilaterally represented if they are apt to need to be deployed to either side of space within the natural environment. Thus, it comes as no surprise that visual pattern discrimination is bilateralized in nonhuman primates. But for mental operations in focal vision, such as face discrimination, bilateral representation is unnecessary and tends not to be found. The same applies to discriminations such as the decoding of adaptively relevant acoustic messages, which can be accomplished in free field prior to orienting attention to any particular place.

If animal lateralization for domains comparable to those that characterize left- and right-hemisphere specializations (e.g., left focal/analytic vs. right spatial/relational) in humans do not clearly emerge from the available data, that does not necessarily mean that an analogous complementarity is absent in nonhuman species. It may exist but not be organized by hemisphere. Ungerleider and Mishkin (1982) described a dorsal–ventral "where/what" complementarity in apes' visual system. This complementarity is not limited to vision, however. Fuster (1989) described an apparently analogous complementarity between dorsomedial frontal and orbital frontal cortex. It may be that humans and apes differ not so much in the functional complementarity but in the anatomical disposition of the relevant brain regions. Evidence from comparative anatomy shows that the what-versus-where distinction, embodied in a bilateral complementarity between piriform (olfactory) cortex and the hippocampus and elaborated by vast but separate (ventral vs. dorsal) additional areas of neocortex along the phylogenetic scale, is fundamental (Sanides, 1970). In humans, some of this complementarity has also established itself across the lateral dimension (Kinsbourne & Duffy, 1990). In nonhuman primates, it may have done so too but not always on the corresponding side of the cerebrum.

The Adaptive Role of Animal Laterality

From the previous perspective, animal laterality represents at most an economy in the use of brain space. It arises from the relaxation of the need for bisymmetry (perhaps mostly within the what system) when the evolving ability is one that does not have to be represented bilaterally to be maximally efficient. It certainly is not limited to the control of midline output mechanisms, such as bird song. This is important to keep in mind when interpreting human lateralization. Nothing in the now extensive animal research literature even addresses the proposition that lateralization lends additional efficiency to any mental operation.

The most specific test for any benefit of lateralization in animals is rarely reported. This is to compare the efficiency with which individuals, who have the majority lateralization and those in whom laterality is aberrant or absent, function (analogous to the many studies comparing the orthodox lateralized right-handers with the more diversely lateralized left-handers in the human population). Such studies would generally require greater sample sizes than those typically available in order to have adequate statistical power and would be premised on demonstrated stability of individual lateralization from test to retest within individual animals, also evidence that is not generally available at this time. Also, a situation comparable to that in humans, in which a substantial minority of the general population differs reliably from the majority in peripheral and/or central laterality, has not as yet been uncovered in any animal species. If anything, it is symmetry that is advantageous, at least at the somatic level, for morphological traits. Symmetry of such characteristics predicts fecundity, growth, and survival in animals and even a mating selection advantage in humans (Thornhill & Gangestad, 1994).

ONTOGENETIC ASPECTS OF LATERALIZATION

Two Models of Developing Laterality

A straightforward account of the development of lateralization would relate each lateralized facility to its antecedents and presume that the specialization in question occurs within the same location in the brain. What changes over time would be the degree of elaboration of the processor, not its location within the neural network. This "invariant lateralization" model (Kinsbourne, 1975) is probably essentially correct, but a more complicated view had until recently been entertained. This is that initially the two hemispheres are "equipotential" for lateralized mental functions and that these functions originate from a bilateral cerebral base. Mental operations lateralize to their proper hemispheres over a considerable period of time, held to be as long as the whole of prepubertal childhood by Lenneberg (1967), the theorist who most clearly formulated this model of "progressive lateralization." This idea was fueled as early as the 19th century by the observation that whereas damage of the mature left hemisphere regularly leads to disorders such as aphasia, apparently comparable damage in early childhood usually results in little or no enduring language deficit. If so, either the left hemisphere has remarkable recuperative properties in the child, or the right hemisphere can adapt its own circuitry to language and can effectively replace the left as the site of language processing at that early age. Observations assembled by Basser (1962) supported the second alternative, in that, although aphasia was quite probable after left-hemisphere lesions in the child, it was also probable after right-hemisphere lesions. But the cases Basser included in his meta-analysis must have included many whose involvement was in fact bilateral (Woods & Teuber, 1978; see later). It is essential to distinguish between right-hemisphere language compensation after left-brain injury and right-hemisphere language as a normal stage in language development. The notion that the right hemisphere participates in early language suits those who view child language as imperfect or not yet a true language (comparable, for instance, to language skills credited to specially educated nonhuman primates). In contrast, continuity theorists, for whom language emerges from preverbal antecedents, and is a refinement, albeit to a momentous degree, of skills available to other animals, have nothing to gain from the hypothesized right-hemisphere role in early language.

Even if normal language development were not to involve the right hemisphere, compensatory language development might still occur in it. If so, when the right hemisphere compensates for a left language area lesion, does it do so completely or only to a limited extent? For contemporary psycholinguistic theory, the latter outcome would be congenial. The notion that there is a uniquely human specialized "language acquisition device" without phylogenetic antecedents (Chomsky, 1966) is weakened if traditionally nonlanguage cortex, as in the right hemisphere, can completely replace the function of the left-sided language module. Thus, neurologists have been predisposed to accept claims for the inadequacy of right-hemisphere language, and research that seems to support this view was not initially scrutinized. For the same reason, the same applies to the progressive lateralization claims. Claims for early right-hemisphere involvement in language (Lenneberg, 1967) and for the limited nature of right-hemisphere language compensation (Dennis & Kohn, 1975) were each initially met with general assent and only seriously challenged years later (Bishop, 1983; Kinsbourne, 1975).

Evidence From Early Hemisphere Lesions

On reanalysis, the childhood data on which Basser (1962) so heavily relied proved to be potentially misleading. Claims for right-hemisphere language were based on little more than the coincidence of aphasia and a left hemiplegia. However, although left hemiplegia implicates the right brain, it does not exclude coexisting damage on the left by the same disease, which could account for aphasia without assuming right-hemisphere language. The improved precision of more recently developed diagnostic tools, as well as a reduction in the incidence of infectious diffuse brain disease, has changed the pattern of apparent right and left involvement in childhood aphasia (Kinsbourne & Hiscock, 1977; Woods & Teuber, 1978). The more recent better documented series show little evidence of aphasia as a result of right-hemisphere damage at any age.

Normative Studies

Evidence from studies of normal children supports the contention that lateralization is invariant across age. Numerous studies using diverse methodologies have demonstrated asymmetries in a variety of apparent preverbal tasks, including conditioning to verbal as opposed to nonverbal stimuli, to changes in speech sounds, and to the conjunction of speech sound and facial movement while speaking (reviewed in Witelson, 1987). The outcomes always favor the right side (left hemisphere). The opposite has generally been the case for nonverbal stimuli.

Also possibly relevant is a general response bias to the right that is evident as early as the first day of life, when the newborn shows a marked rightward turning tendency. As motor skills progressively differentiate, corresponding right-sided biases emerge in grasping and reaching (Hawn & Harris, 1983). Right biases in pointing (deixis) may have some role in the left lateralization of the neural basis for the first words, which are names for the things that the child indicates (Kinsbourne & Lempert, 1979).

Beginning with the third year of life, it is feasible to assess central laterality with the same methods as are used in adults, adjusting only task difficulty. It then becomes possible to evaluate two conflicting propositions: that the degree of lateralization, and therefore the degree of corresponding behavioral asymmetry, progressively increases (Lenneberg), or that it remains the same (Kinsbourne) with increasing age. The main sources of evidence are dichotic listening, visual half-field viewing, and dual-task interference (e.g., Hiscock & Kinsbourne, 1995; Kinsbourne & Hiscock, 1977, 1983; Witelson, 1987). The outcomes of the many studies that use verbal material (speech sounds, print, and spoken speech, respectively) endorse the invariance of lateralization of language processes, both receptive and expressive. The lesser amount of corresponding evidence about nonverbal processes is compatible with the same conclusion for the right hemisphere. Thus Trauner, Ballantyne, Friedland, and Chase (1996) reported impaired affective comprehension following early right, but not left, hemisphere damage.

Right-Hemisphere Compensation

Although there is little support for a role of the right hemisphere in the normal development of phonology and syntax (as distinct from semantics and pragmatics, in which it participates at all ages), the evidence is conclusive that it can assume such a role if the left hemisphere is compelled to relinquish it. Thus, Wada studies, in which language lateralization is ascertained by testing the conscious patient while one or the other hemisphere is temporarily anesthetized by intracarotid amytal, have revealed a significant minority of patients with early left-brain damage who rely on their right hemispheres for language representation (Carlsson, Hugdahl, Uvebrant, Wiklund, & Von Wendt, 1992; Rasmussen & Milner, 1977; Rey, Dellatolas, Bancaud, & Talairach, 1988). Convergent evidence comes from callosectomy (split-brain) studies. When disconnected from the left hemisphere, the right hemisphere can comprehend simple spoken instructions (although it cannot program speech output). Also, aphasics often program their speech through the right brain. The right hemisphere can be instrumental in language recovery even well into the adult years. Kinsbourne (1971) reported three adult aphasics who had sustained left-hemisphere injury. During intracarotid amytal testing on the left, which would be expected to cause speech arrest, these patients continued speaking as before. Two also received right-hemisphere anesthesia, and they both stopped speaking. The inference that these patients had compensated, to an extent reflected by their aphasia, based on the right hemisphere, was supported by a more extensive study by Czopf (1972), who found that more than half of his aphasic sample and particularly those with the more severe language disabilities demonstrated evidence of partial or complete right-hemisphere representation of language. It remains to be determined whether such language compensation in the adult can progress to complete restoration of the premorbid level of function. That this can be so is suggested by several case reports of patients who recovered from aphasia caused by left-sided lesions only to suffer permanent relapse when they sustained mirror symmetric lesions on the right. Their apparently complete recovery from the left-sided stroke would therefore had to have been based on right-hemisphere compensation. However, these patients' language abilities were not formally studied after clinical recovery, and it therefore remains possible that some clinically unobvious language disability persisted. Gainotti (1993) provided a recent review of this literature.

The previous findings are all consistent with Lenneberg's proposal that the hemispheres are equipotential for language at birth. This suggests that the fact that language normally develops on the left in more than 95% of people is due not to any right-hemisphere incapacity in principle for language processing but to its inhibition by the left hemisphere. Callosal section does not release this inhibition, but when a sufficiently extensive left-hemisphere lesion occurs, this hypothesized inhibition would be lifted, enabling the right hemisphere to realize its apparently near-normal if not fully normal language potential.

If the right hemisphere compensates for left lesions that involve the language cortex, is the language compensation that results really complete? If it is not, is that because, as many psycholinguists believe, only the left-hemisphere language module can process syntax effectively (even if semantics, not as uniquely restricted to the human species, are amenable to assistance from either side)? To answer this question, we have to study patients who unequivocally cannot program language in the left hemisphere (because they do not have one) and who are tested specifically for their syntactic ability (which the usual psychometric instruments do not test). These are patients who have undergone hemispherectomy because of intractable seizures due to earlier lateralized brain damage. Unlike patients with partial lesions of a hemisphere, the hemispherectomized patient has no opportunity for any language compensation within the injured hemisphere. Any abilities acquired subsequent to the operation must have been based on the intact residual hemisphere.

Children with early left-hemisphere lesions, and even left-hemispherect-omized patients, progress through the several stages of normal language development and achieve verbal IQs within the normal range (Trauner, Chase, Walker, & Wulfeck, 1993). However, Dennis and colleagues (e.g., Dennis & Kohn, 1975) pointed out that verbal intelligence tests may permit the individual to circumvent the need for syntactical processing, which, according to contemporary psycholinguistic theory, is integral to the specialized language function. Using a newly developed test of syntactic skills, they reported higher scores by a small group of right-hemispherect-omized patients than a small group of left-hemispherectomized patients. They reported similar results in a series of subsequent studies and concluded that losing the left hemisphere selectively imposes a ceiling on the level of language and specifically syntactic development.

In a critique of this body of research, Bishop (1983) pointed out numerous methodological shortcomings that render the results uninterpret-able. Given the scarcity of hemispherectomized individuals that are not mentally retarded, the extremely small sample sizes were presumably unavoidable. Inadequate account was taken of diversity in age and general intellectual level, which poses serious problems for tests that lack norms. Even normal controls are generally lacking, so that one cannot tell whether the experimental participants' scores were significantly lower than those of age- and IQ-matched normal peers would have been. It does appear clear from individual cases even within the Dennis research program that the right hemisphere can at least sometimes support fully normal language development, including development of syntax. Subsequent studies from other laboratories, although also interpreted in terms of an inadequacy of the right hemisphere in supporting language development, are equally subject to criticism (Bishop, 1988). In overview, the notion that there is true language equipotentiality between hemispheres in Lenneberg's sense has not been refuted.

Although initially the right hemisphere does appear to have the potential for full language development, whether it continues to have such potential as the nervous system matures is a separate question. Apparently, the later the left hemisphere is lesioned, the lower will be the ultimate level of verbal function. According to Lansdell (1969), there is reciprocity between verbal and spatial IQ such that the later the left-sided lesion occurs, the lower is the verbal IQ but the higher is the spatial IQ. If so, this might be because as it matures, the right hemisphere becomes increasingly dedicated toward spatial function and decreasingly hospitable to the transfer of verbal representation.

CONCLUSIONS

Language development, even in its preverbal stages, originates on the same side of the brain as that in which it will ultimately be represented in the adult. If that hemisphere is injured, the other hemisphere is capable of assuming the role of representing language. The extent of right-hemisphere compensation is clearly variable, and it remains an open question whether one of the determinants is the availability of as yet undedicated territory in the residual intact hemisphere of the young child. Although the human language skill must, of course, depend on highly specialized circuitry, such circuitry is not necessarily confined to the left hemisphere or even lateralized at all. Lateralization is a common attribute of functional localization in the human brain, but it has never been shown to be necessary or even conducive to the fullest development of any such function. Studies that compare the abilities of right-handers and nonright-handers (at least half of whom are bilateralized for language) are outside the scope of this discussion, but they teach the same lesson: In general, they fail to reveal any substantial cognitive advantage for the more lateralized brain of the right-hander (Hardyck, Petrinovitch, & Goldman, 1976; Kinsbourne, 1988).

The situation in phylogeny is similar. Functional lateralization is quite prevalent in a variety of vertebrate species, but no adaptive advantage for a function of being lateralized has been demonstrated. There is no particular type of ability for which uniform lateralization is in evidence across species. There is no general explanation for lateralization beyond the fact that for the functions in question, bilateralization would confer no additional advantage, because they are not targeted at specific locations in ambient space. If it ultimately turns out that humans have a particularly rich repertoire of lateralized cognitive processors, this would most likely be because they have more processors that do not target their activity on specific points in space, rather than because lateralized processing underlies and enables the human aptitude for higher mental function.

REFERENCES

Adams, C. L., Molfese, C., & Betz, J. C. (1987). Electrophysiological correlates of categorical speech perception for voicing contrasts in dogs. *Developmental Neuropsychology, 3,* 175–189.

Arnold, A. P., & Bottjer, S. W. (1985). Cerebral lateralization in birds. In S. D. Glick (Ed.), *Cerebral lateralization in nonhuman species* (pp. 11–39). Orlando, FL: Academic Press.

Basser, L. S. (1962). Hemiplegia of early onset and the faculty of speech with special reference to the effects of hemispherectomy. *Brain, 85,* 427–460.

Beheim-Schwarzbach, D. (1975). Weitere Untersuchungen zur cytoarchitektonischen Gliederung der Dorsalflache der 1. Temporalwindung bei einem Sprachgenie und bei zwei Anthropoiden [Further investigations of the cytoarchitectonic organization of the dorsal plane of the left temporal convolution in a language genius and in two anthropoids]. *Zeitschrift für mikroskopisch-anatomische Forschung, 89,* 759–776.

Bishop, D. V. M. (1983). Linguistic impairment after left hemidecortication for infantile hemiplegia? A reappraisal. *Quarterly Journal of Experimental Psychology, 35A,* 199–208.

Bishop, D. V. M. (1988). Can the right hemisphere mediate language as well as the left? A critical review of recent research. *Cognitive Neuropsychology, 5,* 353–367.

Braitenberg, V., & Kemali, M. (1970). Exceptions to bilateral symmetry in the epithalamus of lower vertebrates. *Journal of Comparative Psychology, 38,* 137–146.

Carlsson, G., Hugdahl, K., Uvebrant, P., Wiklund, L.-M., & Von Wendt, L. (1992). Pathological left-handedness revisited: Dichotic listening in children with left versus right congenital hemiplegia. *Neuropsychologia, 30,* 471–481.

Chomsky, N. (1966). *Cartesian linguistics.* New York: Harper & Row.

Cipolla-Neto, J., Horn, G., & McCabe, B. J. (1982). Hemispheric asymmetry and imprinting: The effect of sequential lesions to the hyperstriatum ventrale. *Experimental Brain Research, 48,* 22–27.

Collins, R. L. (1985). On the inheritance of direction and degree of asymmetry. In S. D. Glick (Ed.), *Cerebral lateralization in nonhuman species* (pp. 41–71). New York: Appleton-Century-Crofts.

Czopf, J. (1972). Über die Rolle der nicht dominanten Hemisphäre in der Restitution der Sprache der Aphasischen [On the role of the nondominant hemisphere in the recovery of speech of asphasics]. *Archiv für Psychiatrie und Nervenkrankheiten, 216,* 162–171.

Denenberg, V. H., Gall, J. S., Berrebi, A. S., & Yutzey, D. A. (1986). Callosal mediation of cortical inhibition in the lateralized rat brain. *Brain Research, 397,* 327–332.

Denenberg, V. H., & Yutzey, D. A. (1985). Hemispheric laterality, behavioral asymmetry, and the effects of early experience in rats. In S. D. Glick (Ed.), *Cerebral lateralization in nonhuman species* (pp. 109–133). Orlando, FL: Academic Press.

Dennis, M., & Kohn, B. (1975). Comprehension of syntax in infantile hemiplegics after cerebral hemidecortication: Left-hemisphere superiority. *Brain and Language, 2,* 475–486.

Dewson, J. H. (1977). Preliminary evidence of hemispheric asymmetry of auditory function in monkeys. In S. Harnad, R. W. Doty, L. Goldstein, J. Jaynes, & G. Krauthamer (Eds.), *Lateralization in the nervous system* (pp. 63–71). New York: Academic Press.

Diamond, M. C. (1985). Rat forebrain morphology: Right–left; male–female; young–old; enriched–impoverished. In S. D. Glick (Ed.), *Cerebral lateralization in nonhuman species* (pp. 1–10). Orlando, FL: Academic Press.

Ebner, F. F., & Myers, R. E. (1962). Corpus callosum and interhemispheric transmission of tactual learning. *Journal of Neurophysiology, 25,* 380–391.

Ehret, G. (1987). Left hemisphere advantage in the mouse brain for recognizing ultrasonic communication calls. *Nature, 325,* 249–251.

Ettlinger, G. (1987). Primate handedness: How nice if it were really so. *Behavioral and Brain Sciences, 10,* 271–273.

Fuster, J. M. (1989). *The prefrontal cortex* (2nd ed.). New York: Raven.

Gainotti, G. (1993). The riddle of the right hemisphere's contribution to the recovery of language. *Journal of Disorders of Communication, 28,* 227–246.

Geschwind, N., & Levitsky, W. (1968). Human brain: Left–right asymmetries in temporal speech regions. *Science, 161,* 181–187.

Glick, S. D., & Shapiro, R. M. (1985). Functional and neurochemical mechanisms of cerebral lateralization in rats. In S. D. Glick (Ed.), *Cerebral lateralization in nonhuman species* (pp. 157–183). Orlando, FL: Academic Press.

Goldberg, E., & Costa, L. (1981). Hemispheric differences in the acquisition and use of descriptive systems. *Brain and Language, 14,* 144–173.

Hamilton, C. R. (1977). An assessment of hemispheric specialization in monkeys. *Annals of the New York Academy of Science, 299,* 222–232.

Hamilton, C. R. (1983). Lateralization for orientation in split-brain monkeys. *Behavioral Brain Research, 10,* 399–403.

Hamilton, C. R., & Vermeire, B. A. (1982). Hemispheric differences in split-brain monkeys learning sequential comparisons. *Neuropsychologia, 20,* 691–698.

Hamilton, C. R., & Vermeire, B. A. (1988). Complementary hemispheric specialization in monkeys. *Science, 242,* 1691–1694.

Hardyck, C., Petrinovitch, L. F., & Goldman, R. D. (1976). Left-handedness and cognitive deficit. *Cortex, 12,* 266–279.

Hauser, M. D. (1993). Right hemisphere dominance for the production of facial expression in monkeys. *Science, 261,* 475–477.

Hauser, M. D. (1996). *The evolution of communication.* Cambridge, MA: MIT Press.

Hauser, M. D., & Andersson, K. (1994). Left hemisphere dominance for processing vocalizations in adult, but not infant, rhesus monkeys: Field experiments. *Proceedings of the National Academy of Sciences, 91,* 3946–3948.

Hawn, P. R., & Harris, L. J. (1983). Hand differences in grasp duration and reaching in two- and five-month-old human infants. In G. Young, S. J. Segalowitz, C. M. Corter, & S. E. Trehub (Eds.), *Manual specialization and the developing brain* (pp. 71–92). New York: Academic Press.

Heffner, H. E., & Heffner, R. S. (1984). Temporal lobe lesions and perception of species-specific vocalizations by macaques. *Science, 226,* 75–76.

Heilbroner, P. L., & Holloway, R. L. (1988). Anatomical brain asymmetries in New World and Old World monkeys: Stages of temporal lobe development in primate evolution. *American Journal of Physical Anthropology, 76,* 39–48.

Hiscock, M., & Kinsbourne, M. (1995). Phylogeny and ontogeny of cerebral lateralization. In R. Davidson & K. Hugdahl (Eds.), *Brain asymmetry* (pp. 535–578). Cambridge, MA: MIT

Press.

Hopkins, W. D., Washburn, D. A., & Rumbaugh, D. (1990). Processing of form stimuli presented unilaterally in humans, chimpanzees (Pan Troglodytes) and monkeys (Macaca mulatta). *Behavioral Neuroscience, 104,* 577–582.

Hubbs, C. L., & Hubbs, L. C. (1964). Bilateral asymmetry and bilateral variation in fishes. *Papers of the Michigan Academy of Arts, Sciences and Letters, 30,* 229–311.

Ifune, C. K., Vermeire, B. A., & Hamilton, C. R. (1984). Hemispheric differences in split-brain monkeys viewing and responding to video-tape recordings. *Behavioral Neurology and Biology, 41,* 231–235.

Jason, G. A., Cowey, A., & Weiskrantz, L. (1984). Hemispheric asymmetry for a visuospatial task in monkeys. *Neuropsychologia, 22,* 777–784.

Kinsbourne, M. (1971). The minor cerebral hemisphere as a source of aphasic speech. *Archives of Neurology, 25,* 302–306.

Kinsbourne, M. (1975). The ontogeny of cerebral dominance. *Annals of the New York Academy of Sciences, 263,* 244–250.

Kinsbourne, M. (1978). Evolution of language in relation to lateral action. In M. Kinsbourne (Ed.), *Asymmetrical function of the brain* (pp. 553–566). Cambridge, England: Cambridge University Press.

Kinsbourne, M. (1988). Sinistrality, brain organization and cognitive deficits. In D. L. Molfese & S. J. Segalowitz (Eds.), *Brain lateralization in children: Brain implications* (pp. 259–280). New York: Guilford.

Kinsbourne, M., & Bruce, R. (1987). Shift in visual laterality within blocks of trials. *Acta Psychologica, 66,* 139–156.

Kinsbourne, M., & Duffy, C. J. (1990). The role of dorsal/ventral processing dissociation in the economy of the primate brain. *Behavioral and Brain Sciences, 13,* 553–554.

Kinsbourne, M., & Hicks, R. E. (1978). Functional cerebral space: A model for overflow, transfer and interference effects in human performance: A tutorial review. In J. Requin (Ed.), *Attention and performance VII* (pp. 345–362). Hillsdale, NJ: Lawrence Erlbaum Associates.

Kinsbourne, M., & Hiscock, M. (1977). Does cerebral dominance develop? In S. J. Segalowitz & F. A. Gruber (Eds.), *Language development and neurological theory* (pp. 171–191). New York: Academic Press.

Kinsbourne, M., & Hiscock, M. (1983). The normal and deviant development of functional lateralization of the brain. In P. Mussen, M. Haith, & J. Campos (Eds.), *Handbook of child psychology* (Vol. 2, 4th ed., pp. 157–280). New York: Wiley.

Kinsbourne, M., & Lempert, H. (1979). Does left brain lateralization of speech arise from right-biased orienting to salient percepts? *Human Development, 22,* 270–276.

Lansdell, H. (1969). Verbal and nonverbal factors in right hemisphere speech: Relation to early neurological history. *Journal of Comparative and Physiological Psychology, 69,* 734–738.

LeMay, M. (1985). Asymmetries of the brains and skulls of nonhuman primates. In S. D. Glick (Ed.), *Cerebral lateralization in nonhuman species* (pp. 233–245). Orlando, FL: Academic Press.

Lenneberg, E. (1967). *Biological foundations of language.* New York: Wiley.

Levy, J. (1969). Possible basis for the evolution of lateral specialization of the human brain. *Nature, 224,* 614–615.

Marler, P. (1970). Bird song and speech development: Could there be parallels? *American Scientist, 58,* 669–673.

Nottebohm, F. (1971). Neural lateralization of vocal control in a passerine bird: I. Song. *Journal of Experimental Zoology, 177,* 229–261.

Nottebohm, F. (1976). Phonation in the orange-winged Amazon parrot, Amazona amazonica. *Journal of Comparative Physiology, 108,* 157–170.

Pearlson, G. D., Kubos, K. L., & Robinson, R. G. (1984). Effect of anterior–posterior lesion location on the asymmetrical behavioral and biochemical response to cortical suction ablations in the rat. *Brain Research, 293,* 241–250.

Peterson, M. R., Beecher, M. D., Zoloth, S. R., Moody, D. B., & Stebbins, W. C. (1978). Neural lateralization of species-specific vocalization by Japanese macaques (Macaca fuscata). *Science, 202,* 324–327.

Pohl, P. (1983). Central auditory processing V: Ear advantages for acoustic stimuli in baboons. *Brain and Language, 20,* 44–53.

Rasmussen, T., & Milner, B. (1977). The role of early left-brain injury in determining lateralization of cerebral speech function. *Annals of the New York Academy of Sciences, 299,* 355–369.

Rey, M., Dellatolas, G., Bancaud, J., & Talairach, J. (1988). Hemispheric lateralization of motor and speech functions after early brain lesion: Study of 73 epileptic patients with intracarotid amytal test. *Neuropsychologia, 26,* 167–172.

Robinson, R. G. (1985). Lateralized behavioral and neurochemical consequences of unilateral brain injury in rats. In S. D. Glick (Ed.), *Cerebral lateralization in nonhuman species* (pp. 135–156). Orlando, FL: Academic Press.

Sanides, F. (1970). Functional architecture of motor and sensory cortices in primates in the light of a new concept of neocortex evolution. In C. R. Norback & W. Montagna (Eds.), *The primate brain: Advances in primatology* (Vol. I, pp. 137–208). New York: Appleton-Century-Crofts.

Thornhill, R., & Gangestad, S. W. (1994). Human fluctuating asymmetry and sexual behavior. *Psychological Science, 5,* 297–302.

Trauner, D. A., Ballantyne, A., Friedland, S., & Chase, C. (1996). Disorders of affective and linguistic prosody in children after early unilateral brain damage. *Annals of Neurology, 39,* 361–367.

Trauner, D. A., Chase, C., Walker, P., & Wulfeck, B. (1993). Neurologic profiles of infants and children after perinatal stroke. *Pediatric Neurology, 9,* 383–386.

Ungerleider, L. G., & Mishkin, M. (1982). Two cortical visual systems. In D. J. Ingle, M. A. Goodale, & R. J. W. Mansfield (Eds.), *Analysis of visual behavior* (pp. 549–586). Cambridge, MA: MIT Press.

Vanclair, J., Fagot, J., & Hopkins, W. D. (1993). Rotation of mental images in baboons when the visual input is directed to the left cerebral hemisphere. *Psychological Science, 4,* 99–103.

Webster, W. G. (1981). Morphological asymmetries of the cat brain. *Brain, Behavior and Evolution, 18,* 72–79.

Witelson, S. F. (1987). Neuropsychological aspects of language in children. *Child Development, 58,* 653–688.

Woods, B. T., & Teuber, H.-L. (1978). Changing patterns of childhood aphasia. *Annals of Neurology, 32,* 239–246.

9 Adolescent Substance Abuse: A Biopsychosocial Perspective

Robert J. McCaffrey
Catherine A. Forneris
University at Albany
State University of New York

Epidemiological data suggests a declining trend in psychoactive substance use beginning during the late 1970s and continuing through the early 1980s. In spite of this, psychoactive substance use among adolescents has continued to pose a significant social problem. In 1990, the National Institute on Drug Abuse (NIDA) reported that 19% of high school seniors surveyed responded that they smoked cigarettes daily, 4% drank alcohol daily, and 3% smoked marijuana daily (Hoover, 1991). More than 50% of high school seniors admitted trying an illicit drug. At some time in their life, greater than 90% reported having had some experience with alcohol, 44% with marijuana, and 10% with cocaine. When asked about substance use within the past month, 60% of responding seniors admitted to using alcohol, and 33% reported having five or more consecutive drinks in the past 2 weeks.

Although illicit drug use appears to be on the decline, the prevalence of alcohol use appears to have remained relatively stable. Perhaps even more alarming is the trend toward earlier initiation of drug and alcohol use. The National Institute on Alcohol Abuse and Alcoholism (NIAAA) reported that the mean age of initial use to be 14 years (Hoover, 1991). There is also a concomitant trend for adolescents to use more than one substance at a time, that is, polysubstance abuse (PSA). A survey of Maryland adolescent users revealed that the typical adolescent used 3.4 drugs simultaneously (Maryland Department of Health and Mental Hygiene–Drug Abuse Administration, 1985).

A key factor in the deterioration of adolescent health is drug and alcohol use. Hoover (1991) reported that it is a major contributor to disability and death for individuals in the 15- to 25-year-old age group. Almost one half of fatal automobile accidents and homicides, as well as a large proportion of suicides, involve alcohol and other drugs. Alcohol and drug use also has a significant impact on the psychological and cognitive well-being of young adults. Substance abuse and dependency syndromes contribute to mental disorders that are estimated to affect 634,000 young adults. Alcohol use is also often involved when adolescents have early sexual experiences. This frequently results in unplanned and unwanted pregnancies and alcohol-related birth defects (Alexander, 1991). Alcohol abuse is often associated with family violence. Youths that abuse alcohol are less likely to complete high school. The ramifications of this include the inability to maintain employment, which can lead to chronic economic problems and adverse effects on the stability of the family unit.

The factors noted previously underscore the importance of understanding the role of substance-induced neuropsychological impairment in adolescents because the consequences may be lifelong and potentially preventable. The goals of this chapter are to review the existing literature on the neuropsychological sequelae of substance abuse among adolescents. Recent findings from our neuropsychological laboratory examining polysubstance abuse are presented. Finally, it is our hope that the substantive questions not addressed by the current literature will serve as a springboard for further research on this topic.

OVERVIEW OF BIOPSYCHOSOCIAL ISSUES

Family Formation and Stability

Following adolescence, young adults are faced with the challenge of establishing a relationship with a significant other and/or maintaining a marriage and family. Marital and family dynamics are quite intricate, and their relationship to drug use has been examined from many perspectives. The majority of data indicates that drug use is negatively associated with being married and having children and positively related to marital separation and divorce. What is difficult to discern is whether drug use precedes the marital problems and contributes to them, or if substances are used to alleviate marital stress and tension. Results of studies examining this issue are mixed. Marijuana use has been associated with delay of marriage and family, increased separation and divorce, and more infidelity and parenting of illegitimate children (Newcomb & Bentler, 1988). On the other hand, high school use of cigarettes, alcohol, and drugs other than marijuana was indicative of early marriage (Newcomb & Bentler, 1985).

Decisions to marry and start a family are crucial steps for young adults. With both of them come changes in lifestyle, stress, and responsibilities.

Individuals who have little life experience may be too immature to cope effectively and make necessary transitions. Early marriage is associated with a lower success rate than marriages occurring later in life, as measured by a high divorce rate and a greater degree of relationship dissatisfaction.

Criminality and Deviant Behavior

There is a well-known relationship between drug use and antisocial attitudes and behaviors. The nature of this relationship is somewhat puzzling. Does drug use itself promote antisocial attitudes and behaviors, or does the rebellious adolescent gravitate toward drug use? Newcomb and Bentler (1988) stated that "although drug use and deviance are significantly correlated at one occasion, they do not affect each other over time" (p. 102). Drug use does not necessarily produce delinquency.

Alcohol use in early adolescence leads to decreased compliance with the law and social conformity 3 years after the initiation of use (Huba & Bentler, 1983), whereas marijuana and hard drug use do not have a similar influence on law abidance. Alcohol use also appears to be correlated with acts of burglary. Over time, problem drinking becomes less associated with other forms of deviance. In comparison, illicit drug use becomes more associated with other forms of deviance. Interestingly, there is a difference between early drug use and gender. There is no correlation between use of cannabis or other narcotics and aggressive behavior or theft among men. Women who use marijuana exhibit increased aggressive behavior, whereas the use of other narcotics is associated with an increased number of thefts.

Sexual Behavior

The ramifications of teenage drug use on attitudes of dating and sexual involvement is not clear. Low doses of certain drugs may facilitate sexual interaction by lowering inhibitions. High doses and/or chronic drug use may produce a variety of sexual dysfunctions.

Attitudes toward dating and sexual activity may reflect more general attitudes. There is a sparse amount of research on the association between drug use and sexual behaviors. According to Newcomb and Bentler (1988), the majority of research in this field is focused on the sexual activities and practices of teenagers such as dating, kissing, petting, masturbation, premarital intercourse, homosexual contact, and birth control. Of the aforementioned behaviors, contraceptive use has received a great deal of attention. Many factors account for the choice of a reliable method of contraception and proper use of the selected method. A consistent finding of these studies is that men are less informed about birth control, are less likely to recognize the risk of pregnancy, and have fewer supportive attitudes about contraceptive use than women. Men who use effective birth control are more flexible, become involved sexually at an older age, are in a committed and stable relationship, and are well informed about birth control methods. Many of these elements appear to be similar to those of a socially conforming individual who is not likely to act in a deviant manner. Thus, it is possible that an indifference to drug use may be related to this type of personality characteristic. As described by Newcomb and Bentler (1988), adult Black men who had previously smoked marijuana in adolescence were significantly more likely to have fathered illegitimate children than individuals who did not smoke marijuana. Women heroin addicts are significantly less likely to use contraception than a national sample of women. Among adolescent girls, there is a negative relationship both between the increasing frequency of cigarette smoking and the age of first intercourse and effective contraception. Ultimately, ineffective use of birth control or no birth control at all may be related to deviance, problem behavior, and drug use.

Impact on Educational Pursuits

Education plays a major role during the adolescent years. Schools not only provide youths with formal learning instruction but function as centers for social relationships and activities. One possible consequence of drug use may be that it interferes with the learning experience and hence impedes future vocational options requiring a solid academic background.

One hallmark of adolescent alcoholism is the negative consequences at school and increasing apathy toward academic endeavors. Newcomb and Bentler (1986) found that cigarette smoking and hard drug use in high school was directly related to dropping out of school before completion. Although substance use did not deter or decrease previously established educational aspirations and/or goals from initial levels, it was identified with a decreased level of involvement in college.

The consequences of drug use among college students appear to be different than those for high school students. Dropping out of college is not related to drug use for most students. The exception is for those individuals who had begun polysubstance use in high school, whose parents were not educated beyond high school, and who had ambivalent feelings about attending college. Students with these types of backgrounds are more likely to leave college before completion.

Chronic marijuana use does not appear to be directly responsible for poor academic performance. Rather, chronic marijuana use may produce negative consequences by promoting avoidance behaviors, such as avoidance of critical life tasks and decisions (e.g., maintaining financial self-support and independence).

The seeming discrepancy between the effects of drug use in high school and college can be traced to the almost natural self-selection process that takes place before an individual decides to attend college. Students who are heavy drug users in high school are less likely to attend college.

One potential limitation of data derived from college-age drug users is the limited applicability of the results to other populations. From the afore-mentioned discussion, adolescents who are heavy drug users are less likely to attend college. Thus, drug users in college-based samples are a relatively select group of individuals. College-age drug users may be more mature in their abilities to manage their problems and needs than high-school-age drug users, and this alone may obviate the negative consequences of substance use.

Impact on Livelihood Pursuits

Many teenagers hold their first job while in high school. A job may provide a myriad of personal development opportunities for the adolescent. Among these are a modicum of financial independence, the opportunity to learn a skill or trade, or a chance to save money for future endeavors, such as college or travel.

Substance use may affect livelihood pursuits in several ways. These include initiation of employment, type of employment, stability of employment, work performance and job satisfaction. Newcomb and Bentler (1988) stated that there is little data on the consequences of drug use on employment. Undeniably, substance abuse or alcoholism does affect job performance and job stability. As previously discussed, it is not clear whether drug use is the antecedent to these problems, or whether substance users have more trouble maintaining employment due to more basic characterological factor(s) that are reflected in their drug use.

On the job, substance use has received a great deal of research and media interest. Substance abuse on the job can have a variety of consequences including safety hazards, interpersonal conflicts, and a decrease in produc-tivity. In a comprehensive review of the drug literature, Kandel (1980) consistently found that the unemployed have the highest rates of drug use.

Another alternative form of support is government compensation or assistance. It is possible that substance abuse may be related to, or impact upon, utilization of public assistance programs. Early drug use may impair an individual to such an extent so as to prohibit gainful employment. On the other hand, substance abuse may indicate a lifestyle characterized by indifference, inactivity, and a lack of responsibility. Again, it is difficult to discern the antecedents from the consequences. This area needs to be examined further.

Impact on Mental Health

The relationship between drug use and mental health is a virtual Gordian knot. According to Newcomb and Bentler (1988), the findings are mixed and are typically a function of the substance being examined and duration of use. Certainly there are short-term effects of drug use, but it is not clear if this is sufficient to precipitate long-term changes in an individual's mental status.

The mental health sequelae of adolescent substance abuse are somewhat unclear. Drug-using adolescents may have a number of characteristics that predispose them to develop mental illness in later life. By the same token, the seeds of mental illness may begin to flourish during the adolescent years and be especially responsive to the accompanying elements of teenage drug use.

Impact on Social Integration

Social integration encompasses a multiplicity of desirable human essentials. Among these are relatedness, support, a sense of belonging, assertiveness, self-esteem, and competency. The majority of drug users, both young and old, have trouble with social relationships. There is no clearly defined distinction between whether the social difficulties encountered by drug users result from substance use, or if substance use impedes the formation of social links.

The results of studies designed to examine this notion are mixed. One study found that drug use negatively affected the development of those social skills necessary to successfully integrate into society (Pentz, 1985). By comparison, Newcomb (1986) found the teenage alcoholism increased perceived social support as young adults.

Future research is necessary to elucidate both the direction and potential of a causal relationship between drug use and social skills and functioning. Drugs and alcohol may be used to facilitate social interaction, but it is imperative to resolve the extent of this relationship.

OVERVIEW

The adolescent years lay the ground for continued adult development. Impairment in neuropsychological functioning may have a profound impact on the psychosocial factors discussed previously. In this next section, the neuropsychological sequelae substance abuse and polysubstance abuse are examined with an emphasis on adolescent users/abusers. Given that the literature on this topic with adolescents is quite limited, related research findings with young adults are reviewed selectively.

Methodological Considerations

Before reviewing the literature related to adolescent substance abuse, there are several points that the reader should bear in mind. First, the studies reviewed represent a broad spectrum of reports of heterogeneous scientific quality. As such, the evaluation of individual reports is often difficult. Moreover, the diversity of methodological procedures, neuropsychological assessment instruments employed, and the absence of a uniform standard for defining terms, such as abuse, severely limit direct comparisons among studies. For example, many studies fail to provide an adequate description of the demographic characteristics of the participant groups. The actual neuropsychological assessment procedures are not always listed, and in some cases, authors refer to instruments that do not exist. Another difficulty is that some studies compare substance abuser to matched controls and then to unspecified normative data for some of the assessment instruments. These factors, among others, contribute to the difficulty in evaluating the impact of substance abuse on the neuropsychological functioning of adolescents.

NEUROPSYCHOLOGICAL SEQUELAE OF SUBSTANCE USE/ABUSE

Marijuana

The results of studies designed to assess performance differences measures of neuropsychological functioning for adolescent marijuana users demonstrate few consistent differences among users, abusers, and abstainers. Grant, Rochford, Fleming, and Stuckard (1973) examined the effect of marijuana use on a group of 29 male medical students who by self-report smoked moderately or regularly for at least 3 years. The authors failed to clearly define moderate and regular use. The median age of the participants was 23.5. Participants completed the Halstead Category Test, Tactual Performance Test, Reitan's Trail Making Test, Raven's Advanced Progressive Matrices, and the Goal-Directed Serial Alternation Test. The results showed that there was no difference between marijuana smokers and nonsmokers on seven of the eight measures. The smokers did not perform as well as nonsmokers on the Tactual Performance Test: localization ($M = 5.41$, $SD = 2.09$ and $M = 6.83$, SD 2.59, $p < .05$, respectively). Grant et al. concluded that moderate social usage of marijuana does not impair functioning sufficiently to be detected by the neuropsychological instruments used in their study.

In another study, Carlin and Trupin (1977) assessed 10 participants who smoked marijuana daily for an average of 5 years using the Halstead–Reitan Neuropsychological Battery (HRNB). The participants in their sample were of approximately the same age as those in the Grant et al.'s study ($M = 24.10$, $SD = 2.23$ years). The average level of education was 14.6 years. The average number of years of cannabis use was 5 (range 2.5 to 8). The only significant difference ($p < .05$) found between the smokers and the nonsmokers was on the Trail Making test Part B. Carlin and Trupin concluded that relatively long-term chronic marijuana use does not impair an individual's ability to solve complex cognitive tasks, to manipulate complex visual motor problems, to be accurate in identifying sensory stimuli (both unilaterally and bilaterally), or to answer questions dependent on prior learning.

Two separate studies designed to detect the effect of marijuana specifically on learning and memory show somewhat different results from those described previously. One study conducted by Entin and Goldzung (1973) was comprised of two separate experiments using undergraduate volunteers. The first experiment focused on the effect of long-term marijuana use, defined as daily use for at least 8 months, on a verbal learning task. The results of this procedure indicated that chronic marijuana users recalled fewer items than the nonusing group. In the second experiment, undergraduates were assessed on a verbal recall task and a series of Wendt three-step arithmetic problems. The results indicated the users performed less well statistically on the verbal ($p < .02$) but not on the arithmetic tasks compared to nonusers.

The second study, conducted by Gianutsos and Litwack (1976) examined chronic high-frequency marijuana smokers compared to nonsmoking control participants. The chronic high-frequency smokers were defined as those having smoked twice a week or more for 2 to 6 months. The control participants had never smoked marijuana. All participants performed a verbal memory task with a prerecall interference task. The mean number of words recalled for the chronic marijuana smokers was significantly reduced ($p < .05$) compared to the controls. This reduction was particularly pronounced with greater forced processing between initial word presentation and recall. Gianutsos and Litwack inferred that chronic marijuana smokers have a decreased ability to transfer information from short-term to long-term memory storage.

Hallucinogens

There appears to be little reported research on the effects of hallucinogens on neuropsychological functioning in young adults. Culver and King (1974) conducted a study using three groups of college seniors ages 20 to 25. The marijuana group consisted of participants who had not used marijuana, hashish, LSD, or mescaline before college but had used marijuana or hashish at least twice a month for 12 months. The LSD group (all of whom had used marijuana or hashish) contained participants who had also not used marijuana, hashish, LSD, or mescaline before college but who had used LSD and/or mescaline for at least 12 months with an overall frequency of at least once a month. The control group consisted of participants with no history of marijuana or LSD use. All participants were assessed on several measures. Among these were various subtests of the HRNB including the Category test, Tactual Performance test, Finger Tapping test, Speech Sounds Perception test, Seashore Rhythm test, and the Trail Making test. Additionally, the Wechsler Adult Intelligence Scale (WAIS), Laterality Discrimination Test, three tests of spatial-perceptual abilities from the Educational Testing Service's *Manual for Kit of Reference Tests for Cognitive Factors*, and the Minnesota Multiphasic Personality Inventory (MMPI) were administered. The results indicated that the three groups were significantly different in their performance on the Trail Making test. LSD/mescaline users performed within normal limits but significantly worse ($p < .05$) than either of the other two groups on Trail Making tests Parts A, B, and A + B.

Cocaine

There is little research on the effects of cocaine in adolescents specifically, and the data that has been reported is poorly documented and therefore inconclusive. Heaton, O'Malley, Adamse, and Gawin (cited in O'Malley & Gawin, 1990) conducted a study on the effects of cocaine on intellectual and neuropsychological functioning. The participants in Part I were inpatient, recently abstinent cocaine abusers ($M = 23$ days) with a mean age of 27.6 ($SD = 7.17$) years, a mean educational level of 13.2 ($SD = 1.61$), and an estimated mean use 447.15 g over 4 years. The inpatients were assessed on the Wechsler Adult Category Test [*sic*], Finger Oscillation test, the Neuropsychological Screening Battery, and the Wechsler Adult Intelligence Scale–Revised (WAIS-R). O'Malley, Gawin, Heaton, and Kleber (cited in O'Malley & Gawin, 1990) evaluated outpatients who were abstinent cocaine users ($M = 135$ days) with a mean age of 28.4 and mean use of 522.75 g over 46.9 months. Of the outpatients, 60% were White men who had a mean education of 13.5 years ($SD = 1.7$). Control participants were normal individuals matched for age, education, sex, and race. All participants completed an extensive neuropsychological test battery.

These investigators reported data in their results section that is significantly discrepant with the discussion of it in the body of the paper

(O'Malley & Gawin, 1990). This makes interpretation and further discussion of these results extremely difficult.

Analgesics

The literature on analgesic abuse revealed only one study designed to assess the neuropsychological effects of analgesic abuse on young adults. Rounsaville, Novelly, Kleber, and Jones (1981) conducted a study with 72 opiate addicts (mean age 27.9, mean use = 8.2 years) comparing their performance with that of patients with a seizure disorder matched for age, gender, education, and handedness. According to Rounsaville et al., the neuropsychological assessment measures consisted of tests selected for maximal diagnostic power, portability, brevity of administration, relative freedom from cultural bias, and coverage of a range of cognitive abilities and functions. The results demonstrated that the overall level of neuropsychological impairment was moderate to severe in 53% of the opiate addicts, mild in 26%, and absent in 21%. The performance of the analgesic abusing group, however, was not significantly different than that of the control group with seizure disorders. Rounsaville et al. concluded that analgesic abusers demonstrate evidence of global cerebral dysfunction and are, generally, comparable to patients with a seizure disorder.

Inhalants

A review of the literature on the effects of inhalants on cognitive and intellectual functioning in adolescents revealed that there was a relatively large body of empirical data compared to other commonly abused substances. Overall, the reports in the inhalant literature are equivocal. Two separate studies found no statistically significant results between inhalant abusing and nonabusing youths. Massengale, Glaser, LeLievre, Dodds, and Klock (1963) administered a nonstandardized neuropsychological assessment battery to measure cognitive functioning of 16 chronic glue inhalers (median age = 13). The specific tests administered were not described but were reported to measure the following cognitive functions: ability to focus and maintain attention, fine motor performance with and without disrupting stimuli, detection of small and gradual changes in a given set of data, integration of fragmented designs into a meaningful pattern, and ability to recall and reproduce various geometric figures. The participants had inhaled glue vapors for 1 to 24 months. The control group is described as being of similar age and intelligence to the inhalant abusers. No differences were obtained between the chronic abusers and the control group. Similarly, Dodds and Santostefano (1964) found no significant difference in cognitive functioning of 12 boys of primarily Spanish American descent ($N = 10$) on a nonstandardized neuropsychological assessment test battery. The mean age of the adolescents was 13.8. They had been inhaling glue vapors for 3 to 42 months, with a median number of resulting states of intoxication by self-report of 82 per boy (range = 4 to 1,200). The control group was comprised of 21 Anglo-American male adolescents with a mean age of 12.6. The controls were noted to be of average school performance and social adjustment. Both of these reports failed to support the hypothesis that glue sniffing has a serious impact on the inhalant abusing adolescent's neuropsychological functioning compared to control participants. Nonetheless, the authors noted that there are persuasive arguments in favor of treatment for adolescent inhalant abusers. Dodds and Santostefano suggested that glue sniffing may be indicative of other emotional problems. They also stated that habitual intoxication and loss of self-control may lead to experimentation with other substances and an increase in frequency of misdemeanors.

Several other studies have reported significant differences in the performance of inhalant abusing adolescents and young adults. Fornazzari, Wilkinson, Kapur, and Carlen (1983) and Bigler (1979) examined the effects of chronic solvent abuse on performance on the WAIS and HRNB. Fornazzari et al.'s sample consisted of 24 solvent abusers with a mean age of 23 ($SD = 4.4$) and a mean amount of use of 425 mg ($SD = 366$) of toluene a day for a period of 6.3 years ($SD = 3.9$). Of the sample 65% demonstrated impairment in neuropsychological and neurological test performances. The level of neuropsychological impairment was found to be significantly correlated with cerebellar, ventricular, and cortical sulci enlargement. Bigler's sample contained 10 psychiatric patients (ages 16–20) with a history of chronic solvent abuse. The solvent abusing group consisted of 7 men and 3 women ranging in age from 16 to 19. Participants had been abusing inhalants weekly for an average of 2 years. Three control/comparison groups were utilized: (a) brain damaged, (b) nonbrain damaged/psychotic, and (c) nonbrain damaged/nonpsychotic, all matched for age, gender, and educational history to the inhalant abusers. Bigler's results demonstrated that the inhalant abusers had global neuropsychological deficits compared to the nonbrain damaged/nonpsychotic controls. In general, the inhalant abusing group could not be differentiated statistically from either the brain damaged or the psychotic control groups.

Other studies have found significant performance differences between chronic solvent abusers and matched controls on specific subtests of neuropsychological batteries. Tsushima and Towne (1977) found that chronic paint sniffers with a mean age of 18.5 ($SD = 4.04$) and an average use of 5.85 years performed significantly poorer than control participants (mean age = 18, $SD = 2.85$) on 11 of 13 measures. Among these were: the Finger Tapping test (dominant hand), the Seashore Rhythm test, and the Trail

Making test Part A; the Grooved Pegboard test (dominant hand); the Stroop Color and Word test, Parts A, B, and C; the Memory for Design test; and the Peabody Picture Vocabulary test. Tsushima and Towne stated that one important finding of their study was the relation between sniffing and level of test performance. The longer a person has been abusing inhalants, the lower his or her neuropsychological performance, although the results did not reach the conventional statistical significance level (i.e., $p < .05$).

Allison and Jerrom (1984) assessed a group of 10 delinquent adolescent glue sniffers (mean age 15.45, and use = 4.6 years) with nonglue sniffing control participants matched for age, educational level, and reading age. They were assessed using the Wechsler Intelligence Scale for Children (WISC) Vocabulary and Block Design (BD) subtests, two of seven subtests of the Wechsler Memory Scale (WMS), and the Paced Auditory Serial Addition Task (PASAT). These tests were selected to assess memory, nonverbal intelligence, attention, and concentration. The results indicated that chronic solvent inhalers scored significantly lower on the WISC–BD, the WMS subtests, and PASAT. Allison and Jerrom concluded that long-term solvent abuse does produce neuropsychological impairment.

Solvent users have also been found to score significantly lower on neuropsychological tests involving visual processing compared to matched controls. Zur and Yule (1990) assessed 12 adolescent boys with a history of chronic solvent abuse using the Bexley Maudsley Automated Screening Test, which consists of a series of computerized neuropsychological tests. The adolescents had a history of chronic solvent abuse that was defined as inhalation for an average of five times a week for at least 1 year or an average of three times a week for 2 years. The participants were all male (mean age = 16.4, SD = 3.46 years) and were found to be no different from gender matched controls on education level (M = 9.9 years), days missed from school, SES, or full scale IQ. However, the two groups were found to be significantly different in age. The most striking difference was observed on tests of symbol digit coding, a test that the authors stated is highly correlated with the symbol digit coding subtest of the Wechsler Intelligence Scale. The difference in performance between the experimental and control groups was not, however, statistically significant.

Polysubstance Abuse

Polysubstance abuse (PSA) is not new in the United States. In fact, a series of studies in the 1970s evaluated the impact of PSA on the neuropsychological functioning of young adults utilizing the HRNB with an emphasis on the Global Impairment Index. Adams, Rennick, Schooff, and Keegan (1975), using a modified version of the HRNB, reported impairment in conceptual thinking, simple motoric tasks, and visuomotor performance.

These patients had a mean age of 27.6 and demonstrated some improvement across serial evaluations. Grant, Mohns, Miller, et al., (1976) evaluated PSA with a mean age of 22 and found that fully 50% were impaired on the HRNB. In another study, Grant and Judd (1976) performed serial HRNB assessments and obtained clinical electroencephalograms (EEGs) in a population of PSA with a mean age of 26. At the initial testing, 45% of the patients were impaired on the HRNB, and 43% had abnormal EEGs. At a 5-month follow-up, 27% were impaired on the HRNB, and 25% had abnormal EEGs. These findings suggest that the negative effects of PSA among adults may improve with cessation of abuse. The authors pointed out, however, that the base rates for impaired neuropsychological performance and abnormal EEGs at the 5-month follow-up still exceeded those for nonneurological groups. Although these results suggest that improvement occurs over the span of 5 months, not all studies have reported positive results at follow-up. For example, the results of the Collaborative Neuropsychological Study of Polysubstance Abuse (Grant et al., 1978) indicated that at 3 months, 9% of adult PSA demonstrated improvement in neuropsychological performance, 85% no change, and 5% a worsening in their neuropsychological status. Neither the time course nor the extent of change in neuropsychological status among adult PSAs is clear.

The literature on the neuropsychological sequelae among PSA adolescents receiving formal treatment compared to a peer control group is virtually nonexistent. In an unpublished study, McCaffrey (1989) evaluated 47 PSA adolescents (mean age 15, $SD = 1.8$), who were undergoing formal inpatient treatment for their substance abuse disorder and a peer control group that was not screened for episodic substance use. The PSA adolescents were evaluated 10 to 14 days following the completion of detoxification using a series of neuropsychological instruments that Eson and his colleagues (Eson & Bourke, 1980a, 1980b; Eson, Yen, & Bourke, 1978) used in their clinical work and research projects on the recovery of cognitive functions secondary to traumatic brain injuries. The PSA adolescents were identified by clinical records as abusing two or more substances from the three general categories outlined in Table 9.1. As indicated in Table 9.1, alcohol and cannabis were reportedly abused by 90% of the PSA adolescents in combination with other substances. The peer controls ($n = 31$) were recruited from the community and were not screened for substance use/abuse. All adolescents completed the neuropsychological assessment instruments presented in Table 9.2.

The data were subjected to a MANOVA, which was significant followed by univariate tests. As indicated in Table 9.2, the PSA adolescents' performance was significantly poorer than the peer control group on seven of the nine variables. This finding is all the more interesting given that the peer controls were neither screened for nor excluded for episodic substance use.

TABLE 9.1
Frequency and Percentages of Substances Abused in a Sample of 47 PSA
Adolescents

	Frequency	Percentage
Alcohol use		
Beer/wine/liquor	43	91.5
Cannabis use		
Marijuana/hashish	41	87.2
Hard drug use		
Hypnotic	2	4.2
Cocaine	17	36.2
Stimulant	5	10.6
Psychedelic	16	34.0
Inhalant	5	10.6
Narcotics	5	10.6
PCP	3	6.4

TABLE 9.2
A Comparison of PSA Adolescents Versus Controls on a Select Group of
Neuropsychological Tests

Instruments	PSAs (n = 47) Mean ± SD	Controls (n = 31) Mean ± SD	p*
Trail Making Test			
Part A (sec)	31.9 ± 12.8	24.8 ± 7.7	.783
Part B (sec)	76.5 ± 32.6	53.9 ± 16.7	.001
Symbol Digit Modalities Test			
(Total Correct)	53.5 ± 10.9	61.7 ± 6.7	.013
Stroop Color and Word Test			
Word (errors)	49.9 ± 9.0	41.5 ± 5.9	.032
Colors (errors)	69.6 ± 12.6	57.9 ± 8.6	.104
Word–Color (errors)	131.1 ± 32.9	99.5 ± 17.7	.005
Progressive Random Order (Matrices Test)			
Part A (sec)	42.8 ± 10.2	35.1 ± 4.9	.006
Part B (sec)	106.5 ± 32.3	83.0 ± 13.4	.022
Simplified Symbol Digit Test			
(Total Correct)	92.1 ± 20.1	107.5 ± 10.4	.050

*MANOVA significant at $p < .05$.

Unfortunately, we were unable to obtain follow-up data on the PSA adolescents. Nonetheless, our data clearly indicate that there are neuropsychological sequelae in PSA adolescents undergoing inpatient treatment compared to peer controls. Further research in this area is warranted due to the potential role of PSA-induced neuropsychological dysfunction and the impact on subsequent biopsychosocial functioning of the adolescent population.

REFERENCES

Adams, K. M., Rennick, R. M., Schooff, K. G., & Keegan, J. F. (1975). Neuropsychological measurement of drug effects: Polydrug research. *Journal of Psychedelic Drugs, 7,* 151–160.

Alexander, B. (1991). Alcohol abuse in adolescents. *American Family Physician, 43*(2), 527–532.

Allison, W. M., & Jerrom, D. W. A. (1984). Glue sniffing: A pilot study of three cognitive effects of long-term use. *The International Journal of Addiction, 19*(4), 453–458.

Bigler, E. D. (1979). Neuropsychological evaluation of adolescent patients hospitalized with chronic inhalant abuse. *Clinical Neuropsychology 1,* 8–12.

Carlin, A. S., & Trupin, E. W. (1977). The effect of long-term chronic marijuana use on neuropsychological functioning. *The International Journal of Addictions, 12*(5), 617–624.

Culver, C. M., & King, F. W. (1974). Neuropsychological assessment of undergraduate marihuana and LSD users. *Archives of General Psychiatry, 31,* 707–711.

Dodds, J., & Santostefano, S. (1964). A comparison of the cognitive functioning of glue-sniffers and nonsniffers. *The Journal of Pediatrics, 64,* 565–570.

Entin, E. E., & Goldzung, P. J. (1973). Residual effects of marijuana usage on learning and memory. *The Psychological Record, 23,* 169–178.

Eson, M. E., & Bourke, R. S. (1980a, February). *Assessment of information processing deficits after serious head injury.* Paper presented at the eighth annual meeting of the International Neuropsychological Society, San Francisco.

Eson, M. E., & Bourke, R. S. (1980b, September). *Assessment of long-term information processing deficits after serious head injury.* Paper presented at the NATO Advanced Study Institute of Neuropsychology and Cognition, Augusta, Georgia.

Eson, M. E., Yen, J. K., & Bourke, R. S. (1978). Assessment of recovery from serious head injury. *Journal of Neurology, Neurosurgery, and Psychiatry, 41,* 1036–1042.

Fornazzari, L., Wilkinson, D. A., Kapur, B. M., & Carlen, P. L. (1983). Cerebellar, cortical, and functional impairment in toluene abusers. *Acta Journal Scandinavia, 67,* 319–329.

Gianutsos, R., & Litwack, A. (1976). Chronic marijuana smokers show reduced coding into long-term storage. *Bulletin of Psychonomic Society, 7*(3), 277–279.

Grant, I., Adams, K. M., Carlin, A. S., Rennick, R. M., Judd, L. L., & Schoof, K. (1978). The collaborative neuropsychological study of polydrug users. *Archives of General Psychiatry, 35,* 1063–1074.

Grant, I., & Judd, L. L. (1976). Neuropsychological and EEG disturbances in polydrug users. *American Journal of Psychiatry, 133,* 1039–1042.

Grant, I., Mohns, L., Miller, M., & Reitan, R. M. (1976). A neuropsychological study of polydrug users. *Archives of General Psychiatry, 33,* 973–978.

Grant, I., Rochford, J., Fleming, T., & Stuckard, A. (1973). A neuropsychological assessment of the effects of moderate marihuana use. *The Journal of Nervous and Mental Disease, 156*(4), 278–280.

Hoover, A. (1991). Problems of alcohol and other drug use and abuse in adolescents. *Journal of Adolescent Health, 12,* 606–613.

Huba, G. J., & Bentler, P. M. (1983). Causal models of the development of law abidance and its relationship to psychosocial factors and drug use. In W. S. Laufer & J. M. Day (Eds.), *Personality theory, moral development, and criminal behavior* (pp. 165–215). Lexington, MA: Heath.

Kandel, D. B. (1980). Drug and drinking behavior among youth. *Annual Review of Sociology, 6,* 235–285.

Maryland Department of Health and Mental Hygiene—Drug Abuse Administration. (1985). 1984 Survey of Drug Abuse Among Maryland Adolescents—General Report. Baltimore, MD: Author.

Massengale, O. N., Glaser, H. H., LeLievre, R. E., Dodds, J. B., & Klock, M. E. (1963). Physical and psychological factors in glue sniffing. *The New England Journal of Medicine, 269*(25), 1340–1344.

McCaffrey, R. J. (1989). [Neuropsychological sequelae of polysubstance abuse in a sample of inpatient adolescents]. Unpublished raw data.

Newcomb, M. D. (1986). Sexual behavior of cohabitors: A comparison of three independent samples. *Journal of Sex Research, 22,* 492–513.

Newcomb, M. D., & Bentler, P. M. (1985). The impact of high school substance use on choice of young adult living environment and career direction. *Journal of Drug Education, 15,* 253–261.

Newcomb, M. D., & Bentler, P. M. (1986). Drug use, educational aspirations, and workforce involvement: The transition from adolescence to young adulthood. *American Journal of Community Psychology, 14,* 303–321.

Newcomb, M. D., & Bentler, P. M. (1988). *Consequences of adolescent drug use: Impact on the lives of young adults.* Newbury Park, CA: Sage.

O'Malley, S. S., & Gawin, F. H. (1990). Abstinence symptomatology and neuropsychological deficits in chronic cocaine abusers. In J. W. Spencer & J. J. Boren (Eds.), *Residual effects of abused drugs on behavior* (National Institute on Drug Abuse Research Monograph Series, No. 101). Rockville, MD.

Pentz, M. A. (1985). Social competence and self-efficacy as determinants of substance use in adolescence. In S. Shiffman & T. A. Wills (Eds.), *Coping and substance use* (pp. 117–142). Orlando, FL: Academic Press.

Rounsaville, B. J., Novelly, R. A., Kleber, H. D., & Jones, C. (1981). Neuropsychological impairment in opiate addicts: Risk factors. *Annals of the New York Academy of Sciences, 362,* 79–90.

Tsushima, W. T., & Towne, W. S. (1977). Effects of paint sniffing on neuropsychological test performance. *Journal of Abnormal Psychology, 86*(4), 402–407.

Zur, J., & Yule, W. (1990). Chronic solvent abuse: 1. Cognitive sequelae. *Child: Care, Health, and Development, 16,* 1–20.

10 Age-Related Risk Factors for Cognitive Impairment

Robert W. Keefover
Eric D. Rankin
West Virginia University School of Medicine

Common misuse of the term *senile* as a synonym for *demented* reflects the fact that older people are at greater risk for intellectual impairment than are younger individuals. Although debate continues about whether or not cognitive decline is a normal response to senescence, increased vulnerability to many of the factors that promote mental deterioration is a reality of later life. As a result of observations such as those reported by Tomlinson and colleagues a quarter of a century ago (Tomlinson, Blessed, & Roth, 1970), the vaguely defined concept of *senile dementia* (Robbins & Angell, 1978) has gradually been abandoned. Instead, it is now recognized that severe mental deterioration (i.e., dementia) occurs in the older people only in the presence of specific disease states; Alzheimer's disease (AD) being the most common of these (Katzman, 1986). In this context, we now view older people as more vulnerable to cognitive decline because they are at greater risk of developing many of the illnesses that cause it.

Some older people experience intellectual impairment in the absence of identifiable disease. Although these deficits do not typically justify a diagnosis of dementia, they may, nonetheless, detract from an individual's quality of life. Such cases are often attributed to poorly understood nonillnesses, such as Age-Associated Memory Impairment or may manifest as a consequence of psychosocial factors. In some cases, they appear to reflect the aging process itself. Like the dementing illnesses, however, these more subtle mental impairments occur more frequently in later life because of age-dependent increases in vulnerability to certain risk factors.

The terms *intellectual, mental,* and *cognitive* impairment are used interchangeably here in reference to any deterioration in the proficiency with which an individual is able to utilize neuropsychologic systems involved in the process of "thinking." These may involve subtle disturbances in discrete brain structures such as those subserving language appreciation and expression (*aphasia*), or more severe and diffuse impairment of brain function, such as occurs in delirium or dementia. *Delirium*, as defined by criteria set forth in the *Diagnostic and Statistical Manual of Mental Disorders Third Edition–Revised* (DSM-III–R; American Psychiatric Association, 1987), tends to be a reversible condition with prominent evidence of disorientation and fluctuations in the level of consciousness, whereas dementia is often more enduring and involves memory loss and disturbance in at least one other cognitive domain (e.g., praxis, calculation, or language).

This chapter examines a number of risk factors for cognitive decline that are distinguished by the fact that they tend to affect older rather than younger individuals. Four separate categories of risk factors are explored: (a) neurologic senescence, (b) general or systemic medical conditions, (c) neurological disease, and (d) psychosocial variables.

NEUROLOGIC SENESCENCE

At least one third of all older persons exhibit little or no evidence of intellectual decline (Schaie, 1983), and certain cognitive domains, those of immediate and remote memory as well as most language functions, appear to be especially resistant to senile deterioration (Ferris, Flicker, Reisberg, & Crook, 1989). Still, several lines of evidence support the notion that simply growing older leads to impaired competence in many aspects of mentation. At the cellular level, the human organism appears to be less able to maintain its own viability with advancing age (Hayflick, 1976). Age-related neuronal dropout has been reported in many regions of the otherwise nondiseased brain (Goudsmit, Hofman, Fliers, & Swaab, 1990; Mann, Yates, & Marcyniuk, 1984), and this, in turn, contributes to an overall decrease in gross brain weight (Dekaban & Sadowsky, 1978). These atrophic changes are associated with a deterioration in the efficiency of important neurotransmitter systems (Allard & Marcusson, 1989; Morgan, May, & Finch, 1987). Further, senile plaques and amyloid deposits identical to those typically associated with AD occur with greater frequency in the brains of otherwise normal older people (Morimatsu, Hirai, Muramatsu, & Yoshikawa, 1975; Tomonago, 1981).

Presumably, structural and chemical changes such as these account for the age-related degradation observed in several electrophysiologic parameters. Brainstem auditory and somatosensory evoked potentials exhibit extended latencies and diminished amplitudes (Allison, Wood, & Goff, 1983; Dorfman & Bosley, 1979; Hume, Cant, Shaw, & Cowan, 1982; Jerger & Hall, 1980) in older persons. Visual evoked potential latencies are increased as well (Shaw & Cant, 1980), although conflicting results have been observed regarding age-related decreases in their amplitudes (Celesia & Daly, 1977; Shaw & Cant, 1981). In general, these findings indicate that neural structures involved in both the perception and conduction of sensation become less efficient as we age.

As the electroencephalographic (EEG) literature illustrates, however, problems can arise when electrophysiologic techniques are used to measure the effects of uncomplicated aging on neurologic systems. EEG recordings performed on older individuals frequently disclose slowing in the temporal regions (Obrist, Busse, Eisdorfer, & Kleemeier, 1962), a finding that was previously attributed to normal aging. It now appears that this slowing virtually always indicates an underlying pathologic process (Duffy, Albert, McAnulty, & Garvey, 1984), and it has been associated with verbal memory deficits in otherwise intellectually intact older people (Rice, Buchsbaum, Hardy, & Brugwald, 1991). The caveat is that electrophysiologic changes frequently seen in this population cannot be assumed to reflect benign senescence just because they are common.

On the whole, however, it appears that several neural substrates for cognitive processing undergo functional degeneration as a normal consequence of aging and are accompanied by measurable declines in intellectual proficiency (Crook et al., 1986). Further, some of these losses are similar in character across species (Flicker, Dean, Bartus, Ferris, & Crook, 1985). In human studies, otherwise normal older people have exhibited deficits both in general functions, such as attention, reaction time, and cognitive flexibility, and in more specific domains, such as visuo–spatial perception/praxis and recent memory (Birren & Schaie, 1977; Ferris et al., 1989; Light, 1991; Schaie, 1983). Of these, memory impairment is probably the most widely documented intellectual change in old age.

As already mentioned, serious cognitive disturbance, including significant memory loss, virtually always indicates the presence of disease. For example, even early-stage victims of Alzheimer's disease can be distinguished from age-matched control participants on the basis of memory performance deficits (Welsh, Butters, Hughes, Mohs, & Heyman, 1991, 1992). However, very subtle memory impairment, essentially forgetfulness, is frequently observed in otherwise cognitively intact, healthy, older people. Kral originally characterized such individuals as experiencing "benign senescent forgetfulness" (BSF; Kral, 1962). Others have argued that this term may not be semantically appropriate or sufficiently defined by specific diagnostic criteria. Therefore, the term Age-Associated Memory Impairment (AAMI) has been offered to describe a similar, although possibly milder, form of memory disturbance (Crook et al., 1986) affecting up to one half of all otherwise unimpaired seniors (Ferris et al., 1989).

For research purposes, AAMI has been defined as forgetfulness of sufficient severity to cause performance at or below the minus one standard deviation level for young adults on any standardized test of recent memory for which adequate norms have been established. Additionally, individuals should be at least 50 years of age and exhibit adequate performance on dementia screening instruments as well as on tests designed to assess intellectual function. Finally, they should be free of medical, psychiatric, or pharmacologic factors that might confound memory performance. The important point here is that the stated goal in proposing these criteria was to acknowledge and characterize memory loss that may be seen in healthy, older individuals in the later decades of life.

Observations like these support the conclusion that one of the most important age-related risk factors for mental decline in later years is age itself. Of course, that is not to say that intellectual deterioration is inevitable as we grow older. Because so few of us live beyond 85 years, it may never be possible to prove or disprove the invariability of such a relationship between senility and cognitive impairment.

GENERAL/SYSTEMIC MEDICAL CONDITIONS

The most important negative influence aging exerts on intellectual function is that it enhances an individual's vulnerability to physical events that may lead to cognitive impairment. Prominent among these are accident-related injuries and acute illnesses manifesting secondarily in the presence of physical frailty. Nutritional deficits and the cumulative effects of chronic illnesses represent additional threats to cognitive integrity. Even the treatment of medical illness can diminish mental capacity in older people. In essence, those who are cognitively least resilient in the face of disease are also those who are most likely to become ill.

PHYSICAL SENESCENCE

The potential for aging physiological mechanisms to unfavorably impact on cognition is illustrated by the consequences of altered pharmacokinetics in senescence. Not only are older people prescribed more drugs, they are also more sensitive to the effects of their medications and exhibit different absorption, distribution, and elimination characteristics regarding pharmacologic agents than do younger people (O'Malley, Meagher, & O'Callaghan,

1985). As a result, an increase in the incidence of adverse medication reactions is well documented in older patients (Briant, 1977; Lamy, 1979). These reactions often involve deterioration of mental status, because many of the drugs commonly prescribed in geriatric populations are those with a capacity to negatively affect cognition (Keefover, 1990).

Cognitive performance is also dependent on adequate nutritional status, and although low socioeconomic status is frequently cited as a major cause of deterioration in the nutritional state of older persons (Gupta, Dworkin, & Gambert, 1988), age-related increases in physiologic requirements for certain nutrients (Suter & Russell, 1987) and changes in the absorption characteristics of the gastrointestinal tract (Webster, 1985) may be more important in this regard. An association between impaired intellectual functioning and modest deficiencies in most nutrients has not been established, but there is evidence that such a relationship exists for vitamins B12 and folate. Tissue deficits in both these vitamins have been demonstrated in older populations (Fairbanks & Elveback, 1983; Webster & Leeming, 1979), and vitamin B12 deficiency is a widely recognized cause of dementia and other mental status changes (Damasio & Demeter, 1981; Lindenbaum et al., 1988). Although folate deficiency alone is not ordinarily felt to cause serious intellectual impairment, associations have also been reported between low levels of this vitamin and poor performance on mental status screening instruments (Goodwin, Goodwin, & Garry, 1983; Hanger, Sainsbury, Gilchrist, Beard, & Duncan, 1991).

Postural instability is another physical characteristic of old age that increases an individual's risk for intellectual compromise. An age-dependent diminution in the efficiency of both central and peripheral sensory impulse conduction (Dorfman & Bosley, 1979; Dyck, Schultz, & O'brien, 1975; Hume et al., 1982), compromised functioning of the vestibular apparatus (Teasdale, Stelmach, & Breunig, 1991), and the effects of chronic disease (Lipsitz, Jonsson, Kelley, & Koestner, 1991) are the primary reasons for a well-documented increase in the incidence of falls among older individuals (Gryfe, Amies, & Ashley, 1977). Among the medical sequelae of falling episodes are blows to the head, and the risk of sustaining brain injury during these events is increased in persons over the age of 50 (Levin, Benton, & Grossman, 1982).

The acute and subacute brain insults routinely associated with head injury include contusions, diffuse axonal injury, and epidural and subdural hematomas (Adams & Victor, 1989). The latter may be more common in old age because the brain atrophy mentioned previously as a frequent consequence of senescence leads to stretching of small bridging veins spanning the gap between the inner table of the skull and the brain parenchyma. As a result, these vessels are more disposed to tearing with even minor sudden shifts of the brain within the cranial vault.

The variety of cerebral lesions that may result from head trauma accounts for the fact that such injuries can produce several different patterns of cognitive impairment. These range from the discrete memory or language disturbances typical of focal insults to the temporal regions (Zola-Morgan, Squire, & Mishkin, 1982) or left hemisphere (Geschwind, 1971) respectively, to the more generalized impairments in attention, judgment, and impulse control seen with frontal lobe lesions (Luria, 1969). Even a full dementia syndrome can evolve as a direct consequence of closed head injuries.

An occasional delayed outcome of head trauma is dementia secondary to normal pressure hydrocephalus (NPH; Zander & Foroglou, 1976). In this disorder, slowed efflux of cerebrospinal fluid (CSF) from the intrathecal compartment initially produces increases in pressure throughout the CSF system. Until the process reaches equilibrium and finally arrests, expansion of the ventricles may accommodate this pressure increase, but at the expense of underlying brain structures. Although the mechanism by which these changes compromise cognitive performance is not clear, the presence of ventriculomegaly suggests that disruption of white matter tracts and/or microcirculation, particularly in the diencephalon and deep forebrain, accounts for the gait instability, incontinence, and dementia-like mental status changes that characterize the condition (Adams & Victor, 1989; Matsuda, Nakasu, Nakazawa, & Handa, 1990). NPH is one of the more common potentially treatable causes of dementia (Mahler & Cummings, 1988; Rhymes, Woodson, Sparage-Sachs, & Cassel, 1989) and may also develop as a result of conditions other than head trauma (Bradley et al., 1991). The dementia seen with NPH often typifies the *subcortical dementia syndrome*; a phenomenon that is discussed later in association with Parkinson's disease (Albert, Feldman, & Willis, 1974).

ACQUIRED ILLNESSES

Medical illness in general is more common in old age (U.S. Department of Health and Human Services, 1981), and most illnesses have the capacity to negatively influence cognition. Factors such as diminished endocrine and cardiac function (Abrass, 1991), along with the cumulative effects of chronic pathologic processes, such as atherosclerosis, hypertension, and emphysema, all contribute to an increased occurrence of chronic illness in senescence. The presence of these enduring, and sometimes progressive, diseases may represent the greatest threat of all to the intellectual integrity of older individuals.

This problem is further aggravated by the fact that the treatment of illnesses in older people may pose an even greater threat to mental function than do the illnesses themselves. As has already been noted, the use of medications in geriatric patients is associated with an increased risk of adverse reactions, including the impairment of cognition. Surgical treatment too, particularly that used in the management of cardiac disease, is more likely to produce mental status changes in these individuals (Dubin, Field, Gastfriend, 1979; Tufo, Ostfeld, & Shyekelle, 1970). Finally, regardless of the treatment modality employed, simply hospitalizing an older person increases his or her risk for developing delirium (Lipowski, 1980; Roth, 1955).

The chronic and/or progressive medical conditions that are both more common in old age and are known to represent a threat to intellectual function in this age group can be divided into two categories: (a) those that primarily afflict of the nervous system (e.g., brain diseases) and (b) those that occur systemically or result specifically from disease processes in nonnervous tissue. This classification is somewhat arbitrary, because some neurological ailments, such as stroke, are actually focal manifestations of systemic disease and also because illnesses that produce cognitive impairment necessarily exert their effects by interfering with normal brain function. Nonetheless, distinguishing the neurologic from systemic diseases that compromise intellectual function is a useful way of organizing the topic and has a precedent in the clinical literature (Adams & Victor, 1989).

Systemic Illnesses

In considering generalized disease processes that produce mental dysfunction, it is appropriate to start with a discussion of alcohol abuse, one of the most common health problems in the United States (West, Maxwell, Noble, & Soloman, 1984). Several neurobehavioral syndromes can develop as a result of chronic alcohol use (American Psychiatric Association, 1987). Conditions such as Alcohol Intoxication, Alcohol-Induced Psychotic Disorder (Alcohol Hallucinosis), and Alcohol-Induced Persisting Amnestic Disorder (Korsakoff's Psychosis) manifest primarily as a function of the recency and/or the intensity of alcohol consumption and may, therefore, be considered age-related by virtue of the fact that the lifetime incidence of alcoholism exhibits a bimodal pattern, with the second peak representing persons in their 60s and 70s (Zimberg, 1987). By contrast, the development of alcoholic hepatitis with secondary hepatic encephalopathy is more likely to occur in older people simply because the greater the duration of heavy alcohol consumption, the more likely an individual is to experience this malady (Podolsky & Isselbacher, 1991).

An intriguing phenomenon particularly deserving of attention here is the so-called alcohol dementia syndrome. Computerized tomographic (CT) studies revealing generalized cortical atrophy in the brains of chronic alcoholics (Cala & Mastaglia, 1981; Lishman, 1981) suggest that the deleterious effects of this substance on neural tissue are, to some extent, cumulative. Although a direct relationship between brain atrophy per se, occurring on this or any other basis, and intellectual competence has not been established, these observations are at least consistent with the general impression that long-term alcohol abuse can result in cognitive impairments of sufficient magnitude to justify the diagnosis of dementia. If this is true, alcoholism can be regarded as an age-related risk factor for intellectual decline, because the longer one's exposure history, the more likely it is that one will exhibit the mental manifestations of its toxic effects on the brain. It should be noted, however, that despite the demonstration of cognitive impairments in chronic alcoholics (Grant & Mohns, 1976) and the energetic attempts of some authors to define alcoholic dementia as a specific entity (Cutting, 1978; Seltzer & Sherwin, 1978), conceptualizing the condition as a distinct illness or syndrome remains problematic (Adams & Victor, 1989).

Although not usually recognized as such, sleep apnea is another common medical disorder exhibiting an increased incidence with age (Hayward et al., 1992). In its most common form, obstructive sleep apnea, narrowing or closure of the oropharynx occurs repeatedly throughout the night and results in episodes of breathing cessation that may last 90 seconds or longer. As a result of these events, patients may fully awaken or at least arouse from deeper to lighter stages of sleep, experience significant drops in blood oxygen concentration with concomitant elevations in carbon dioxide levels, and eventually develop chronic cardiovascular disorders such as hypertension and heart failure (Krieger, 1989).

Intellectual disturbances such as impaired attention and recall have been documented in older individuals who exhibit sleep apnea (Hayward, et al., 1992; Yesavage, Bliwise, Guilleminault, Carskadon, & Dement, 1985). One explanation offered for these cognitive changes is that they reflect decreases in alertness due to repeated sleep disruption (Morris & Singer, 1966; Sloan, Craft, & Walsh, 1989; Telakivi et al., 1988). Other authors have suggested that it is recurrent brain hypoxia that accounts for this diminution in mental efficiency (Berry, Webb, Block, Bauer, & Switzer, 1986; Findley et al., 1986). Still other studies indicate that the apneics who develop neuropsychological abnormalities are those who experience elevations in blood carbon dioxide levels (Findley et al. 1986).

Low blood oxygen and high carbon dioxide levels are often even more pronounced in cardiopulmonary diseases such as congestive heart failure (CHF) and chronic obstructive pulmonary disease (COPD), both of which occur with greater frequency in old age (Ingram, 1991; Klainer, Gibson, & White, 1965). Although acute confusional episodes secondary to cerebral hypoxia and/or hypercarbia are common during acute exacerbations and the latter stages of both these illnesses, it is only in COPD that the impact of chronic alterations in blood gas concentrations on cognitive function has been systematically studied. These investigations suggest that performance on tasks assessing higher level intellectual skills, such as abstraction, as well as more basic functions, such as memory and motor dexterity, vary in direct relation to baseline blood oxygen levels (Fix, Golden, Daughton, Kass, & Bell, 1982; Grant, Heaton, McSweeny, Adams, & Timms, 1982; Prigatano, Parsons, Wright, Levis, & Hawryluk, 1983). One finding of particular relevance to older people is that the combination of increased age and decreased oxygen level best predicts impaired performance on measures of perceptual, learning, and problem-solving skills (Grant et al., 1987).

In general, two conclusions are suggested by these studies. The first is that any long-term cognitive deficits observed in individuals who experience chronic disorders of blood gas regulation (e.g., sleep apnea, COPD, CHF) are more likely to result from persistent or recurrent cerebral hypoxia than from hypercarbia. This issue deserves more study, however. Secondly, hypoxia appears to represent a greater threat to the mental capacities of older patients than to those of the younger victims of these diseases. Again, the illnesses that produce this condition are not only more likely to occur in later life but will also have had more time to exert their deleterious effects on the brain.

Of the metabolic diseases representing a significant threat to intellectual capabilities in later life, the most common is diabetes mellitus (DM). Primary DM may present in one of two major forms: Type 1 (often referred to as juvenile or insulin-dependent diabetes), with onset typically very early in life and characterized by reliance on exogenous sources of insulin for survival, and Type 2 (also known as adult-onset or noninsulin dependent diabetes), which frequently occurs in obese individuals and which may respond readily to treatment with oral hypoglycemic agents or even to simple weight loss (Foster, 1991).

Over time, both Types 1 and 2 DM can result in complications primarily involving neural, vascular, and renal tissues. Because evidence of these complications usually manifests 15 to 20 years after the onset of the diabetes, it is likely that their development is more closely related to the duration and severity of the hyperglycemic state than to the type of DM experienced. Assuming this to be the case, DM can be considered an age-related risk factor for the development of any of the secondary medical problems arising as complications of the primary disease, including those with an unfavorable impact on intellectual function. One study found that 17% of all diabetics who had been diagnosed with the disease for 15 years or longer scored within the brain damaged range on a word list learning task (Wilkinson, 1981).

There are numerous mechanisms by which DM can alter mental status. Acutely, both excessively high and low glucose levels can produce confusional states. Over the long term, vascular complications of the primary disease can contribute to the development of stroke and cardiac disease, each of which can have its own negative effect on cognition. Renal failure is another frequent outcome of long-standing DM, which can have a detrimental impact on brain functioning. Given evidence discussed earlier, which suggests that a modest compromise in cognitive function may be inherent in the aging process, it seems likely that even minor brain insults occurring as a result of an illness such as DM will have a greater negative impact in older patients than in younger individuals with the disease.

Another hormonal disturbance widely recognized for its capacity to disrupt brain function is thyroid disease. Thyroid metabolism is quite complex (Guyton, 1991), and there are so many age-related physiologic changes that can either increase or decrease the production and utilization of the active form of thyroid hormone that it is difficult to know what represents "normal" in these individuals. Further, the interpretation of thyroid tests in older people is complicated by the fact that many of the illnesses that occur frequently in this population, as well as the medicines used to treat them, can influence thyroid activity levels. Nonetheless, the prevalence of thyroid disease in general appears to be relatively high in older persons, with hypothyroidism being approximately five to six times more common than hyperthyroidism (Green, 1985).

Both high and low levels of thyroid hormone can produce cognitive or psychiatric behavioral change, and it is standard practice in the evaluation of both acute and chronic mental status disturbance to measure its activity (Cummings, 1985). Typically, excessive thyroid activity produces anxiety, affective disturbance, psychosis, and/or confusion, whereas lower activity levels are associated with psychomotor slowing, inattentiveness, or even stupor (Adams & Victor 1989). However, older people appear particularly prone to a form of thyroid dysfunction referred to as *apathetic thyrotoxicosis*. In this condition, hyperthyroidism may produce some of the subdued behaviors more typical of the hypothyroid state. This manifestation of excessive thyroid activity may actually account for more cases of dementia in older people than does hypothyroidism, even though the latter is the more common metabolic disturbance in this population (Fairclough & Besser, 1974; Lahey, 1932).

One of the most ubiquitous medical problems identified in the adult population of the United States is hypertension. It reportedly affects at least 50% of older persons (Lindholm, 1990) and, if left untreated, can lead to lethal complications (Williams & Braunwald, 1991). Because of its contribution to the development of cerebrovascular disease, hypertension is a principle antecedent to multi-infarct dementia and other neuropsychological disorders that occur as a consequence of stroke (Fisher, 1968; Hachinski, 1990). Much less frequently, severe hypertension alone may produce an acute or subacute global cerebral disturbance. Although this latter phenomenon, referred to as *hypertensive encephalopathy*, can be observed in the context of an evaluation of the dementia syndrome (Mahler & Cummings, 1988), it more commonly manifests as a diffuse neurologic crisis (Adams & Victor, 1989).

It is not unusual for hypertension to indirectly contribute to alterations in mental status through the adverse effects of antihypertensive medication use. Because many patients with high blood pressure are treated with diuretic medications that facilitate the excretion of sodium and potassium during renal filtration, they may be at risk to develop confusional states due to excessively low serum levels of these electrolytes (Mahler & Cummings, 1988). Although this is seldom a problem in patients who are reasonably cooperative and well managed, it is not a rare occurrence in older individuals who may be more prone to noncompliance due to socioeconomic and other factors.

Neurologic Disease

In any discussion of age-related primary neurologic diseases that may cause intellectual decline, it is appropriate to begin by addressing the phenomenon of Alzheimer's disease. Evidence that AD affects more than just nervous tissue notwithstanding (Piletz, Sarasua, Whitehouse, & Chotani, 1991; Zebrower, Beeber, & Kieras, 1992), it is the brain that bears the brunt of the illness (Ishii, 1966; Khachaturian, 1985). Among the small number of diseases that are virtually synonymous with dementia, indeed among all diseases that produce severe intellectual impairment in older people, AD is by far the most common (Evans et al., 1989; Zhang et al., 1990). In fact, the concept of senile dementia might never have evolved if it were not for AD.

It is, therefore, ironic that it was AD's capacity to cause dementia in presenile populations that first drew attention to its distinctive neuropathological features (Alzheimer, 1907) and initially maintained its importance in medical textbooks (Robbins & Angell, 1978). In more recent years, epidemiologic studies have revealed that it is very much an age-related phenomenon, with prevalence rates for clinically diagnosed AD rising from less than 1% among persons in their early 60s to nearly 50% by the ninth decade of life (Evans, et al., 1989). Neuropathological confirmation of these rates is problematic, however, because it requires the detection of so-called senile plaques and neurofibrillary tangles at autopsy or via biopsy during life (Khachaturian, 1985). Because, as mentioned earlier, these lesions are also found in the brains of deceased older people who were intellectually intact at the time of death, the quantity representing a necessary or sufficient condition for the manifestation of AD remains unsettled (Breteler, Claus, van Duijn, Launer, & Hofman, 1992).

Assuming that all individuals who develop plaques and tangles and who live long enough will ultimately become demented, it is probably less pertinent to discuss AD as a risk factor for late-life cognitive decline than to explore potential risk factors for the initiation of processes leading to AD itself. Probably the most widely debated of these is exposure to aluminum (Glick, 1990). However, although several studies have reported an association between this element and occurrence of the disease, their methodologies have been criticized, and a consensus regarding the role of aluminum in the development of AD has not been forged (Lord Walton of Detchant, 1991). Serious head injury (Heyman et al., 1986; Mortimer, 1990; Van Duijn et al. 1992), myocardial infarcts (Aronson et al., 1990), and genetic factors (Heston, Orr, Rich, & White, 1991) have also drawn attention as possible etiologic variables in the disease.

Of the previous factors, genetic/familial factors have generated the most intense investigation efforts to date. Chromosome 21 has been found to include a specific locus that when altered, may facilitate the occurrence of AD. Initially, this chromosome was studied because of its association with Down syndrome, a condition in which AD virtually always appears. More recently, a genetic marker located on Chromosome 21 has been found to be closely associated with a familial form of AD. Finally, a segment of this chromosome coding the production of amyloid precursor protein (APP) has been found altered in many AD patients in such a way as to facilitate the accumulation of amyloid, the core substance of senile plaques (Esch et al. 1990; Levy et al., 1990). Although the role of this substance in the evolution of the disease is not clear, it has been shown to be toxic to neurons and conceivably provides the cellular insult that ultimately leads to the development of dementia (Mattson et al., 1992). In addition to these findings implicating Chromosome 21 in AD pathogenesis, loci on both Chromosomes 14 and 19 have been suggested as sites at which genetic events that promote development of the disease may occur (Katzman, 1986).

Two other factors that do not play etiologic roles but that have, nonetheless, been advanced as risk factors for the clinical emergence and progression of AD are age and limited formal education. The first of these has already been discussed. The second raises questions that will be extremely difficult to answer, given the obvious problem of developing a meaningful cross-cultural definition of education. A particularly fascinating aspect of the discussion engendered by this issue, however, relates to observations that the severity of cognitive disturbance in AD is proportional to the degree of neuronal synaptic disruption found in the cortex of autopsied brains taken from individuals with AD (Masliah et al., 1992). Therefore, synaptic density could represent a "brain reserve" that develops in response to enriching experiences such as education and that may provide a buffer against the ravages of AD (Katzman, 1986, Zhang et al., 1990).

After AD, the most frequently diagnosed cause of dementia is cerebral infarction or so-called multi-infarct dementia (MID), also referred to as vascular dementia (VaD; Rhymes et al., 1989; Schoenberg, Kokmen, & Okazaki, 1987). In addition, strokes producing less widespread brain injury can result in more discrete cognitive deficits such as aphasia, amnesia, and various forms of agnosia. The incidence of stroke in general more than doubles with each decade of life above the age of 35 (Wolf, Kannel, & McGee, 1986), so that it is very much a health problem of advanced years. Further, the factors most predictive of a poor outcome following stroke are old age and living alone (Kotila, Waltimo, Niemi, Laaksonen, & Lempinen, 1984).

With specific regard to dementia due to stroke, an adult incidence rate of 28 cases/100,000/year has been reported for VaD (Schoenberg et al., 1987) and virtually all cases occur in persons over 55 years. The age-related character of the problem is even more dramatically illustrated by the results of a longitudinal study conducted in Sweden, which indicated an almost 1,000 fold greater incidence of VaD in those in their middle 70s than in individuals 20 years younger (Schoenberg, 1988).

However, in the absence of generally accepted guidelines for establishing the diagnosis of VaD, the validity of figures such as those just noted remains unsettled (Brust, 1988; O'brien, 1988). Even though the volume of infarcted brain tissue can be accurately quantified at autopsy, this information alone is not sufficient for establishing the diagnosis, because it does not take into account the location of the lesion(s) (Tomlinson et al., 1970). Clinical guidelines for detecting the disorder on the basis of historical and examination findings (Hachinski et al., 1975) have also been found lacking (Bennett, Wilson, Gilley, & Fox, 1990; Erkinjuntti, 1987; Zubenko, 1991). Even the availability of "high tech" brain imaging has failed to resolve the problem, because questions remain regarding which radiographic findings actually reflect ischemic changes (Braffman et al., 1988) and how much evidence of infarction is necessary on a scan to determine that a patient's dementia is due to ischemic injury (Kozachuk et al., 1990). In view of these difficulties in accurately diagnosing VaD *in vivo*, consensus-based guidelines that rely on clinical and radiographic information have been proposed (Chui et al., 1992). Because VaD is the most common dementing process with any foreseeable potential for treatment responsiveness, this problem will undoubtedly receive further attention.

As a category of illness, brain tumors probably represent the third most common neurological illness leading to dementia in older people (Rhymes et al., 1989). Their ranking might be higher but for the fact that several aggressive primary brain tumors such as medulloblastomas and glioblastomas, as well as metastatic brain tumors such as lung and breast cancer, become less prevalent in the very old (Cairncross, Kim, & Posner, 1980; Schoenberg, Christine, & Whisnant, 1978). Even though the incidence of these malignant tumors is rising in older populations (Greig, Ries, Yancik, & Rapoport, 1990), patients who develop them seldom survive to very old age. In contrast, individuals with less aggressive tumors, such as meningiomas and pituitary adenomas, may live to be quite old. It is, therefore, the latter category of brain tumor that accounts for more cases of dementia in older people (Schoenberg, et al., 1978).

Typically, tumors exert their deleterious effects on brain function by one of two mechanisms: (a) focal tissue destruction via direct pressure or invasion of the parenchyma, or (b) generation of increased intracranial pressure due to obstruction of cerebrospinal fluid outflow (obstructive hydrocephalus) or increased tissue volume within the skull ("mass effect"; Adams & Victor, 1989). In the first case, the cognitive changes produced are often discrete deficits in the intellectual domain normally mediated by the damaged portion of the brain. The second mechanism is more likely to produce generalized cognitive failure consistent with the diagnosis of dementia.

It is also this latter process that is more likely to develop in the presence of noninvasive tumors such as those noted previously to be more common in the very old. Because the evolution of symptoms is often protracted and subtle, older patients exhibiting mental decline secondary to these slow-growing brain tumors may be presumed by friends, family, and physicians to be experiencing an irreversible dementia like Alzheimer's disease and may, therefore, be provided a less rigorous diagnostic evaluation. Physicians may place undue reliance on their belief that individuals with brain tumors can usually be detected by the manifestation of other signs and symptoms besides intellectual decline. Although other clinical features are indeed frequently present, they typically involve vague complaints of headache, unsteadiness of gait, and urinary incontinence, all of which may be overlooked because they are also found in other more common dementias. In view of the previous comments, it is perhaps surprising that the role of routine cranial imaging (CT/MRI) in the evaluation of dementia in older people continues to be debated (Clarfield, 1990; Katzman, 1990; Larson, Reifler, Sumi, Canfield, & Chinn, 1986). In any case, there is little doubt that an inverse relationship exists between the age of a patient with dementia and the likelihood that his or her evaluation will include brain imaging. For this reason, among others, the risk for serious intellectual deterioration represented by brain tumors is an age-related phenomenon.

Parkinson's disease (PD) is yet another neurologic disease commonly implicated in the manifestation of dementia (Rhymes et al., 1989). It typically begins between the ages of 50 and 65 and exhibits a prolonged course of deterioration, so that more than half of those exhibiting its symptoms are over the age of 70 (Godwin-Austin, Lee, Marmot, & Stern, 1982; Kurland, Kurtzke, & Goldberg, 1973). In fact, the prevalence of PD has been reported to increase from 2.3 cases per 100,000 for those age 50 or less to 1,144.9 cases per 100,000 for those age 80 or over (Mayeux et al., 1992). Clearly, it is an age-related illness.

For the majority of individuals with Parkinson's disease, PD is essentially a profound disturbance of motor function characterized by diffuse rigidity and a variable degree of tremor. Other commonly described clinical features include cogwheel rigidity, bradykinesia, festinating gait, micrographia, and hypophonia (Adams & Victor, 1989). However, these may simply represent variations in the manifestation of the two primary characteristics of the illness. Bradyphrenia, literally "slow thought," is a seldom used but very descriptive term that conveys the essence of the most common mental changes observed in these patients (Agid, Ruberg, Dubois, & Javoy-Agid, 1984). That is, they appear more delayed than actually impaired in the exercise of intellectual functions such as memory retrieval, information processing, and cognitive flexibility. In many cases, the problem is so subtle that it is viewed simply as a consequence of slowed motor performance.

Approximately 25% of PD patients, however, will ultimately experience intellectual difficulties of sufficient severity to be considered demented (Brown & Marsden, 1984). As with PD in general, the prevalence rate for Parkinson-related dementia increases dramatically with age; rising from 41.1 cases per 100,000 in those up to 50 years old to 787.1 cases per 100,000 in those 80 years or older (Mayeux et al., 1992). Because the deficits observed, even in severely impaired individuals, are primarily those reflecting diminished cognitive efficiency, they have been said to suffer a distinct neuropsychological syndrome referred to as subcortical or fronto-limbic dementia (Albert, 1979; Albert et al., 1974)

Subcortical dementia prominently features a diminution in initiative, increased irritability, and difficulty processing and manipulating information. These impairments suggest disruption of neural systems located in the diencephalon and deep frontal lobes (Oyebode, Barker, Blessed, Dick, & Britton, 1986; Taylor, Saint-Cyr, & Lang, 1986), whereas dysfunction in other brain loci is often not as clinically obvious (Cooper, Sagar, Jordan, Harvey, & Sullivan, 1991; Huber & Paulson, 1985; Levin et al., 1991). This pattern of intellectual decline is also seen in cases of multi-infarct dementia resulting from the accumulation of small strokes predominantly affecting deep white matter areas (Bennett et al., 1990) and in several other diseases that, like PD, reflect disturbance in basal ganglia function (Adams & Victor, 1989). Of the latter, progressive supranuclear palsy (PSP) is particularly relevant here because of its clinical similarity to PD and because it tends to emerge in older populations (Duvoisin, Golbe, & Lepore, 1987). Also known as the Steele–Richardson–Olszewski syndrome, PSP is somewhat distinctive in that it features progressive ophthalmoplegia in addition to generalized rigidity. Up to 80% of those individuals who develop the disorder will ultimately show signs of a mild to moderate dementia (Maher & Lees, 1986).

Both PD and PSP may also indirectly contribute to disruptions in mental function because of the effects of medications used to treat them. In virtually all cases, these agents act by increasing the availability of the neurotransmitter dopamine or by blocking the activity of acetyl choline; either of these actions can produce acute confusion. In addition, dopamine sparing agonists can promote the emergence of psychosis and depression (Cedarbaum & Schleifer, 1991).

One final neurological illness with the capacity to produce severe mental status change and with a clear tendency to develop more frequently in older populations is *Progressive Multifocal Leucoencephalopathy* (PML). Caused by a viral agent (JC virus), PML virtually never manifests in individuals with an intact immune system (Adams & Victor, 1989). The greater incidence of PML in later life can, therefore, probably be explained by an increased exposure risk for older people to diseases and medications that diminish immunocompetence.

PSYCHOSOCIAL VARIABLES

Cognitive impairments need not, of course, occur exclusively on the basis of disease. The quality of intellectual performance depends on attitude and motivation as much as it does on the physical condition of the brain. Therefore, although individuals do not develop aphasias or dyspraxias because of depression or anxiety, they may, nonetheless, experience difficulty in following conversation, recalling detail, or balancing a checkbook as a consequence of these psychological states.

The phenomenon of Pseudodementia (Pdm) is one in which disturbances in attitude are so severe that they mimic global disruption of neurobehavioral systems. Typically observed as a complication of depression in older people, Pdm not only features sadness, guilt, and other signs of affective illness but also impairments in attention/concentration, recall, and initiative (Caine, 1981; Wells, 1979). These latter characteristics may be so prominent that the clinical impression is one of dementia rather than affective disorder. Indeed, the presentation is very similar to the subcortical dementia syndrome previously described as a manifestation of fronto-limbic pathology (Albert et al., 1974). That these dementia-like behaviors reflect the influence of motivation on cognitive functioning becomes apparent with careful observation. Unlike individuals with diseases that produce true amnesia, patients with Pdm do not "forget that they can't remember." In fact, they often complain bitterly of memory problems.

Further, their impaired performance on neuropsychological tasks is often inconsistent and results from poor effort and "I don't know" responses.

Mood also exerts less profound effects on cognitive proficiency. For example, individuals who are depressed perform more poorly on word recall tasks than do matched control participants (Weingartner & Silberman, 1984). Again, however, such apparent diminutions in intellectual prowess could reflect amotivation or "learned helplessness." Because individuals who are depressed may not perceive that a relationship exists between the intensity of their effort and the quality of their performance (Seligman, Klein, & Miller, 1976), they may be less motivated during testing. Interestingly, animals exposed to experimental conditions that promote "learned helplessness" also exhibit reductions in catecholamine neurotransmitters (Weiss, Stone, & Harrell, 1970). The fact that these neurotransmitters are predominantly utilized by neural pathways projecting to frontal and limbic regions of the brain (Pickel & Milner, 1987) and that successful treatment of depression often involves the use of medications that increase brain catecholamine activity suggests that fronto-limbic dysfunction represents a common pathway leading to the amotivation so characteristic of depression. The role of the frontal lobes in mediating motivation is well recognized (Stuss & Benson, 1984), and the clinical similarity between Pdm and the subcortical or fronto-limbic dementia syndrome has been mentioned earlier. Further, studies using positron emission tomography (PET) imaging have demonstrated relatively lower metabolic activity in the frontal lobes of individuals who are depressed compared to normal controls (Baxter et al., 1989; Martinot et al., 1990). Therefore, although experiences that promote learned helplessness may ultimately result in amotivation such as that seen in depression, the mechanism by which this occurs probably involves disturbances in fronto-limbic brain physiology.

While Pdm is usually observed in older individuals, it has not been established that depression itself is an age-related phenomenon. Nor is it clear that older individuals are more vulnerable to the cognition—inhibiting effects of depression (Niederehe, 1986; Sugar & McDowd, 1992). They are, however, exposed to a greater number of life-events that have the potential to inflict psychological trauma (Shraberg, 1978) and older people account for 25% of all suicide attempts, although representing only 9% of the population (Resnick & Cantor, 1970). These findings suggest that serious depression, at least, may be more prevalent in old age.

It is not necessary that attitude and motivation disturbances reach the pathologic proportions seen in depression for these factors to exert a negative influence on intellectual proficiency in old age. One study involving older people found that depression scores did not predict performance on recall tasks as well as did those on an instrument measuring the

participants' self-perceptions of their own memory acuity (West & Bramblett, 1990). Because older individuals tend to gauge their current memory
competence on the basis of an idealized notion of how good it "used to be"
(Sugar, 1988), diminished efficiency in this domain could simply represent
a self-fulfilling prophecy.

Observations that older people who participate in activities that utilize
cognitive skills such as working memory and reasoning are better able than
nonparticipants to perform other tasks requiring similar skills (Clarkson-
Smith & Hartley, 1990) lends credence to the adage that "you use it or lose
it." Therefore, social disengagement may represent yet another risk factor
for intellectual deterioration in the aged. For example, although older
people are capable of developing and employing strategies that compensate
for performance deficits related to age-dependent decreases in reaction time
(Salthouse, 1987; Schaie, 1989), the motivation to do so may not be
sufficiently encouraged in a society that expects older people to perform less
effectively and to assume fewer challenging roles (Heise, 1987). Further, the
complexity and richness of the environment in which an individual exists
appears to have a proportionately invigorating influence on intellectual
proficiency, even in later life (Kohn & Schooler, 1983; Owens, 1966). If so,
retirement and a shift to a less demanding low-stimulation environment
could represent a threat to cognitive vitality in old age.

In addition to the previously mentioned diminutions in their physical
vigor, the loss of friends who can share activities and a tendency for society
to view older persons as nonparticipants may encourage older people to
adopt relatively sedentary lifestyles. This retreat to a less physically
demanding daily routine might, in turn, contribute to deterioration in
cognitive proficiency. Although little research has thus far focused on this
subject, there is evidence to suggest that sustained regular exercise may
confer at least some protection against an age-related deterioration in
reaction time (Blumenthal et al., 1991; Botwinick & Storandt, 1974). At this
point, however, there is insufficient information available on which to base
conclusions regarding the impact of physical activity on other cognitive
processes such as memory or praxis.

SUMMARY

Although physical disabilities may be a source of frustration or even
genuine hardship for individuals who find themselves at a later point in the
lifespan, intellectual decline often represents a much greater concern. It not
only diminishes one's ability to participate in social and self-care activities,
it can also deprive an individual of the capability and privilege of exercising
self-determination. Therefore, although dependency due to physical infir-

mity may diminish our sense of dignity, severe mental impairment literally strips us of our humanity. Fortunately, although most of us will become senile, that does not necessarily mean that we will become demented. What is abundantly clear, however, is that our exposure to risk factors for diminished cognitive proficiency increases in old age. In fact, age itself may represent just such a risk factor. Other threats to intellectual integrity in later life include physical frailty, systemic and neurologic medical illness, and alterations in the psychological domains of attitude and motivation. Questions regarding which of these can be mitigated represent important public policy issues for our aging society.

REFERENCES

Abrass, I. B. (1991). Biology of aging. In J. D. Wilson, E. Braunwald, K. J. Isselbacher, R. G. Petersdorf, J. B. Martin, A.S. Fauci, & R. K. Root (Eds.), *Harrison's principles of internal medicine* (12th ed., pp. 73–76). New York: McGraw-Hill.

Adams, R. D., & Victor, M. (1989). *Principles of neurology.* New York: McGraw-Hill.

Agid, Y., Ruberg, B., Dubois, B., & Javoy-Agid, F. (1984). Biochemical substrates of mental disturbances in Parkinson's disease. In R. G. Hassler & J. F. Christ (Eds.), *Advances in neurology* (Vol. 40, pp. 211–218). New York: Raven.

Albert, M. L. (1978). Subcortical dementia. In R. Katzman, R. D. Terry, & K. L. Bick (Eds.), *Alzheimer's disease: Senile Dementia and Related Disorders* (pp. 173–180). New York: Raven.

Albert, M. L., Feldman, R. G., & Willis, A. C. (1974). The subcortical dementia of progressive supranuclear palsy. *Journal of Neurology, Neurosurgery, and Psychiatry, 37,* 121–130.

Allard, P., & Marcusson, J. O. (1989). Age-correlated loss of dopamine uptake sites labeled with (3H)GBR-12935 in human putamen. *Neurobiology of Aging, 10,* 661–664.

Allison, T., Wood, C. C., & Goff, W. R. (1983). Brain stem auditory, pattern-reversal visual, and short-latency somatosensory evoked potentials: Latencies in relation to age, sex, and brain and bodysize. Electroencephalography and *Clinical Neurophysiology, 55,* 619–636.

Alzheimer, A. (1907). Über eine eigenartige erkankung der hirnrinde [Regarding an unusual disease of the cortex]. *Allgemeine Zeitschrift fuer Psychiatrie und Psychisch-Gerichtliche Medicine, 64,* 146.

American Psychiatric Association. (1987). *Diagnostic and Statistical Manual of Mental Disorders Third Edition–Revised.* Washington, DC.

Aronson, M. K., Ooi, W. L., Morgenstern, H., Hafner, A., Masur, D., Crystal, H., Frishman, W. H., Fisher, D., & Katzman, R. (1990). Women, myocardial infarction and dementia in the very old. *Neurology, 40,* 1102–1106.

Baxter, L. R., Schwartz, J. M., Phelps, M. E., Mazziotta, J. C., Guze, B. H., Selin, C. E., Gerner, R. H., & Sumida, R. M. (1989). Reduction of prefrontal cortex glucose metabolism common to three types of depression. *Archives of General Psychiatry, 46,* 243–250.

Bennett, D. A., Wilson, R. S., Gilley, D. W., & Fox, J. H. (1990). Clinical diagnosis of Binswanger's disease. *Journal of Neurology, Neurosurgery, and Psychiatry, 53,* 961–965.

Berry, D. T. R., Webb, W. V., Block, A. J., Bauer, R. M., & Switzer, D. A. (1986). Nocturnal hypoxia and neuropsychological variables. *Journal of Clinical and Experimental Neuropsychology, 8,* 229–238.

Birren, J. E., & Schaie, K. W. (1977). *Handbook of the psychology of aging.* New York: Van

Nostrand Reinhold.

Blumenthal, J. A., Emery, C. F., Madden, D. J., Schniebolk, S., Walsh-Riddle, M., George, L. K., McKee, D. C., Higginbotham, M. B., Cobb, F. R., & Coleman, R. E. (1991). Long-term effects of exercise on psychological functioning in older men and women. *Journals of Gerontology, 46,* 352-361.

Botwinick, S., & Storandt, M. (1974). Cardiovascular status, depressive affect, and other factors in reaction time. *Journals of Gerontology, 29,* 543-548.

Bradley, W. G., Whittemore, A. R., Watanabe, A. S., Davis, S. J., Teresi, L. M., & Homyak, M. (1991). Association of deep white matter infarction with chronic communicating hydrocephalus: Implications regarding the possible origin of normal-pressure hydrocephalus. *American Journal of Neurological Radiology, 12,* 31-44.

Braffman, B. H., Zimmerman, R. A., Trojanowski, J. Q., Gonatas, N. K., Hickey, W. F., & Schlaepfer, W. W. (1988). Brain MR: Pathological correlation with gross and histopathology: I. Lacunar infarction and Virchow-Robin spaces. *American Journal of Neurological Radiology, 9,* 621-628.

Breteler, M. B., Claus, J. J., van Duijn, C. M., Launer, L. J., & Hofman, A. (1992). Epidemiology of Alzheimer's disease. *Epidemiologic Reviews, 14,* 59-82.

Briant, R. H. (1977). Drug treatment in the elderly: Problems and prescribing rules. *Drugs, 13,* 225-229.

Brown, G. R., Marsden, C. D. (1984). How common is dementia in Parkinson's disease? *Lancet, 2,* 1262-1265.

Brust, J. C. M. (1988). Vascular dementia is overdiagnosed. *Archives of Neurology, 45,* 799-801.

Caine, E. D. (1981). Pseudodementia. *Archives of General Psychiatry, 38,* 1359-1364.

Cairncross, J. G., Kim, J. H., & Posner, J. B. (1980). Radiation therapy for brain metastases. *Annals of Neurology, 7,* 529-541.

Cala, L. A., & Mastaglia, F. L. (1981). Computerized tomography in chronic alcoholics. *Alcoholism (NY), 1,* 87-90.

Cedarbaum, J. M., & Schleifer, L. S. (1991). Drugs for Parkinson's disease, spasticity and acute muscle spasms. In A. G. Gilman, T. W. Rall, A. S. Nies, & P. Taylor (Eds.), *Goodman & Gilmans's: The pharmacologic basis of therapeutics* (pp. 463-490). New York: Pergamon.

Celesia, G. A., & Daly, R. F. (1977). Effects of aging on visual evoked responses. *Archives of Neurology, 34,* 403-407.

Chui, H. C., Victoroff, J. I., Margolin, D., Jagust, W., Shankle, R., & Katzman, R. (1992). Criteria for the diagnosis of ischemic vascular dementia. *Neurology, 42,* 473-480.

Clarfield, A. M. (1990). Should a major imaging procedure (CT or MRI) be required in the workup of dementia?: An opposing view. *The Journal of Family Practice, 31,* 401-410.

Clarkson-Smith, L., & Hartley, A. (1990). The game of bridge as an exercise in working memory and reasoning. *Journals of Gerontology, 45,* 233-238.

Cooper, J. A., Sagar, H. J., Jordan, N., Harvey, N. S., & Sullivan, E. V. (1991). Cognitive impairment in early, untreated Parkinson's disease and its relationship to motor disability. *Brain, 114,* 2095-2122.

Crook, T., Bartus, R. T., Ferris, S. H., Whitehouse, P., Cohen, G. D., & Gershon, S. (1986). Age-associated memory impairment: Proposed diagnostic criteria and measures of clinical change—Report of a NIMH work group. *Developmental Neuropsychology, 2,* 261-271.

Cummings, D. L. (1985). *Clinical neuropsychiatry.* New York: Grune & Stratton.

Cutting, J. (1978). The relationship between Korsakov's syndrome and "alcoholic" dementia. *British Journal of Psychiatry, 132,* 240-251.

Damasio, A. R., & Demeter, S. (1981). Dementia due to systemic illness. *Resident and Staff Physician, 7,* 36-41.

Dekaban, A. S., & Sadowsky, D. (1978). Changes in brain weight during the span of human life: Relation of brain weight to body height and body weight. *Annals of Neurology, 4,* 345–356.

Dorfman, L. J., & Bosley, T. M. (1979). Age-related changes in peripheral and central nerve conduction in man. *Neurology, 29,* 38–44.

Dubin, W. R., Field, N. L., & Gastfriend, D. R. (1979). Postcardiotomy delirium: A critical review. *Journal of Thoracic and Cardiovascular Surgery, 77,* 586–594.

Duffy, F. H., Albert, M. S., McAnulty, G., & Garvey, A. J. (1984). Age-related differences in brain electrical activity of healthy subjects. *Annals of Neurology, 16,* 430–438.

Duvoisin, R. C., Golbe, L. I., & Lepore, F. E. (1987). Progressive supranuclear palsy. *Canadian Journal of Neurological Science, 14*(Suppl. 3), 547–554.

Dyck, P. J., Schultz, P. W., & O'brien, P. C. (1972). Quantitation of touch-pressure sensation. *Archives of Neurology, 26,* 465–473.

Erkinjuntti, T. (1987). Differential diagnosis between Alzheimer's disease and vascular dementia: Evaluation of common clinical methods. *Acta Neurologica Scandinavia, 76,* 433–442.

Esch, F. S., Keim, P. S., Beattie, E. C., Blacher, R. W., Culwell, A. R., Oltersdorf, T., McClure, D., & Ward, P. J. (1990). Cleavage of amyloid beta peptide during constitutive processing of its precursor. *Science, 248,* 1122–1124.

Evans, D. A., Funkenstein, H., Albert, M. S., Scherr, P. A., Cook, N. R., Chown, M. J., Hebert, L. E., Hennekens, C. H., & Taylor, J. O. (1989). Prevalence of Alzheimer's disease in a community population of older persons. *Journal of the American Medical Association, 262,* 2551–2556.

Fairbanks, V. F., & Elveback, L. R. (1983). Tests for pernicious anemia: Serum vitamin B12 assay. *Mayo Clinic Proceedings, 58,* 135–137.

Fairclough, P. D., & Besser, G. M. (1974). Apathetic T-3 toxicosis. *British Medical Journal, 1,* 364–365.

Ferris, S. H., Flicker, C., Reisberg, B., & Crook, T. (1989). Age-associated memory impairment, benign forgetfulness and dementia. In M. Bergener & B. Reisberg (Eds.), *Diagnosis and treatment of senile dementia* (pp. 72–82). Berlin: Springer-Verlag.

Findley, L. J., Barth, J. T., Powers, D. C., Wilhoit, S. C., Boyd, D. G., & Suratt, P. M. (1986). Cognitive impairment in patients with obstructive sleep apnea and associated hypoxemia. *Chest, 90,* 686–690.

Fisher, C. M. (1968). Dementia in cerebrovascular disease. In J. F. Toole, R. G. Siekert, & J. P. Whisnant (Eds.), *Cerebral Vascular Disease: Sixth Conference* (pp. 232–236). New York: Grune & Stratton.

Fix, A. J., Golden, C. J., Daughton, D., Kass, I., & Bell, C. W. (1982). Neuropsychological deficits among patients with chronic obstructive pulmonary disease. *International Journal of Neurosciences, 16,* 99–105.

Flicker, C., Dean, R. L., Bartus, R. T., Ferris, S. H., & Crook, T. (1985). Animal and human memory dysfunctions associated with aging, cholinergic lesions, and senile dementia. *Annals of the New York Academy of Science, 444,* 525–527.

Foster, D. W. (1991). Diabetes mellitus. In J. D. Wilson, E. Braunwald, K. J. Isselbacher, R. G. Petersdorf, J. B. Martin, A. S. Fauci, & R. K. Root (Eds.), *Harrison's principles of internal medicine* (12th ed., pp. 1739–1759). New York: McGraw-Hill.

Geschwind, N. (1971). Current concepts in aphasia. *New England Journal Medicine, 284,* 654–656.

Glick, J. L. (1990). Dementias: The role of magnesium deficiency and an hypothesis concerning the pathogenesis of Alzheimer's disease. *Medical Hypotheses, 31,* 211–225.

Godwin-Austen, R. B., Lee, P. N., Marmot, M. G., & Stern, G. M. (1982). Smoking and Parkinson's disease. *Journal of Neurology, Neurosurgery, and Psychiatry, 45,* 577–581.

Goodwin, J. S., Goodwin, J. M., & Garry, P. J. (1983). Association between nutritional status and cognitive functioning in a healthy elderly population. *Journal of the American Medical*

Association, 249, 2917-2921.

Goudsmit, E., Hofman, M. A., Fliers, E., & Swaab, D. F. (1990). The supraoptic and paraventricular nuclei of the human hypothalamus in relation to sex, age and Alzheimer's disease. *Neurobiology of Aging, 11,* 529-536.

Grant, I., & Mohns, L. (1976). Chronic cerebral effects of alcohol and drug abuse. *International Journal of Addictions, 10,* 833-920.

Grant, I., Heaton, R. K., McSweeny, A. J., Adams, K. M., & Timms, R. M. (1982). Neuropsychologic findings in hypoxemic chronic obstructive pulmonary disease. *Archives of Internal Medicine, 142,* 1470-1476.

Grant, I., Prigatano, G. P., Heaton, R. K., McSweeny, A. J., Wright, E. C., & Adams, K. M. (1987). Progressive neuropsychologic impairment and hypoxemia: Relationship in chronic obstructive pulmonary disease. *Archives of General Psychiatry, 44,* 999-1006.

Green, M. F. (1985). The endocrine system. In M. S. J. Pathy (Ed.), *Principles and practice of geriatric medicine* (pp. 173-180). Chichester: Wiley.

Greig, N. H., Ries, L. G., Yancik, R., & Rapoport, S. I. (1990). Increasing annual incidence of primary malignant brain tumors in the elderly. *Journal of the National Cancer Institute, 82,* 1621-1624.

Gryfe, C. I., Amies, A., & Ashley, M. J. (1977). A longitudinal study of falls in an elderly population: I. Incidence and morbidity. *Age-Ageing, 6,* 201-210.

Gupta, K. L., Dworkin, B., & Gambert, S. R. (1988). Common nutritional disorders in the elderly: Atypical manifestations. *Geriatrics, 43,* 87-89, 95-97.

Guyton, A. C. (1991). *Textbook of medical physiology* (8th ed.). Philadelphia: Harcourt Brace Jovanovich.

Hachinski, V. C., Iliff, L. D., Zilhka, E., Du Boulay, G. H., McAllister, V. L., Marshall, J., Russell, R. W. R., & Symon, L. (1975). Cerebral blood flow in dementia. *Archives of Neurology, 32,* 632-637.

Hachinski, V. C. (1990). The decline and resurgence of vascular dementia. *Canadian Medical Association Journal, 142,* 107-111.

Hanger, H. C., Sainsbury, R., Gilchrist, N. L., Beard, M. E. J., & Duncan, J. M. (1991). A community study of vitamin B12 and folate levels in the elderly. *Journal of the American Geriatric Society, 39,* 1155-1159.

Hayflick, L. (1976). The cell biology of human aging. *New England Journal of Medicine, 295,* 1302.

Hayward, L., Mant, A., Eyland, A., Hewitt, H., Purcell, C., Turner, J., Goode, E., LeCount, A., Pond, D., & Saunders, N. (1992). Sleep disordered breathing and cognitive function in a retirement village population. *Age-Ageing, 21,* 121-128.

Heise, D. (1987). Sociocultural determination of mental aging. In C. Schooler & K. Schaie (Eds.), *Cognitive functioning and social structure over the life course* (pp. 247-261). Norwood, NJ: Ablex.

Heston, L. L., Orr, H. T., Rich, S. S., & White, J. A. (1991). Linkage of an Alzheimer disease susceptibility locus to markers on human chromosome 21. *American Journal of Medical Genetics, 40,* 449-453.

Heyman, A., Wilkinson, W. E., Stafford, J. A., Helms, M. J., Sigmon, A. G., & Weinberg, T. (1986). Alzheimer's disease: A study of epidemiologic aspects. *Annals of Neurology, 15,* 335-341.

Huber, S. J., & Paulson, G. W. (1985). The concept of subcortical dementia. *American Journal of Psychiatry, 142,* 1312-1317.

Hume, A. L., Cant, C. R., Shaw, N. A., & Cowan, J. C. (1982). Central somatosensory conduction time from 10 to 79 years. *Electroencephalography and Clinical Neurophysiology, 54,* 49-54.

Ingram, R. H. (1991). Chronic bronchitis, emphysema, and airways obstruction. In J. D. Wilson, E. Braunwald, K. J. Isselbacher, R. G. Petersdorf, J. B. Martin, A. S. Fauci, & R.

K. Root (Eds.), *Harrison's principles of internal medicine* (12th ed., pp. 1074–1082). New York: McGraw-Hill.

Ishii, T. (1966). Distribution of Alzheimer's neurofibrillary changes in the brainstem and hypothalamus of senile dementia. *Acta Neuropathology, 6,* 181–187.

Jerger, J., & Hall, J. (1980). Effects of age and sex on auditory brainstem response. *Archives of Otolaryngology, 106,* 387–391.

Katzman, R. (1986). Medical progress: Alzheimer's disease. *New England Journal of Medicine, 314,* 964–973.

Katzman, R. (1990). Should a major imaging procedure (CT or MRI) be required in the workup of dementia?: An affirmative view. *The Journal of Family Practice, 31,* 401–410.

Keefover, R. W. (1990). Alzheimer's disease as a diagnosis of exclusion. *West Virginia Medical Journal, 86,* 51–55.

Khachaturian, Z. S. (1985). Diagnosis of Alzheimer's disease. *Archives of Neurology, 42,* 1097–1104.

Klainer, L. M., Gibson, T. C., & White, K. L. (1965). The epidemiology of cardiac failure. *Journal of Chronic Disease, 18,* 797–814.

Kohn, M., & Schooler, C. (with Miller, J., Miller, K., Schoenbach, C., & Schoenbach, R.). (1983). *Work and personality: An inquiry into the impact of social stratification.* Norwood, NJ: Ablex.

Kotila, M., Waltimo, O., Niemi, M. L., Laaksonen, R., & Lempinen, M. (1984). The profile of recovery from strokes and factors influencing outcome. *Stroke, 15,* 1039–1044.

Kozachuk, W. E., DeCarli, C., Schapiro, M. B., Wagner, E. E., Rapoport, S. I., & Horwitz, B. (1990). White matter hyperintensities in dementia of Alzheimer's type and in healthy subjects without cerebrovascular risk factors. *Archives of Neurology, 47,* 1306–1310.

Kral, V. A. (1962). Senescent forgetfulness: Benign and malignant. *Canadian Medical Association Journal, 86,* 257–260.

Krieger, J. (1989). Breathing during sleep in normal subjects. In M. H. Kryger, T. Roth, & W. C. Dement (Eds.), *Principles and practice of sleep medicine* (pp. 257–180). Philadelphia: Saunders.

Kurland, L. T., Kurtzke, J. F., & Goldberg, I. D. (1973). *Epidemiology of neurologic and sense organ disorders.* Cambridge, MA: Harvard University Press.

Lahey, F. H. (1932). Management of severe and of atypical hyperthyroidism. *Annals of Internal Medicine, 5,* 1123–1128.

Lamy, P. P. (1979). Considerations in drug therapy of the elderly. *Journal of Drug Issues, 9,* 27–45.

Larson, E. B., Reifler, B. V., Sumi, S. M., Canfield, C. J., & Chinn, N. N. (1986). Diagnostic tests in the evaluation of dementia: A prospective study of 200 elderly outpatients. *Archives of Internal Medicine, 146,* 1917–1922.

Levin, B. E., Llabre, M. M., Reisman, S., Weiner, W. J., Sanchez-Ramos, J., Singer, C., & Brown, M. C. (1991). Visuospatial impairment in Parkinson's disease. *Neurology, 41,* 365–369.

Levin, H. S., Benton, A. L., & Grossman, R. G. (1982). *Neurobehavioral consequences of closed head injury.* New York: Oxford University Press.

Levy, E., Carman, M. D., Fernandez-Madrid, I. J., Power, M. D., Lieberburg, I., VanDuinen, S. G., Bots, G. T., Luyendijk, W., & Frangione, B. (1990). Mutation of the Alzheimer's disease amyloid gene in hereditary cerebral hemorrhage, Dutch type. *Science, 248,* 1124–1126.

Light, L. L. (1991). Memory and aging: Four hypotheses in search of data. *Annual Review of Psychology, 42,* 333–376.

Lindenbaum, J., Healton, E. B., Savage, D. G., Brust, J. C., Garrett, T. J., Podell, E. R., Marcell, P. D., Stabler, S. P., & Allen, R. H. (1988). Neuropsychiatric disorders caused by cobalamin deficiency in the absence of anemia or macrocytosis. *New England Journal of*

Medicine, 318, 1720–1728.

Lindholm, L. (1990). Hypertension and ageing. *Clinical and Experimental Hypertension, 12,* 745–759.

Lipowski, Z. J. (1980). *Delirium: Acute brain failure in man.* Springfield, IL: Thomas.

Lipsitz, L. A., Jonsson, P. V., Kelley, M. M., & Koestner, J. S. (1991). Causes and correlates of recurrent falls in ambulatory frail elderly. *Journals of Gerontology, 46,* M114–M122.

Lishman, W. A. (1981). Cerebral disorder in alcoholism: Syndromes of impairment. *Brain, 104,* 1–20.

Lord Walton of Detchant (1991). *Alzheimer's disease and the environment. Round table series 26.* London: Royal Society of Medicine Services Ltd.

Luria, A. R. (1969). Frontal lobe syndromes. In P. J. Vinken, & G. W. Bruyn (Eds.), *Handbook of clinical neurology* (Vol 2, pp. 725–757). New York: Elsevier.

Maher, E. R., & Lees, A. J. (1986). The clinical features and natural history of the Steele–Richardson–Olszewski syndrome (progressive supranuclear palsy). *Neurology, 36,* 1005–1008.

Mahler, M. E., & Cummings, J. L. (1988). Dementia: Look for the treatable cause. *Diagnosis, 10,* 64–76.

Mann, D. M. A., Yates, P. O., & Marcyniuk, B. (1984). Monoaminergic neurotransmitter systems in presenile Alzheimer's disease and in senile dementia of Alzheimer type. *Clinical Neuropathology, 3,* 199–205.

Martinot, J. L., Hardy, P., Feline, A., Huret, J. D., Mazoyer, B., Attar-Levy, D., Pappata, S., & Syrota, A. (1990). Left prefrontal glucose hypometabolism in the depressed state: A confirmation. *American Journal of Psychiatry, 147,* 1313–1317.

Masliah, E., Ellisman, M., Carragher, B., Mallory, M., Young, S., Hansen, L., DeTeresa, R., & Terry, R. D. (1992). Three-dimensional analysis of the relationship between synaptic pathology and neuropil threads in Alzheimer disease. *Journal of Neuropathology and Experimental Neurology, 51,* 404–414.

Matsuda, M., Nakasu, S., Nakazawa, T., & Handa, J. (1990). Cerebral hemodynamics in patients with normal pressure hydrocephalus: Correlation between cerebral circulation time and dementia. *Surgical Neurology, 34,* 396–401.

Mattson, M., Cheng, B., Davis, D., Bryant, K., Lieberburg, I., & Rydel, R. (1992). B-Amyloid peptides destabilize calcium homeostasis and render human cortical neurons vulnerable to excitotoxicity. *Journal of Neuroscience, 12,* 376–389.

Mayeux, R., Denaro, J., Hemenegildo, N., Marden, K., Ming-Xin, T., Cote, L. J., & Stern, Y. (1992). A population-based investigation of Parkinson's disease with and without dementia. *Archives of Neurology, 49,* 492–497.

Morgan, D. G., May, P. C., & Finch, C. E. (1987). Dopamine and serotonin systems in human and rodent brain: Effects of age and neurodegenerative disease. *Journal of the American Geriatric Society, 35,* 334–345.

Morimatsu, M., Hirai, S., Muramatsu, A., & Yoshikawa, M. (1975). Senile degenerative brain lesions and dementia. *Journal of the American Geriatric Society, 23,* 390–406.

Morris, G. O., & Singer, M. T. (1966). Sleep deprivation: The context of consciousness. *Journal of Nervous and Mental Disease, 143,* 291–304.

Mortimer, J. A. (1990). Epidemiology of dementia: Cross-cultural comparisons. *Advances in Neurology, 51,* 27–33.

Niederehe, G. (1986). Depression and memory impairment in the aged. In L. W. Posn (Ed.), *Handbook for clinical memory assessment of older adults* (pp. 226–237). Washington, DC: American Psychological Association.

O'brien, M. D. (1988). Vascular dementia is underdiagnosed. *Archives of Neurology, 45,* 797–798.

Obrist, W. D., Busse, E. W., Eisdorfer, C., & Kleemeier, R. W. (1962). Relation of the electroencephalogram to intellectual function in senescence. *Journal of Gerontology, 17,*

197-206.

O'Malley, K., Meagher, F., O'Callaghan, W. (1985). The pharmacology of ageing. In M. S. J. Pathy (Ed.), *Principles and practice of geriatric medicine* (pp. 181-193). Chichester: Wiley.

Owens, W. (1966). Age and mental abilities: A second adult follow-up. *Journal of Educational Psychology, 57,* 311-325.

Oyebode, J. R., Barker, W. A., Blessed, G., Dick, D. J., & Britton, P. R. (1986). Cognitive functioning in Parkinson's disease. *British Journal of Psychiatry, 149,* 720-725.

Pickel, V. M., & Milner, T. A. (1987). Electron microscopy of central catecholamine systems. In H. Y. Meltzer (Ed.), *Psychopharmacology: The third generation of progress* (pp. 49-59). New York: Raven Press.

Piletz, J. E., Sarasua, M., Whitehouse, P., & Chotani, M. (1991). Intracellular membranes are more fluid in platelets of Alzheimer's disease patients. *Neurobiology of Aging, 12,* 401-406.

Podolsky, D. K., & Isselbacher, K. J. (1991). Cirrhosis of the Liver. In J. D. Wilson, E. Braunwald, K. J. Isselbacher, R. G.Petersdorf, J. B. Martin, A. S. Fauci, & R. K. Root (Eds.), *Harrison's principles of internal medicine* (12th ed., pp. 73-76). New York: McGraw-Hill.

Prigatano, G. P., Parsons, O. A., Wright, E., Levis, D. C., & Hawryluk, G. (1983). Neuropsychologic test performance in mildly hypoxemic patients with chronic obstructive pulmonary disease. *Journal of Consulting Clinical Psychology, 51,* 108-116.

Resnick, H., & Cantor, J. (1970). Suicide and aging. *Journal of the American Geriatric Society, 18,* 152.

Rhymes, J. A., Woodson, C., Sparage-Sachs, R., & Cassel, C. K. (1989). Nonmedical complications of diagnostic workup for dementia. *Journal of the American Geriatric Society, 37,* 1157-1164.

Rice, D. M., Buchsbaum, M. S., Hardy, D., & Brugwald, L. (1991). Focal left temporal slow EEG activity is related to a verbal recent memory deficit in a non-demented elderly population. *Journals of Gerontology, 46,* P144-P151.

Robbins, S. L., & Angell, M. (1978). *Basic pathology.* Philadelphia: Saunders.

Roth, M. (1955). The natural history of mental disorder in old age. *Journal of Mental Science, 101,* 281-301.

Salthouse, T. (1987). Age, experience and compensation. In C. Schooler & K. Schaie (Eds.), *Cognitive functioning and social structure over the life course* (pp. 142-157).. Norwood, NJ: Ablex.

Schaie, K. W. (1983). *Longitudinal studies of adult psychological development.* New York: Guilford.

Schaie, K. (1989). Late life potential and cohort differences in mental abilities. In M. Perlmutter (Ed.), *Late life potentials* (pp. 43-61). Washington, DC: Gerontological Society of America.

Schoenberg, B. S. (1988). Epidemiology of vascular and multi-infarct dementia. In J. S. Meyer, H. Lechner, J. Marshall, & J. F. Toole (Eds.), *Vascular and multi-infarct dementia* (pp. 47-59). Mount Kisco, NY: Futura.

Schoenberg, B. S., Christine, B. W., & Whisnant, J. P. (1978). The resolution of discrepancies in the reported incidence of primary brain tumors. *Neurology, 28,* 817-823.

Schoenberg, B. S., Kokmen, E., & Okazaki, H. (1987). Alzheimer's disease and other dementing illnesses in a defined United States population: Incidence rates and clinical features. *Annals of Neurology, 22,* 724-729.

Seligman, M., Klein, D., & Miller, W. (1976). Depression. In H. Leitenberg (Ed.), *Handbook of behavior modification and behavior therapy* (pp. 168-210). Englewood Cliffs, NJ: Prentice-Hall.

Seltzer, B., & Sherwin, I. (1978). Organic brain syndromes: An empirical study and critical review. *American Journal of Psychiatry, 135,* 13-21.

Shaw, N. A., & Cant, B. R. (1980). Age-dependent changes in the latency of the pattern visual evoked potential. *Electroencephalography and Clinical Neurophysiology, 48,* 237–241.

Shaw, N. A., & Cant, B. R. (1981). Age-dependent changes in the amplitude of the pattern visual evoked potential. *Electroencephalography and Clinical Neurophysiology, 51,* 671–673.

Shraberg, K.D. (1978). The myth of pseudodementia: Depression in the aging brain. *American Journal of Psychiatry, 135,* 601–603.

Sloan, K., Craft, S., & Walsh, J. K. (1989). Neuropsychological function in obstructive sleep apnea with and without hypoxemia. *Sleep Research, 18,* 304.

Stuss, D. T., & Benson, D. F. (1984). Neuropsychological studies of the frontal lobes. *Psychological Bulletin, 95,* 3–28.

Sugar, J., & McDowd, J. (1992). Memory, learning, and attention. In J. Birren, R. Sloane, & G. Cohen (Eds.), *Handbook of mental health and aging* (pp. 307–337). San Diego, CA: Academic Press.

Sugar, S. (1988). *A comparison of questionnaire and diary methods for studying forgetting.* Paper presented at the meeting of the *Psychometric Society, Chicago.*

Suter, P. M., & Russell, R. M. (1987). Vitamin requirements of the elderly. *American Journal of Clinical Nutrition, 45,* 501–512.

Taylor, A. E., Saint-Cyr, J. A., & Lang, A. E. (1986). Frontal lobe dysfunction in Parkinson's disease. The cortical focus of neostriatal outflow. *Brain, 109,* 845–883.

Teasdale, N., Stelmach, G. E., & Breunig, A. (1991). Postural sway characteristics of the elderly under normal and altered visual and support surface conditions. *Journals of Gerontology, 46,* B238–B244.

Telakivi, T., Kajaste, S., Partinen, M., Koskenvuo, M., Salmi, T., & Kaprio, J. (1988). Cognitive function in middle-aged snorers and controls: Role of excessive daytime somnolence and sleep-related hypoxic events. *Sleep, 11,* 454–462.

Tomlinson, B. E., Blessed, G., & Roth, M. (1970). Observations on the brains of demented old people. *Journal of Neurological Science, 11,* 205–242.

Tomonago, M. (1981). Cerebral amyloid angiopathy in the elderly. *Journal of the American Geriatric Society, 29,* 151–157.

Tufo, H. M., Ostfeld, A. M., & Shyekelle, R. (1970). Central nervous system dysfunction following open-heart surgery. *Journal of the American Medical Association, 212,* 1333–1340.

United States Department of Health and Human Services. (1981). *The need for long-term care, a chartbook of the Federal Council on Aging* (DHHS Publication No. (OHDS) 81–20704). Washington, DC: Office of Human Development Services.

Van Duijn, C. M., Tanja, T. A., Haaxma, R., Schulte, W., Saan, R. J., Lameris, A. J., Antonides-Hendriks, G., & Hofman, A. (1992). Head trauma and the risk of Alzheimer's disease. *American Journal of Epidemiology, 135,* 775–782.

Webster, S. G. P. (1985). Absorption of nutrients in old age. In M. S. J. Pathy (Ed.), *Principles and practice of geriatric medicine* (pp. 291–296). Chichester: Wiley.

Webster, S. G. P., & Leeming, J. T. (1979). Erythrocyte folate levels in young and old. *Journal of the American Geriatric Society, 27,* 451–454.

Weingartner, H., & Silberman, E. (1984). Cognitive changes in depression. In R. Post & J. Ballenger (Eds.), *Neurobiology of mood disorders* (pp. 121–135). Baltimore: Williams & Wilkins.

Weiss, J. M., Stone, E. A., & Harrell, N. (1970). Coping behavior and brain norepinephrine in rats. *Journal of Comparative and Physiological Psychology, 72,* 153–160.

Wells, C. E. (1979). Pseudodementia. *American Journal of Psychiatry, 136,* 895–900.

Welsh, K., Butters, N., Hughes, J., Mohs, R., & Heyman, A. (1991). Detection of abnormal memory decline in mild cases of Alzheimer's disease using CERAD neuropsychological measures. *Archives of Neurology, 48,* 278–281.

Welsh, K. A., Butters, N., Hughes, J., Mohs, R., & Heyman, A. (1992). Detection and staging of dementia in Alzheimer's disease: Use of the neuropsychological measures developed for the Consortium to Establish a Registry for Alzheimer's Disease. *Archives of Neurology, 49,* 448–452.

West, L. J., Maxwell, D. S., Noble, E. P., & Soloman, D. H. (1984). Alcoholism. *Annals of Internal Medicine, 100,* 405–416.

West, R., & Bramblett, J. (1990). *Path analysis of the relationship among aging, depression, memory performance and memory self evaluation.* Paper presented at the *Cognitive Aging Conference, Atlanta, GA.*

Wilkinson, D. G. (1981). Psychiatric aspects of diabetes mellitus. *British Journal of Psychiatry, 138,* 1–9.

Williams, G. H., & Braunwald, E. (1991). Hypertensive vascular disease. In J. D. Wilson, E. Braunwald, K. J. Isselbacher, R. G. Petersdorf, J. B. Martin, A. S. Fauci, & R. K. Root (Eds.), *Harrison's principles of internal medicine* (12th ed., pp. 1001–1015). New York: McGraw-Hill.

Wolf, P. A., Kannel, W. B., & McGee, D. L. (1986). *Prevention of ischemic stroke: Risk factors.* In H. J. M. Barnett, J. P. Mohr, B. M. Stein, & F. M. Yatsu (Eds.), *Stroke: Pathophysiology, diagnosis, and management* (pp. 967–988). New York: Churchill Livingstone.

Yesavage, J., Bliwise, D., Guilleminault, C., Carskadon, M., & Dement, W. (1985). Preliminary communication: Intellectual deficit and sleep-related respiratory disturbance in the elderly. *Sleep, 8,* 30–33.

Zander, E., & Foroglou, G. (1976). Post-traumatic hydrocephalus. In P. J. Vinken, & G. W. Bruyn (Eds.), *Handbook of clinical neurology* (Vol 24, pp. 231–253). Amsterdam: North-Holland.

Zebrower, M., Beeber, C., & Kieras, F. J. (1992). Characterization of proteoglycans in Alzheimer's disease fibroblasts. *Biochemical and Biophysical Research Communications, 184,* 1293–1300.

Zhang, M. Y., Katzman, R., Salmon, D., Jin, H., Cai, G. J., Wang, Z. Y., Qu, G. Y., Grant, I., Yu, E., Levy, P., Klauber, M. R., & Liu, W. T. (1990). The prevalence of dementia and Alzheimer's disease in Shanghai, China: Impact of age, gender, and education. *Annals of Neurology, 27,* 428–437.

Zimberg, S. (1987). Alcohol abuse among the elderly. In L. Carstenson & B. Edelstein (Eds.), *Handbook of clinical gerontology* (pp. 57–65). New York: Pergamon.

Zola-Morgan, S., Squire, L. R., & Mishkin, M. (1982). The neuroanatomy of amnesia: Amygdala-hippocampus versus temporal stem. *Science, 218,* 1337–1339.

Zubenko, G. (1991). Progression of illness in the differential diagnosis of primary dementia. *American Journal of Psychiatry, 147,* 435–438.

Author Index

Subject Index

A

Age-Associated Memory Impairment
(AAMI), 217–218
Alcohol, 201–202, 222
Alcohol dementia syndrome, 221
Altruism, 4
Alzheimer's disease, 56–57, 215, 217,
225–226, 228
Analgesics, 208
Anoxia, 144
Anxiety, 64–65
Aphasia, 191, 218
Asphyxia, 144–146
Attention deficit disorder (ADD), 150
Auditory evoked responses (AER), 72, 79,
81–83, 85–91

B

Bayley Mental Development Index, 72–73,
76, 78
Bayley Scales of Infant Development, 52,
71
Behaviorism, 2
Brain dysfunction, 135
Brain Electric Source Analysis (BESA),
125–126
Brainstem evoked responses (BSER), 78–79
Brazie Perinatal Scale, 72

C

California Verbal Learning Test, 53
Canalization, 7
Central nervous system (CNS) dysfunction,
137, 139, 142
Child developmentalists, 16
Childrearing, 8, 12
Children, 17, 60
Chronic obstructive pulmonary disease
(COPD), 222
Cocaine, 207
Cognitive impairment, 215, 230
Cognitive proficiency, 232
Congestive heart failure (CHF), 222
Culture, 4
Current Source Denisty Analysis (CSDA),
125–126

D

Developmental theory, 12
Diabetes mellitus (DM), 223–224
DZ pairs, 10, 15, 39

E

Electroencephalograph (EEG), 217
Environment, 3 – 4, 6